Divine Protocol

The Order of God's Kingdom

By William Owens

Owens, William, 1964
Divine Protocol - The Order of God s Kingdom
william@higherstandard.net

p. cm.
ISBN: 0-9-658629-9-2

1. Owens, William 1964 2. Clergy
1st Printing 1998; 2nd Printing 2000; 3rd Printing 2002; 4th Printing 2002
5th Printing 2003

All Scripture quotations are taken from the Holy Bible King James Version

Published by:
HIGHER STANDARD PUBLISHERS, LLC
P.O. Box 440131
Kennesaw, GA 30160
770-621-4686

http://www.higherstandardpublishers.com

Table of Contents

Words evade me in expressing my depth of awareness of how God has blessed me in inscribing the truths of His Kingdom as expressed on the following pages. I am truly humbled.

It is obvious to me, one unlearned in the natural arena of men, as to why God would anoint this pitiful soul who has been saved to the uttermost by His grace; so that He would get the glory! From the core of my being, I surrender all the glory to God my Father, Christ my Savior and The Holy Spirit my Teacher. I have simply obeyed and shall continue to do so.

God is moving. Man wants to move with God, yet many times, he is moving with a system, a religion, men or the devil. There is, however, a definite protocol to ensure that man moves with God. This order cannot be controlled in any form or fashion. There is only one orchestrator; God the Father only one door; Jesus Christ; and only one Performer of the work; The Holy Spirit. Divine Protocol is, "The Order of God's Kingdom" or express another way, God's official order that is correct in the dealings of His Kingdom". It is this order that will move you in the way God is moving. It will keep you in sync with God, keep you relevant with God and keep you anointed by God.

The Body of Christ is at the threshold of a demonstration of God that will be Canaan for some and Egypt for others. Those who have prepared themselves in character will experience a great thrust in being used of God in the next millennium. Those who have resisted God and established homes of pleasures and carnality will be brought to severe chastisement. Divine Protocol is a word of instruction for the unprepared to get prepared and for the prepared on how to move forward.

This word is non-conclusive and though the message is perfect, its delivery, I am sure, will fall short in one way or the other. I pray that the truth that I have attempted to express is clear and concerning that which you do not understand or simply disagree with, pray both for you and I that God would speak so profoundly as to do away with the speculations regarding His truth that we may apprehend all that He apprehends of us.

It has been 15 years since I accepted the call to the ministry and since that time, I have written 10 books. This has called for many trials in my life. More failures than successes. More rejection than acceptance. It has been a true discipleship and mentoring process that I am so thankful to God for allowing me to experience. I can truly say, "I know Him and His ways".

Through these 17 years, I have not been alone. I have had one of heaven's handmaidens given to me to be my HELPmate. Selena, I love you with the love of Christ, and I honor you with the highest praise save that which belongs to Him. You have demonstrated that God can and will establish protocol in the life of a woman to fulfill her greatest role; that of woman, wife and mother.

A woman who reflects the character of God the way a man never could. A woman who appreciates her uniqueness and the power she has been given to HELP. A woman who, through God's wisdom, is building up women to be women.

A wife who knows the needs of her husband and ensures that they are fulfilled. A wife who cherishes every aspect of her husband's growth through trials and sufferings. A wife who bears the cross as her own. A wife such as this is who I have.

A mother who has mothered the seed of my loins. A mother who labors to keep our children warm. A mother who gives father the support so necessary to be effective. A mother who has birthed much more than my children.

I love you Mrs. Owens, with the love of Christ and thank you for loving me by obeying Him.

To my children who have patiently endured the process and have allowed me to teach them Divine Protocol through my life. They are the fruit of our labors and the single most profound evidence of God's order. No work that your mother and I have done shall surpass the work that we have done in you. This is God's order and the reality of His kingdom in your life will ensure the quality of work in ours. I love you dearly.

To all the people who have supported my writings and have encouraged my faith. Your continual prayers and words of encouragement have been a source of my strength to persevere and overcome the most intense warfare imaginable. Regardless of where the Lord takes me, I will always be in need of your fervent prayers for humility, holiness and boldness.

Finally, to you, the reader of this inscribed work of God, may you strive to incorporate Divine Protocol in every area of your life, for it is for you that this word has been published and shall be declared.

INTRODUCTION

As we behold the turn of the century come upon the beings of mankind and of all creation, there awaits a great expectation that time has groaned for since the fall of man. This expectation has baffled the soul of man so that many have written it off as "wishful thinking", "religious beliefs" and the like.

In the midst of billions of souls that doubt and do not believe, there are yet only millions who do. They have such hope in this great expectation that they have given their lives for it. Sufferings and persecutions, coupled with untold victories, provide the evidence that their expectation is real - not an imaginary hope, religious expression or even an intellectual decision. Rather, it is a demonstrative reality that truly reveals this expectation as that which shall consume all that was, all that is, and all that shall be.

The greatest event of all history, which in itself is history, shall be the consummation of salvation for all mankind who have placed an unswerving trust in He Who is none other than Jesus Christ, Immanuel, the [only] Way, the [only] Truth, and the [only] Life, the I Am, the Resurrection and the Life, the Alpha and Omega, the Beginning and the End.

This remnant of "called out" souls, known as the Body of Christ, has received a most profound gift of the grace of God that has yet to be revealed by Him to us. I shall now communicate a most urgent message to those who are partakers of this prized expectation that is waiting to be expressed.

Between each second, we, the Body of Christ, have arrived that much closer to our soon redemption. Within the passing of each minute, we have or have not accomplished the will of our Father which is in heaven. Every hour has witnessed our efforts to bring forth fruit met with repentance, or to have toiled in vain.

It has always been time for the children of righteousness to know the will of God and the way that it must be fulfilled. Unfortunately, many have been ignorant of the ways of God, and therefore have gone about to establish their own (Rom. 10:2,3). There comes a time when God no longer winks at willful ignorance (Acts 17:30), but demands that all righteousness be fulfilled.

Divine Protocol can be interpreted and expressed in many ways. I shall endeavor to share it in the most simplest fashion in order to bring the point directly to your heart: Divine Protocol is "The Order of God's Kingdom".

Shall we humbly seek for boldness to remove the ideas of men? Shall we admit to our various prejudices and repent of this sin? It is obvious to us all that there are problems amongst us, yet the greatest problem of all is the intentional ignoring of where we really are.

From our families at home to our fellowship at our churches, God is demanding Divine Protocol - "The Order of God's Kingdom". Away with the traditions and commandments of men that are comprised of opinions, prejudices and sins ranging from willful sin, racism, unforgiveness toward one another, and contempt toward the Holy Ghost.

May we now embark upon a glimpse of God's order, God's plan, God's way, known as Divine Protocol.

William Owens

October 2004

CHAPTER 1

Understanding Divine Protocol

God's way is like the wind;
you perceive it, yet never can predict it.

***The wind bloweth where it listeth, and thou hearest the sound thereof, but canst not tell whence it cometh, and whither it goeth: so is everyone that is born of the Spirit.* Jo 3:8**

n order to have a clear revelation of Divine Protocol, one must have a clear revelation of God.

Allow me to emphatically declare that God has revealed Himself to man through the revelation of His Son, Yeshua, Jesus Christ (Heb.1:2). There is no other way for man to obtain access to God but through His Son. Most religions accept that we must have a mediator between man and God, yet only Christianity declares there is only one God and one mediator between Him. As well, Christ is the only Man recognized as God, Who gave Himself as a ransom for His subjects. Other religions demand that the subjects be given as their own ransom through humanistic ideals that are always without divine representation. Christianity alone has the divine 'program' that declares a divine order represented by the Divine Himself which is woven throughout scripture as well as history.

***For [there is] one God, and one mediator between God and men, the man Christ Jesus; Who gave himself a ransom for all, to be testified in due time.* 1 Ti 2:5,6**

Therefore, our quest must be through Jesus Christ as we persist in asking, seeking, and knocking while believing that this mystery shall be revealed to those who, through a rebirth of their spirit, are qualified by His righteousness and enabled supernaturally by His Spirit to be enlightened concerning God's order.

***But God hath revealed them unto us by his Spirit: for the Spirit searcheth all things, yea, the deep things of God.* 1 Co. 2:10**

God is a Spirit, and therefore must be worshipped in spirit. God is Truth, thus worship must be in truth. This is the axiom of all beginnings. Coming into an honest and pure fellowship with God through His Son, Jesus Christ, establishes a relationship that brings a true liberty to the spirit, soul and body of man. As one grows in this newly found freedom, even as a child grows in its physical freedom, both the spiritual and physical realms must learn to respect the protocol of their respective place in order to be effective in God's kingdom within the realm of the earth.

This revelation of God is made known to man through Jesus Christ alone. We all have access to God, for God is no respecter of persons. No matter how different our callings may be, we all have been given the freedom to grow in the knowledge of God through the acceptance of His Son, Jesus Christ. As a result, those who understand Divine Protocol and those who do not are both the result of the effort that they made in seeking it. This understanding of God is therefore readily made available to all who have the Spirit of the Lord by way of a relationship; not by works, but by grace.

***Now we have received, not the spirit of the world, but the spirit which is of God; that we might know the things that are freely given to us of God.* 1 Co. 2:12**

On the basis of this relationship, we are granted access to know the things that are freely given to us of Our Father. God's ways are revealed to us by His Spirit and we can all know them.

There are far too few saints who are laboring in their relationship, while far too many are observing the motions of spirituality around them. In other words, we go to church, attend conferences and are close enough to the things of God to where we compare it to being with God. There are far too few who demonstrate their faith, while many others choose simply to observe them. This very imbalance has been instrumental to false prophets and teachers who work out their deceptive schemes among God's flock of our day. It has raised up fol-

lowers of men rather than followers of God. Many have regarded it easier to live off of the revelation granted to someone else rather than extend themselves to God and be enlightened through a personal relationship founded on love. As a result of this immature state, they depend on those who are only able to sow and add water, not realizing all the seeds and water that one can handle will never bring growth. Only God can give the increase.

This type of ignorance and imbalance has caused divisions and denominational barriers. Because we have left the revelation of God up to but a few to "discover", many sheep know little or nothing! Thus, they believe whatever they are told, unable to discern good from evil.

There is an individual impartation that must be experienced in order for the revelation of God to be embraced. Regardless of how much one studies God's Word, be it by seminary, Bible college, correspondence course, etc., this impartation that I speak of is experienced on a level separate from the "observing" of God's Word. God's ways are not "learned" in the natural. Rather, they are discerned in the spiritual. The simplicity of knowing God becomes a reality when one follows the straight and narrow way. It consists of a condition that is a prerequisite to receiving the revelation of God's Word and His way. It is the heart which has the soil of sincerity, purity and honesty, and the soul that has grasped the feet of the Savior before reaching for the words of the Savior. They have come to He Whom the Word testifies of, and not just the word itself. In their most profound and sought after desire, they find their fulfillment in the Messiah alone speaking through His Word to their spirit.

Those who have an understanding of Divine Protocol have simply found the Prince of Peace, the Bright Morning Star. They sup with the Father and the Son, and the order of God is a natural experience that evolves with time (Mt 13:31,32). As a newborn baby strains through the process of building the strength to hold up its head, likewise the children of God learn divine order with each step of painful growth that builds the necessary strength for longevity. Such growth is purely a result of a faith that exceeds natural limits, the seen, and the comprehensible. However, it is cautious of the foolish and the presumptuous way. This faith responds to the beckoning of the Spirit and through experience and growth, begins to comprehend the Divine Protocol of God.

The comprehension of God's way is not possible with the mind of man. On the contrary, the way of God is rejected by the natural man for again, God is a spirit:

But he that is spiritual judgeth all things, yet he himself is judged of no man. **1Cor. 2:15**

Many Christians have experienced the frustrations of trying to see God through the facilities of their common sense and if not careful, they will begin to reason away many divine possibilities due to the natural man's inability to receive the ways of the Lord. The contrary effect is not to altogether reject God (it would appear), but to establish their own way while assuming it is God's way. Such is the result of the lack of scriptural discipleship in many of our churches. We fall into the vices of presumption, tradition and doctrines of devils. Even to this day, man has walked in such an air of pride and self exaltation. These thwarted views grow to levels of contempt toward God and those who bear such contemptible fruit take a most perverse pleasure in lording over God's heritage. What saith the scriptures?

Ye hypocrites, well did Esaias prophesy of you saying, This people draweth nigh unto me with their mouth, and honoureth me with their lips; but their heart is far from me. But in vain they do worship me, teaching for doctrines the commandments of men. **Mt 15:7-9**

The Pharisee stood and prayed thus with himself, God, I thank thee, that I am not as other men are, extortioners, unjust, adulterers, or even as this publican. **Luke 18:11**

For they being ignorant of God's righteousness, and going about to establish their own righteousness, have not submitted themselves unto the righteousness of God. **Ro. 10:3**

Has not history testified of the truth's greatest enemy the religiosities of men which are none other than the commandments and doctrines of men? Such professors of the Gospel have not submitted themselves to the One True Teacher. He demands for self to die that He may live in each of us. Because they reject the standard of God, they come in by some other means to proclaim a gospel that is no gospel at all. Who can know the Word of God but he who does the will of the Father (Jo 7:17)? Ultimately, such deliberate resistance of God's way without repentance can lead to detrimental extremities as departing from the faith, or teaching things that they do not know and thus yield themselves to doctrines of devils (Col. 2:8; 1Tim. 4:1). Such is the sin of rebellion (1 Sam. 15:23).

May I express the urgent need that I have to shed light on the results of not following the move of God's Spirit? To fall short in any measure of unbelief is a serious issue indeed (Heb. 3:12). God is not pleased when we doubt His beckoning. Such apprehension or deliberate doubting fully deserves the rebuke of our loving Father, for His soul will have no pleasure in those who draw back (Heb.10:38).

Striving to Comprehend

We must strive to comprehend in our spirit the ways of God through His Spirit. Understanding the rebellion of our carnal mind against our spiritual mind will simplify our growth process toward understanding Divine Protocol.

A great portion of understanding Divine Protocol is to know the order of your person. Man is made up of three distinct persons; spirit, soul and flesh. From the day you were born, there has been an intense warfare between these three. Our spirit cries out for rebirth, our soul desires the pride of life, and our flesh lusts after carnal pleasures. There is a godly order and place for each of these, for they were made by God for His purpose. Very simply stated, our spirit man is king, our soul is servant, and our flesh is slave. Protocol, as it pertains to our person, will further enhance protocol as it pertains to God.

May we grasp the divine principle that relationship precedes revelation, for through our intimacy with the Father and Son, we shall know of His ways. Each member of the Body of Christ has been given the liberty as well as the admonition to walk with God to the fullest of their desire and to seek Him till they be found of Him.

> ***Wherefore, beloved, seeing that ye look for such things, be diligent that ye may be found of him in peace, without spot, and blameless.*** **2 Pe 3:14**

Divine Protocol is a result of divine relationship. Becoming aware of divine order is a process of growth from the inward man. This experience is dependent on the pureness of one's motives along with a most fervent desire to truly want the things of God for themselves. It is exercising an unfeigned faith to solely love God.

FAITH

Faith is beautiful. There is nothing that can be compared with its likeness, nor can anything replace its ability. Genuine faith responds to God, whereas feigned faith responds to self, to man, and to all that is seen.

There is, however, a "faith" among Christians that seeks to name it, claim it and outright demand it all in Jesus' name. This type of twisted belief finds its roots being strengthened with the powerful source of self, satan and the world. Such faith seeks its own good rather than that of the kingdom of God and others. This wave of "quick fix" Phosophy and motivational jargon has led thousands into vain pursuits and the giving of their money in hopes of buying a blessing (Col. 2:8). Such acts of impulsiveness have left far too many believers hurt, dazed and confused as they frantically attempt to get a grip on the real genuine move of God for His glory.

Those who claim such a faith are out of touch with the protocol of God. In essence, they have established their own law of faith by becoming a law unto themselves. They declare, "let everything be done in decency and in order" without considering the order of God. Whether or not they are unintentional victims of such a warped and void faith, does not excuse the fact that they are most incapable of knowing Divine Protocol through such a repugnant channel of all that is marred with the carnal man.

Now the end of the commandment is charity out of a pure heart, and of a good conscience, and of faith unfeigned. **1 Ti. 1:5**

God's ways are pure and holy and His requirements are no less the same in order to behold and comprehend them. Divine Protocol, God's Official Order that is Correct in the Dealings of His Kingdom, is a gradual increase of awareness which is revealed within the spirit of those who walk in reverence and obedience to God. It is impossible to know God without faith which is built upon a life of obedience. This same principle holds true for knowing His protocol.

A person's level of revelation, as it pertains to Divine Protocol, will directly correspond to their level of experienced faith. God does not just unload His wisdom upon immature saints. He requires the proving of one's faith and life prior to the receiving of any divine treasures which are most precious indeed. Without the fire of God to purge impure motives, hidden sins, and an array of fleshly lusts, the kingdom of God is unable to grow and flourish from within. True faith allows all righteousness to be fulfilled. A very distinct and most significant prerequisite part of this process is the testing of an individual's faith prior to and during the true enlightenment of the mystery of the kingdom of God.

As human beings, we are quite hasty in allowing our carnal man to interpret the ways of God. When relating to the various triumphant experiences of Shadrach, Meshach, and Abednego in the fiery furnace, of Daniel in the lion's den, of Joseph cast into prison, and of our Lord being tried through and through, we are slow to behold the profound results of testing and endurance that occurred within the testing of their faith.

For we have not an high priest which cannot be touched with the feeling of our infirmities; but was in all points tempted like as we are, yet without sin. **Heb. 4:15**

We should be awestruck at the realization that Jesus, Who is God, had to experience our infirmities in order to be touched by them. His understanding of His Father's protocol came out of what He experienced as Jesus, the man. As God-man, He was well acquainted with being God. Nevertheless, He had to dwell among mankind. This dwelling was to become likened unto them to the point that it was personal. He was tempted with temptation in order to learn obedience through suffering. Through this process which was ordained before the foundation of the world, He overcame the sting of death and is fit to be hailed as Savior and Lord (Heb.2:10).

Our faith must be exercised in the realm of obedience toward conformity to the image of Christ as well as the mind of Christ. As we partake of the sufferings of which we have been found worthy to endure, we must grasp with our hearts and understand with our renewed minds the implications before us. The testing of our faith is the invitation to comprehend Divine Protocol. It is God appearing to us with the desire to bring us to the height of life which is a personal revelation of Himself and His way. The trials and sufferings that we endure are not only for our maturity in this life, but they also work for us a rich reward in the life to come.

Divine Protocol requires a divine faith in order to comprehend it. Therefore, it is to our advantage to yield to God's leading that faith may be molded in our lives. Those who are faithful with little will be made rulers seemingly overnight. This reveals a profound principle pertaining to faith; it must be found true in every believer's life.

How quick we are to interpret trials, persecutions and the like as attacks from the devil, while denying them as chastening and purging from the hand of the Lord. While enjoying the precious gift of his son who was the result of a promise of God, Abraham was confronted by the Lord in a totally unexpected way. No doubt he could have labeled such a request as from the devil or out of order.

> ***And it came to pass after these things, that God did tempt Abraham, and said unto him, Abraham: and he said, Behold, here I am. And he said, Take now thy son, thine only son Isaac, whom thou lovest, and get thee into the land of Moriah; and offer him there for a burnt offering upon one of the mountains which I will tell of thee.*** ***Gen. 22:1,2***

The children of Israel experienced such a humbling and trying time of testing, that many of them wanted to return back to Egypt prior to

them even crossing the Red Sea. They desired bondage rather than liberty, Pharaoh instead of God, and the way of ease and complacency rather than that of conflict and growth.

And thou shalt remember all the way which the Lord thy God led thee these forty years in the wilderness, to humble thee, and to prove thee, to know what was in thine heart, whether thou wouldest keep his commandments, or no. Deut. 8:2

Many of us receive opportunities from the Lord to exercise our choice even as Solomon did. Such decisions prove our faith to be genuine and our motives pure. True faith will keep its affections on things above, whereas fleshly faith focuses on the rudiments of worldly treasures.

And Solomon loved the Lord, walking in the statutes of David his father: only he sacrificed and burnt incense in the high places.

In Gibeon the Lord appeared to Solomon in a dream by night: and God said, Ask what I shall give thee.

Give therefore thy servant an understanding heart to judge thy people, that I may discern between good and bad: for who is able to judge this thy so great a people? And the speech pleased the Lord, that Solomon had asked this thing. 1 Kings 3:3,5,9,10

How many of us would believe that God would require us to give our last morsel of bread to a rugged prophet? Certainly, God would not require us great preachers to go to a widow and request the last portion of her food. But this Negro Sidonian woman, in the village of Zidon which was founded by the first born of Canaan, son of Ham, was aware that God was trying her faith. Elijah was quite familiar with the providential ways in which God works. He did not allow his pride to hinder his faith from responding to God's Divine Protocol.

These examples, and countless others, reveal to us that our God is a proving God. He accepts us the way we are, only to make us into who He has ordained for us to be. This process is solely attainable through our demonstration of faith. It is for this reason that faith is given by God that we may respond to Him. Our common sense tells us to stop at a red light and to proceed at a green light. Likewise, it is through our spiritual sense coupled with faith that we walk on the waters of challenges and overcome the contrary winds of adversity. To know that you must stop at a red light yet choose to keep going, is to become a menace to yourselves and others. Likewise, to understand what God requires of you and to yet fall short because of unbelief, will destroy ones perception of God as well as forfeit experiencing His order known as Divine Protocol.

To capture the differences of reactions from man's being, the following is true indeed:

- Faith is a response from our spirit,
- fear is a reaction from the mind,
- and foolishness is a reaction from the flesh.

Only by the revelation of God's Word and the exercising of ones faith will the dividing asunder of soul and spirit, joint and marrow and the discerning of thoughts and intents of the heart become a reality (Heb 4:12).

God's Official Order that is Correct in the Dealings of His Kingdom is an ever unfolding knowledge which is discerned by our spirits and responded to by our faith. The process of getting our faith to perform must not be equated with negative notions or ideas, but rather as the purging hand of our Father (Jo 15:2).

Now no chastening for the present seemeth to be joyous, but grievous: nevertheless afterward it yieldeth the peaceable fruit of righteousness unto them which are exercised thereby.
Heb. 12:11

May we not be hasty in passing judgment on ourselves or even others during times of chastening. An incorrect or surface verdict can and will easily return to serve as a rebuke of one's ignorance to the unnoticeable progression which is taking place in the midst of exceeding conflict. We are promised that after such correction we shall yield the peaceable fruit of righteousness and understanding of God's way - Divine Protocol. The process of tearing down the old man and building up the new may only hurt the flesh and the intellect, however, it is yet a genuine edification for our spiritual man.

Jesus asked His followers several times, "Are you offended by my words? Are you ashamed of suffering for me?" Anyone who refuses to endure their fiery furnace of purification, and the correcting hand of God has been offended by the Gospel and may never come to know Divine Protocol in this life.

OBEDIENCE

The call for obedience has not been sounded by the majority of our preachers as the scriptures demand. Doctrines which are not altogether false, are nonetheless imbalanced in their delivery. It takes a strong spirit in the preacher to declare the whole counsel of God while not being moved by the reaction of the people and especially other preachers. When obedience is not being uttered, God's people fail to bear fruit unto perfection. Therefore, multitudes of Christians are not walking in obedience to His commandments and leading. Most of our preaching today has maintained a great proclaiming of God's faithfulness toward us regardless of how difficult it may get. Yet the preacher must also make clear God's demands for our faithfulness to Him under the same difficulty. We have been assured that whatever the extent of our trial, He has already assured us that it will not be above what we are able to bear.

> ***There hath no temptation taken you but such as is common to man: but God [is] faithful, who will not suffer you to be tempted above that ye are able; but will with the temptation also make a way to escape, that ye may be able to bear [it].*** **1Co 10:13**

While attempting to establish the fact that we are saved by grace, which is received by faith in our hearts, many have cast out the command to obey which is exercised by our will. Never should a person attempt to separate faith and obedience for in doing so, one destroys the very foundation on which faith is built...to love God with all your mind, your soul, and your strength, and as Jesus said, "those who love me keep my commandments" (Jo 14:21).

If there was a specific word which describes the whole aspect of Divine Protocol from beginning to end, it would be obedience. Before one can begin to understand the depth of God's way, they must first understand obedience. One begins to abound in the knowledge of God and His Divine Protocol due to an exercising of continual obedience. When the fulfillment of Divine Protocol in ones life is a continual process, it is again only an experienced reality by those who are continually obeying.

The haughty notion that a shallow belief in God, or even faith in grace alone is sufficient enough for an individual to inherit the kingdom of God must be purged from the minds of countless individuals who claim to know Christ, but indeed deny Him by their works as well as by their fruit. Satan has used this deceptive Phosophy to defeat and deceive millions from beholding the pearly gates of heaven. Many a soul has plunged into the awaiting chambers of hell thinking that they could be redeemed by faith alone. I must, with all authority of the scriptures and the Spirit of the Living God, exercise my office of a prophet to expose this cancerous heresy which stifles the branch and causes it to be unproductive, as well as hinders the dire need of revival in this land.

Obedience is not a condition; it is a command. Grace is not a command; it is a condition. When God said, "Obey", He spoke to your will. When He said "Grace has saved you", He spoke to your heart. A command spoken to your will cannot be believed with your heart, nor can a condition spoken to your heart be believed with your will. It requires faith to believe in our hearts the redemptive work of grace. Likewise, a choice of the mind or will is necessary to carry out obedience.

> ***That if thou shalt confess with thy mouth the Lord Jesus, and shalt believe in thine heart that God hath raised him from the dead, thou shalt be saved. For with the heart man believeth unto righteousness; and with the mouth confession is made unto salvation.*** **Ro. 10:9,10**

Take notice that we came to believe on the Lord Jesus with our hearts and not with our minds. The Word says, "the natural man receiveth not the things of God, neither can he for they are spiritually discerned" (1 Cor. 2:14).

When God redeems a person, He saves their entire being. What He requires of our hearts is faith which we readily give. Yet too often, what we fail to give is obedience from our wills that is demonstrated in and through our body not through our mouths in lip service. This is why Christians who do not obey God's commands deem those who do as self righteous. They are responding from a conviction because they themselves have ignored His demand and requirements of willful obedience.

> ***For he that is dead is freed from sin. Now if we be dead with Christ, we believe that we shall also live with him.***
>
> **Ro. 6:7,8**

> ***Neither yield ye your members [as] instruments of unrighteousness unto sin: but yield yourselves unto God, as those that are alive from the dead, and your members [as] instruments of righteousness unto God.*** **Ro 6:13**

Our wills are linked to our souls which in turn determine the action of our bodies. Our hearts are linked to our faith which determines what we believe or disbelieve. This is the very principle by which Christ Himself will determine those who said, "Lord, Lord", from those who willfully obeyed Him by "doing" what He has said. This is why there are liars who profess, "I'm a Christian" with their mouth, while their fruit shows them a deliberate servant of sin. Did not the mouth of our Lord utter, "Ye shall know them by their fruit?"

The Gospel is the good news of being set free from the law of sin and death in order to serve the law of righteousness. What saith the scriptures? ...*but where sin abounds grace did much more abound* (Rom. 5:20) . This scriptural evidence supports the standard of Divine Protocol as it pertains to the workings of salvation. The word, "abound" is translated in the Greek to mean, "super abounded" over the works of sin.

For this reason was Christ manifested that He might destroy the works of the devil, which, simply stated, is the very fruit of disobedience. Whether or not we occasionally stumble is not the issue. What baby is born walking? God's grace is so sufficient and the work of Calvary so complete, that not only can He succor us completely (Heb. 2:18), but also restore us as we work out our salvation by choosing not to sin (Heb.10:26). For an individual to premeditate adultery, fornication or any act which is contrary to all righteousness and to believe that Christ has died for such a display of ungodliness is to do despite to the Spirit of grace, trod under foot the Son of God and count the blood of the covenant as unholy (Heb. 10:29).

It is through the obedience of God's command that Divine Protocol is perceived and received. Through a continual progression of doing God's will while believing His promises, a clean vessel shall be blessed in his deeds.

> ***For if any be a hearer of the word, and not a doer, he is like unto a man beholding his natural face in a glass: For he beholdeth himself, and goeth his way, and straightway forgetteth what manner of man he was. But whoso looketh into the perfect law of liberty, and continueth therein, he being not a forgetful hearer, but a doer of the work, this man shall be blessed in his deed.***
>
> ***Jas. 1:23-25***

Divine Protocol is imparted as a result of fulfilling God's written protocol. As I have previously explained, it is not possible to believe a written command apart from the involvement of our will. This is a process of our intellect in choosing between what God has spoken or what the flesh, the world, or the devil has spoken. Through exercising our wills, we will do the works of righteousness or of sin. There is no middle ground, for to omit what we know to do is sin, as even doing what we know we should not do.

We all desire for God to personally reveal to us specifics regarding every area of our lives. This mark of maturity is attained through child-like obedience to God's commandments from the scriptures as well as our conscience. There is no other way to experience Divine Protocol other than through the established order of God's covenant: observing to do all that is written therein. Such is not grievous, for we are born of God and His Spirit works in and through us which shall fulfill all righteousness. For this is the love of God, that we keep His commandments: and His commandments are not grievous.

For whatsoever is born of God overcometh the world: and this is the victory that overcometh the world, [even] our faith.
1Jo 5:3,4

How much more could be expressed upon this vital issue of obedience? What then is the need for order in God's kingdom if His subjects are allowed to remain in gross disobedience? Furthermore, why would Christ even die and rise from the grave if He could not completely set at liberty those who are the servants of sin? I submit to you that obedience is not only the mark of godliness, but the core of Divine Protocol, for a house divided against itself cannot stand. If sin and righteousness can dwell in the same vessel as equals possessing the throne of that person, then Christ's kingdom has an end and we have been most gravely deceived.

It is imperative that we make our calling and election sure (2 Peter 1:10), and examine ourselves whether we be in the faith. Let us prove ourselves by acknowledging the presence of Christ, Who is light. Some believe that they are of the faith even though they walk in darkness. This is the fruit of a reprobate (2 Cor. 13:5); unable to acknowledge wrong because they have exchanged the truth for a lie. God has given them over that they would believe a lie (Rom. 1:25,26,28). May we realize that Christ has become the author of salvation to a particular remnant of people. It is not those who have faith alone that will be justified, but those who show their faith by obedience that shall behold Him face to face (Heb. 5:9, Rom. 2:13).

Sacrifice

No man can serve two masters: for either he will hate the one, and love the other; or else he will hold to the one, and despise the other. Ye cannot serve God and mammon. **Mt 6:24**

The power of faith and the strength of obedience is only relevant because of sacrifice. What use are these essential attributes which have been granted by His grace, if we are not desirous to conform to His purpose which He hath purposed in Himself before the foundation of the world? Every act of obedience is a result of sacrifice, in that we yield to do His will and not our own.

Faith and obedience are means of interaction with God. Be this of a truth, interaction requires an exercising of these attributes in order to bear fruit that will remain. To properly understand their relation to Divine Protocol, we definitely must have a working knowledge of sacrifice.

Truly, it is heartbreaking to behold the many Christians who have a degree of understanding of God, yet due to their unwillingness to sacrifice, their knowledge is not effectively producing fruit nor does it go from glory to glory. Disobedience is a most stubborn hindrance that can only be dealt with by obedience. You cannot "Greek and Hebrew" it away. You cannot annul it with some doctrine from a popular Bible scholar. When you lay down at night upon your own bed and begin to just think about God, your conscience immediately begins to convict you of disobedience, or it confirms your obedience.

The absurd teaching that our sacrifice toward obedience is not good enough is a weak and beggarly attempt to avoid surrendering to God what He requests from us. History has proven that we are unable to earn the gift of salvation. Has not the Word of God declared all our righteousness "as filthy rags" (Isa. 64:6), and that none of us are righteous, "no, not one" (Rom. 3:10)? Certainly then, it is understood that our sacrificial service to God is not to "earn" our salvation nor justify our sin. Christ alone has done both of them for all who call upon His name. The response of your obedience is the testimony of God's grace in our life. This act, which is more valuable than all sacrifices and offerings, reveals the genuineness of your repentance and thus the acceptance of His justifying you before a Holy God.

Then said Jesus unto his disciples, If any man will come after me, let him deny himself, and take up his cross, and follow me. **Mt 16:24**

And that he died for all, that they which live should not henceforth live unto themselves, but unto him which died for them, and rose again. **2 Co. 5:15**

I am crucified with Christ: nevertheless I live; yet not I, but Christ liveth in me: and the life which I now live I live by the faith of the Son of God, who loved me, and gave himself for me.
Gal. 2:20

What Christ has done for us, we must in turn do for Him and others. He has revealed in Himself the very life that He desires us to live. He is Lord of lords, King of kings, the Alpha and Omega, and Life itself. Why should we expect Him to require anything less than what He has given? Even the rulers of this world expect their subjects to serve them obediently. Our military does not provide healthcare, food, shelter and a future to people who work or perform whenever they feel like it. No!! They are the property of the United States government. Willingly, they obey their commanding officer. If this is so regarding earthly things, how much more does this principle operate in the heavenly realm?

Shall we endeavor, by the grace of God, to bring perspective to this most essential area of serving God that we may have a further understanding of Divine Protocol; God's Order that is Correct in the Dealings of His Kingdom.

The Greatest Sacrifice: Death

As we behold the very life that our Savior lived, we witness the greatest sacrifice that has ever been made. Though He possessed the very essence of faith and revealed obedience to the fullest, without the surrendering of His will to His Father to become a servant (Ph. 2:6-8), His mission would have been in vain.

Who gave himself for our sins, that he might deliver us from this present evil world, according to the will of God and our Father.
Gal. 1:4

And walk in love as Christ also hath loved us, and hath given himself for us, an offering and a sacrifice to God for a sweetsmelling savour. ***Eph. 5:2***

Hereby perceive we the love of God, because he laid down his life for us: and we ought to lay down our lives for the brethren.
1 Jo 3:16

Divine Protocol is a heavenly order that requires an entire surrendered life of those who purpose to walk in it. This is a process that takes time and God is clearly aware of it. For this reason, He is tremendously patient with us.

I beseech you therefore, brethren, by the mercies of God, that ye present your bodies a living sacrifice, holy, acceptable unto God, which is your reasonable service. ***Ro. 12:1***

However, the watchman on the wall, the preacher, the prophet and the prophetess, all have the distinct responsibility to declare one thing: "prepare the way of the Lord and make His paths straight." The obvious hindrance is neglect amongst those called in declaring the necessity for sacrificial living. We have emphasized too many of the blessings of God and not enough of the conditions by which those blessings are realized. In essence, we have said, "God loves you, do what you feel, He understands. Just flow, He will bring it to pass."

There is a deceptive Phosophy in our pulpits that is robbing people of their reward (Col. 2:18). "By good words and fair speeches" they are deceiving the hearts of the simple (Rom. 16:18). These are such that do not serve our Lord, but rather their own bellies. Such manipulators only serve to cause divisions and offenses which are contrary to the fruit of God's Word - sacrifice (Rom. 16: 17-18).

The truth of the matter is that many ministers do not want believers to live for Christ more than they want them to follow after themselves. This is precisely why the scribes and Pharisees hated Jesus. Our Lord liberated the people from the control and manipulation of men that they may freely worship the Father in Spirit and in truth without the intervention of man other than Jesus Himself.

You must see and believe that knowing Christ is an individual choice and responsibility. Unfortunately, many of our large denominations are not presenting the full scope of sacrifice that Christ requests, thus hindering the laborers from coming forth.

 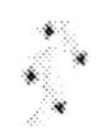

Now the parable is this: The seed is the word of God. Those by the wayside are they that hear; then cometh the devil, and taketh away the word out of their hearts, lest they should believe and be saved. They on the rock are they, which, when they hear, receive the word with joy; and these have no root, which for a while believe, and in time of temptation fall away. And they which fell among thorns are they, which, when they have heard, go forth, and are choked with cares and riches and pleasures of this life, and bring no fruit to perfection. But that on the good ground are they, which in an honest and good heart, having heard the word, keep it, and bring forth fruit with patience.

Luke 8:11-15

This powerful declaration of our Lord Jesus Christ reveals the primary reason why individuals who are receiving the Word are yet not bearing fruit. We readily affirm that faith cometh by hearing, however, we ignore that even though hearing comes by the Word of God, one has to possess the correct motives to genuinely hear. This very concern of His disciples prompted them to ask why He spoke in parables. His reply should serve to sober us, lest we be puffed up by vain knowledge.

And he said, Unto you it is given to know the mysteries of the kingdom of God: but to others in parables; that seeing they might not see, and hearing they might not understand.

Luke 8:10

There are many methods of studying the Bible in our time and day. Courses ranging from memorizing Scriptures to historically analyzing the setting of the scriptures. You can study Greek and Hebrew at hundreds of theological institutes throughout the land. However, without sacrifices by which God's Word and revelation of His protocol grows and produces fruit, all attempts to gain wisdom and insight are in vain. Indeed, we should be thankful to God for everything that is good which allows us to learn of Him in a deeper and more profound way through the many ministries that exist today. However, we are showing insult to Almighty God when we take our refuge in the systems of men. Though the systems of men will always exist and the Lord does work through them to accomplish His will and work, we yet need the wisdom of God to know the distinct ways of His Spirit for ourselves.

There are many institutions in our time that have had a profound impact on the lives of God's people in furthering their effectiveness spiritually. Yet, never should the people of God expect any vessel to bring them into face to face communion with God but God Himself.

THE WAYSIDE

As it pertains to knowing the protocol of God, one cannot know it while abiding on the outskirts of where the reality of the Gospel really is. The wayside is a place where a person is found clinging to irrelevant and dormant issues that are disguised as good works or religious efforts. These only serve as distractions away from true spiritual progression that comes through being where God is; in conflict with spiritual darkness and overcoming. Waysiders are double minded individuals in regards to the service of God, and sacrifice is not a way of life to them. In essence, the wayside is a "hangout" for Christians who begin the race of faith and salvation, but somehow find reason to simply relax for a minute by taking on these non-spiritual issues. This minute turns into an hour and then a few days and before long, they have retreated to the isles of complacency which leads compromise, then finally contempt. It will take circumstances to bring those who abide on the wayside out, and God knows how to stir the nest of His people who have chosen to be at ease in Zion.

Naturally, there are those who are on the wayside and sincerely do not realize it. Satan truly knows how to appear as an angel of light especially in the form of distracting God's people through false spiritual labor. Such labor has much to do with emotionalism and spiritualism. Its focus is on spirituality but not Christ. It seeks for signs and wonders and amusement without a pure hunger for simple truth.

When we observe the standard of the Church today, such a standard is lower than most sororities. Christians are not expected to do anything but show up, get preached happy, eat, retreat and sleep. In return, they pay the preacher and are insured a preacher's sermon at their funeral. The wayside is real in our generation and many of our churches are established to cater to such Christians. Wayside churches can be no more than a thriving business because the people have gathered unto themselves teachers that will say what they want to hear. They have itching ears that desire words that will soothe their conscience which stands convicted by the Holy Ghost. There are even those who are preaching the outright truth, and yet the waysiders remain. Such can be a danger to a ministry because waysiders like company. As a result, they search for potential recruits to join them in their spiral to spiritual decay and confusion. Instead of yielding themselves to God, they do so to the devil and cause friction amongst those who are trying to press into God's kingdom. Those who are bent on forever living on the wayside will sooner or later have to be confronted and placed out of your church or the whole church is placed in a position of being hinderred in it's spiritual progress.

The Bible explicitly declares,"then cometh the devil..." Any and all wayside experiences involve the devil coming. This is very important for Christians to understand. Once you are saved, it will only be a matter of time before the devil "cometh." The successful Christian will be discipled between their salvation experience and the devil's "coming" time to a degree that they will be able to stand against and rebuke him with all authority. Jesus put into perspective the importance of preparing ones self for a hostile takeover. It is written:

> ***Then goeth he, and taketh with himself seven other spirits more wicked than himself, and they enter in and dwell there: and the last [state] of that man is worse than the first. Even so shall it be also unto this wicked generation.*** **Mt 12:4**

Therefore, the wayside consists of those who, through neglect of spiritual preparation, have allowed the devil to simply storm back into their lives and take the Word out of their heart. The ultimate goal that satan has in mind is to keep you from being determined to hold onto your salvation. In other words, he realizes that "he" cannot take your salvation. Yet, through your neglect of retaining the Word in your heart, you will frustrate its progression by falsely assuming that salvation simply means believing. Even the devils believe and tremble (Jas. 2:19). As a result, you have believed a gospel that is no gospel at all because their is no conforming to obedience. Therefore, the real truth goes unheeded until you take notice that where you are headed is not good, or until you arrive at what you are not expecting - issues that create difficulty and even hell itself.

How many people have gotten on the wrong bus and did not realize it until it arrived at the wrong location? Yet all the while you could see signs that caused you to wonder if you were going in the right direction. These signs are the warnings that God gives us that we are going the wrong way! Do you expect God to welcome people into heaven who have the excuse, "I thought?" If the bus driver does not give you a refund when you ride the wrong bus, why does society expect God to give one on the day of judgment? People have all kind of tricks when it comes to trying to get over for free and God knows them all.

Allow me to reiterate that this is the Divine Protocol of God's Kingdom and not anyone's point of view. These are real issues which affect the life of the Christian every day. Many are being defeated at this first line of attack by the devil. The Word declares....and [the devil] taketh away the word out of their hearts, lest they should believe and be saved (Luke 8:12).

The Word of God is explicitly declaring that between salvation and the wayside experience, ones salvation is very sensitive and vulnerable. The vulnerability does not stem from God's commitment, but from ours. It is the word within the heart that brings about Divine Protocol, and satan will allow you to retain your testimony, your experience, your ministry and even your idea of salvation. Yet he realizes that if he inhibits the Word of God from taking root in your heart, whatever you do have will not develop to full maturation. It will be found without the spirit of the Word and thus powerless in the effect of your character as well as in spiritual realm of God to advance His Kingdom in the earth.

This is a key reason why there are many people dabbling in the occult in and outside of the ministry. When we discover that our chants for God to do this and do that are not working, we begin to seek means and methods that are not supported by scripture. When there is no fear of being deceived, it is because deception is already present. When there is no evidence of an earnest desire for the will of God, it reveals the fruit of deception. Of course, you hear the words, "Thy will be done", but there is no corresponding action in the body. Without the body being presented acceptable to the Lord and the mind being renewed, God's will will never be known.

> ***I beseech you therefore, brethren, by the mercies of God, that ye present your bodies a living sacrifice, holy, acceptable unto God, [which is] your reasonable service. And be not conformed to this world: but be ye transformed by the renewing of your mind, that ye may prove what [is] that good, and acceptable, and perfect, will of God.*** **Ro 12:1-2**

These are several reasons why there is much humanism in the pulpit and fleshly presentations of the Gospel which all reveal that somewhere along the line, the Word was not securely established in their lives, in their spirits and in their minds. Keep in mind that this humanism sounds good to the natural man. It appears that nothing seems to be wrong. This is precisely why it is called deception. The devil knows how to appeal to the intellect in such a way as to lift it up and provide just enough emotional satisfaction to make a people think it is the Lord because they "feel" it. If it does not bear witness with your spirit and manifest the fruit in your body, you are being misled, deceived and set up for a sting.

You must face and endure the wayside experience. It is going to come and if you avoid it, you will be held captive by it until you confront it and obtain the victory. The only sure way to forever put the issues of God's Word being removed from your heart is to allow the times of temptation to come and have their part. Divine Protocol evolves within the realm of experience and as you embrace these experiences, you will then come forth perfect and entire wanting nothing.

> ***But let patience have [her] perfect work, that ye may be perfect and entire, wanting nothing.*** ***James 1:4***

No Root

Due to the absence of depth of true spiritual life, such hearers of the Word "believe" only when times are good. When there are not any conditions present to demand a choice based on their free will sacrifice, there is rejoicing and dancing that can be heard across town! To their misfortune however, when the trials come to prove ones faith, the musicians pack up, the sound system is broken down, and they simply fall away from that which they have heard. In reality, they never had any roots to begin with. Rather, they had an appearance of unity with Christ, yet are standing by themselves in shallow soil unable to take root.

> ***They on the rock [are they], which, when they hear, receive the word with joy; and these have no root, which for a while believe, and in time of temptation fall away. Lk 8:13***

This is a powerful axiom that the person who has purposed to fulfill the will of God in their life must adhere to. The will of God is the result of following the order of God. Once you know the will of God, there then must be a process toward beholding it develop step by step. This is "The Order of God's Kingdom" that we are slow and hesitant toward understanding. We simply want to... just do it. God's kingdom does not operate like a sports shoe slogan.

God's kingdom is eternal and therefore the laborers and the manner in which they labor are based upon eternal principles. You cannot operate within the scope of God's kingdom with humanistic, opinionated and self centered views. Nor can one expect God to operate through any other channel than their spirit. There is nothing in the flesh that will contribute toward you flowing with God's order. Divine Protocol is only accessible through the divine nature by which all things have been given us for life and godliness.

CHOKED

What else has deceived 21st century Christians like no other attraction other than the cares, riches and pleasures of this life? I am disturbed at the vain attempts of many Christian leaders to make everything in this life appear to be acceptable in spite of what Jesus has said regarding the trouble that we will have. While certainly being a believer of God's financial prosperity, I am also an advocate of walking with God without money. We have built fires to keep ourselves warm while we wait for our idea of prosperity to fall down from heaven. We even believe that every Christian should be financially blessed without a care in the world and they should not move forward until they get their money taken care of by God. We believe that if the Christians that we know are not expecting a financial breakthrough, then something is seriously wrong with their doctrine. We do not expect to find them being content with what God has provided as they advance His kingdom with joy in the Holy Ghost.

From my own personal struggles, I realize the temptation that preachers face in having to choose between an earthly career or their heavenly calling. For God's servants to minimize their potential by holding onto this world's idea of success, is to fall short of Divine Protocol. In the end, they regret for settling for what has appeared to be prosperity. Though a career might be permissible for a season, eventually it is going to take all that is within you to major in the things of God. Take a job building tents somewhere so that you will not become entangled in the affairs of this life. Many Christians forfeit the joy of doing God's will for high salaries. Move when God says move, or else you will wonder why, for some unexplainable reason, everyone at your job does not like you anymore. God is going to get His man one way or the other! However, if you stubbornly insist on having it your way, God will move on and just wait for you on judgment day.

> ***No man that warreth entangleth himself with the affairs of [this] life; that he may please him who hath chosen him to be a soldier.***
> ***2Ti 2:4***

Because of a person's unwillingness to sacrifice their cares to the Lord, they inhibit themselves from beholding His heavenly order through an enlightened perspective. Does not the Holy Writ declare to us, *take no thought for your life, but seek ye first the kingdom of* God (Mt 6:25a, 33a)? How beautifully it assures us that His providential care, which is a part of His protocol, has directly seen to our needs already (v.33).

Oh, the depths and the riches of His work! You see, beloved, the mystery of sacrifice cannot readily be seen in the mere presentation of the Word itself. It is revealed as we partake of it. What we interpret as "giving up our rights", God views as an opportunity to reveal Himself to us. What we view as denying ourselves of a "deserved" career, God beholds our surrendering as a demonstration of a true sacrifice for His kingdom which shall not go unrewarded.

The obvious implication before us is that there is nothing that we can give up for Him and the gospel's sake that He will not reward up to 100 times over.

> ***And every one that hath forsaken house, or brethren, or sisters, or father, or mother, or wife, or children, or lands, for my name's sake, shall receive an hundredfold, and shall inherit everlasting life.*** **Mt 19:29**

Let it be readily understood that sacrifice is a painful experience and our Lord is well acquainted with it. Three times He prayed with such an earnest fervor for His cup to be removed, yet it was His Father's will that He partake of it. Therefore, He endured it (Mt26:36-44), and how blessed we are that He did.

As this mystery is unveiled, we come closer to understanding the power of God toward us when we sacrifice. The position of which Jesus Christ has been given was not free, yet through the sacrifice of Himself for the entire world, He gained an immeasurable return. He is hailed not only as Lord of all, but He also reaps the redemption of mankind being reconciled to Himself and thus to God.

Presenting your body, soul, and mind to God is a choice. That is why it is called a "living sacrifice". We must be placed in various situations in order to determine who we are going to serve; God or mammon. As we exercise ourselves in choosing God over anyone and anything else, named or unnamed, whether in heaven, hell, or on this earth, we are exercising ourselves toward understanding Divine Protocol to the same level of our sacrifice. The day that we cease from sacrificing is the day that we cease to understand God. All such living sacrifices shall receive a reward that has not been seen nor heard, neither has it entered into our hearts the things that God has prepared for those that love Him (1 Cor. 2:9). We shall live forever in His presence enjoying all of heaven and the mansions inside our Father's house throughout the universe and beyond.

Go On Unto Perfection

Therefore leaving the principles of the doctrine of Christ, let us go on unto perfection; not laying again the foundation of repentance from dead works, and of faith toward God,

> ***Of the doctrine of baptisms, and of laying on of hands, and of resurrection of the dead, and of eternal judgment. And this we will do if God permit.*** ***Heb. 6:1-3***

Once a vessel has been prepared for a voyage, all that remains is to cast off. Once the student has studied and gained credentials, the most fulfilling accomplishment at that time is to be found worthy to enter into higher heights of his or her chosen field of study.

When we, as children of the Most High God, are exercising our portion of faith by fulfilling the call of obedience and presenting ourselves as living sacrifices, then, "Bon Voyage" - it is time to go on unto perfection.

Once a person has an understanding of the foundational workings of Divine Protocol, namely, faith, obedience and sacrifice, there is a necessary process toward the actual exercising of this knowledge. Many people have a "head" knowledge of God and an understanding that they can verbally communicate. However, true Divine Protocol exceeds talk. The possessors of God's gifts are those who administer them.

> ***Then he which had received the one talent came and said, Lord, I knew that thou art an hard man, reaping where thou hast not sown, and gathering where thou hast not strawed: And I was afraid, and went and hid thy talent in the earth: lo, there thou hast that is thine. His lord answered and said unto him. Thou wicked and slothful servant, thou knewest that I reap where I sowed not, and gather where I have not strawed:***

Thou oughest therefore to have put my money to the exchangers, and then at my coming I should have received mine own with usury. Take therefore the talent from him, and give it unto him which hath ten talents. **Mt 25:24-28**

The individual who has a talent and refuses to go on unto perfection is labeled as a slothful and wicked servant. Such a person wanted to receive revelations, gifts and talents from the Lord while yet remaining dormant and unproductive. He attempted to justify his state with excuses based on fear of failure (v.25). In like manner, many Christians today are attempting to glory in the doctrine of Christ. Valuable time and energy is being spent on discussing Greek and Hebrew, speaking in tongues, water baptisms and the laying on of hands just to name a few. These are basically avenues by which God can work among us, but they are not the work of God. They are used to get the work of God's kingdom accomplished, not to become the focus in and of themselves. When a mechanic reaches for a set of pliers, does he just look at them and open and close them? Or does he place them around something to accomplish a specific task? We have a handle on the gifts and the principles of the doctrines of Christ, but we must place them around a tangible purpose of God and move forward in true spiritual labor.

One does not operate a lawn mower just by observing it. It is a piece of machinery by which we accomplish the "work" of cutting grass. When you purchased it, your grass was still standing tall, wasn't it? It was not until you cranked the lawnmower up and pushed it on the grass that your yard became a work of art. On the same token, you cannot accomplish the work of God by merely observing the principles by which His kingdom operates. Rather, you must operate them until you become the spiritual masterpiece that God has ordained you to be.

The reason why many are failing to attain an ultimate working knowledge of Divine Protocol is because there is a refusal to become experienced and sharpened through exercising these principles. Many shrink back from "taking the lawn mower out and cutting the grass", which in essence is taking the knowledge of God and performing what His knowledge has revealed. A great pleasure is derived among noninvolved Christians in just observing the things of God, while never really purposing to become useful or profitable for His kingdom.

 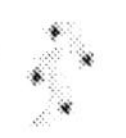

And cast ye out the unprofitable servant into outer darkness: there shall be weeping and gnashing of teeth. ***Mt 25:30***

There are many advertisements regarding seminars, conference and workshops, that are conducted nationwide. Some of them receive endorsements which attempt to expound upon a "new teaching" of possessing the land or beholding the glory of God like never before. Such propaganda has prompted a "sign seeking" spirit right in the midst of the Body of Christ. Emphasis has shifted from seeking God's Divine Protocol in regards to the gifts of the Spirit and the glory of God, to seeking what one can acquire by way of these attributes of God. This prevalent temptation to turn God's house of prayer into a den of thieves must be overcome through watchfulness and earnest prayer. While there are always those who are truly blessing the sheep of His pasture, we must be very discerning in regards to what we are going to and why we are going. Magazines and seminars are not the focus, for such avenues can be quite effective for the kingdom of God. Rather, it is the motives and intents of the heart which breeds spiritual idolatry.

The cry of concern which I am attempting to present to the people of God must be adhered to with all sincerity. Going on unto perfection does not consist of remaining on the observing dock of the principles of Christ, while refusing to exercise your faith to obey God through daily sacrifice. How else might you grow up and become the teachers that you ought to be by now (Heb. 5:12)? It is high time to be weaned from milk and to mature by partaking of the meat of the kingdom of God. God's meat is going on to perfection which is savored, not by observing or even discovering His Word, but rather in performing the observation and new discovery.

But, beloved, we are persuaded better things of you, and things that accompany salvation, though we thus speak. For God is not unrighteous to forget your work and labour of love, which ye have shewed toward his name, in that ye have ministered to the saints, and do minister. ***Heb. 6:9-10***

Can we understand that every aspect of Divine Protocol serves for one ultimate realization; a furthering of ones salvation within the divine purposes of God and to share this treasure with men?

We notice here in Hebrews that the things which accompany salvation consist of work and labor. The word "work" in the Greek means to "toil". Have we, the Body of Christ, effectively toiled in taking the principles of the doctrine of Christ to the world instead of to ourselves? What good is it to have on the armor of God, the helmet of salvation, the breastplate of righteousness, the sword of the Spirit, loins girded about with truth, and your feet shod with the preparation of the gospel of peace, if it is forsaken for the laying again of the foundation of repentance from dead works, and for heeding to the cares, pleasure and riches of this life?

As individuals, we have attempted to avoid the hard facts about the gospel of our Savior, Jesus Christ. The facts are that it demands that you no longer live for yourself, but that you surrender your all to the purpose of your Lord and Savior that others might be saved.

Those who behold the mystery of Divine Protocol also behold the mystery of true riches.

> ***Now if any man build upon this foundation gold, silver, precious stones, wood, hay, stubble; Every man's work shall be made manifest: for the day shall declare it, because it shall be revealed by fire; and the fire shall try every man's work of what sort it is. If any man's work abide which he hath built thereupon, he shall receive a reward. If any man's work shall be burned, he shall suffer loss: but he himself shall be saved; yet as by fire.***
>
> ***1 Co. 3:12-15***

Going on unto perfection means being a laborer together for God (v.9). It means being used to usher sinners into His kingdom, to stir up the Body of Christ to render pure services and worship unto God, while first and foremost growing more through an intimate relationship with Him. It is exemplified in those who were the sheep and not the goats; those who had "done it unto Him" not those who "did it not" (Mt 25:31-46), and the son who repented and went to work, not those who said, "Yes, Lord" but did nothing (Mt 21:28-32). It is also reflected in those who came to the wedding banquet when asked, not those who heard yet made light of it and instead, pursued their interests and concerns (Mt 7:21). Those who are doers of the law, not those who are merely hearers (Rom. 2:13). Those who are working their faith, not those who idly possess it. Those who are yielding themselves as instruments of righteousness unto God through faith and by grace, not those who are workers of iniquity in spite of grace (Rom. 6:13-16; Eph. 2:8-10). Those who fight the fight of faith unto the end, not those who start and fall away (1 Tim. 6:12; 2 Tim. 4:1).

Oh, how obvious and glorious are His ways revealed to those who truly desire to see! Shall we fight against God and even those who speak the truth? Certainly not. Let us humble ourselves unto the Lordship of Christ, and do that which He requires of us. Let us go on unto perfection, ceasing from childish ways that we may behold and comprehend the Divine Protocol of God. With all diligence, we shall partake of the very meat that our Lord partook of, for His meat was to do the will of Him that sent Him and to finish it (Jo 4:34). Through such surrendered lives, we will abound in our knowledge of God through an ever increasing revelation of God's Official Order that is Correct in the Dealings of His Kingdom.

Chapter 2

The Order of Divine Protocol

There is an order of man and an
order of God; Only one matters

In our course of labors for the kingdom of our Lord, we must, with a brightening awakening, be ever so careful of how we build upon this foundation of holiness. It is His desire to express through me, not only His revelation of Divine Protocol, but also His order of it. It is with this understanding that we shall seek His perspective for this issue and not the vanities of our own ideas and opinions.

The simplicity of order has complicated its application as well as the delegation of it. We easily behold the natural order of earthly things; i.e. what goes up must come down, A comes before B, and 2 before 3. Before you build a work with its many aspects, you must first "ginoskeo" or "knoweth" the foundation on which it shall be built.

Even so, there is a spiritual order to protocol which is given by His Spirit and not our minds. It is an order which first must be apprehended that Divine Protocol may be effective. To behold a portion of God's will is only effective if you likewise possess the knowledge of what to do with it.

Shall we acknowledge the spiritually immaturity which assail many of our churches and affirm the imminent demand for attention to this issue? It is to the benefit of our souls, and those we watch over, to understand the mystery of God's order, known as Divine Protocol.

We shall explore important aspects of Divine Protocol as it pertains to areas of our lives. Our families, jobs, ministries and church relationships are but a few areas which need vital attention.

Many ministers have falsely or presumptiously assumed that just because they have a revelation, graduated from seminary, wrote books, or conferred with this or that person, that they have a "right" to take their ministry and do what they esteem to be correct or just. But it is quite the contrary if we see through the mind of the Spirit. We should be desirous to discover, with stupendous clarity, the exact order that God has ordained for His revelation, His ministry and for all which He has given to go forth and bear fruit.

The true authenticity of a thing can be proven by its fruit. Both the true and false will indeed grow (Mt 13:26), however, growth alone does not reveal Divine Protocol. The fruit which is being produced will, without respect of persons, unveil the order by which one is building - that which is of men, or that which is of God.

And Jesus answering said unto him, Suffer it to be so now: for thus it becometh us to fulfil all righteousness. Then he suffered him. ***Jo 3:15***

We, as the Body of Christ, must arise to fulfilling all that God has required of us rather than attempting to avoid the unavoidable. That which God has required will not be exempt from His ever watchful eye. Besides this, it behooves us to readily accept His way, for it serves to build our lives as well as to ensure our labors. Those who seek to carry out the will of God apart from the way of God have yielded to the inclinations of "an evil heart of unbelief in departing from the living God" (Heb. 13: 12). The beauty of establishing the order of Divine Protocol is to experience God's unceasing provision of wisdom and power in all areas of our life. It is to humble ourselves and allow all righteousness to become a reality rather than a distant hope which is hindered by our unwillingness to empty our closet of frail excuses.

The apparent difficulty of allowing God's order of protocol to reign in our lives is readily understood. In this computerized, intellectualized and rationalized society, we are tempted to conform the things of God

into the image of this sinful and adulterous generation, rather than to be conformed into the image of Christ. Many times, it is seemingly effortless for us to receive from God great visions, but to respond to the visions in the way that He has ordained for their fulfillment invites offenses. The straight and narrow path fails to meet the requirements of what we can see and comprehend. It requires a road of suffering, trials and afflictions which we dare not expose ourselves to. This is the way of rich discipleship that mature laborers vitally need in order to understand the very essence of Divine Protocol. Until repentance is sought after regarding out last act of refusal to carry out God's order, we will only veer further and further away from the truth and the order of Divine Protocol. All such labor is vain and vexation of spirit.

Except the Lord build the house, they labor in vain that build it: except the Lord keep the city, the watchman waketh but in vain.
Psalms 127:1

Shall we be wise unto ourselves and heed to God's order lest we kindle His judgment? Let us diligently hearken to His will and way that we may live the abundant life that He has promised as we strive to comprehend this. "We ought to give the more earnest heed to the things which we have heard lest at any time we should let them slip" (Heb. 2:1).

As we pierce behind the veil of God's order, we take notice of the first order of things; the family. When our hearts and minds are open to God and we seek His order for Divine Protocol, we will experience the mystery of the Groom and His Bride which is founded and established within the confines of our homes.

The Spirit of the Lord is speaking to the Church, "Order, order! Order in My house!" And the first house He will be inspecting is yours.

Chapter 3

Your Foundation is Your Family

The person who does not build
up their home, the same has torn it down.

And if a house be divided against itself, that house cannot stand.
Mark 3:25

t is amazingly difficult to express the love that God has toward the family. The difficult aspect esteems from a warped value system which has unawaringly invaded the dwelling places of God's children, and this while men slept (Mt 13:25). The church has attempted to grow in all wisdom and spiritual understanding in regards to the protocol of our families while touching, tasting and handling the wisdom of this world which are all destined to perish with use. Through allowing the spirit of the world via television, movies, periodicals and now the internet to invade our minds and spirits, Christians are destroying the very thing that they are attempting to build up through the Spirit of the Lord; the family unit.

If you have purposed to have the life, ministry, or any other aspect of what God has purposed for you, it must first be built on the strength of your family whose foundation is Christ and builder is God. If it starts anywhere else, it will last momentarily, and collapse upon the shifting sands of self and the adversities that life will bring. By the mercy of God, some fruit may be borne, but it will lack the fullness of what it could have been. Even if you are single in the natural, you yet possess a family. This fact is proven by the presence of God your Father, Jesus your Savior and the Holy Ghost your Comforter. For that matter, He dwells in all believer's hearts and homes and we must allow His presence to have precedence in the confines of our tents as well as our temples, that His Official Order that is Correct in the Dealings of His

Kingdom might precede further than the pages of our Bibles and the walls of our churches.

THE MYSTERY OF CHRIST AND THE CHURCH - REVEALED IN THE FAMILY

This is a great mystery: but I speak concerning Christ and the church. ***Eph. 5:32***

How marvelous is this revelation to the sons of God, that He would grant to those that are made a little lower than the angels to express to one another the love that He has toward us. Does not this constitute a true order of Divine Protocol? A resounding "Yes!"

As the blood of bulls and goats and the priesthood of the old covenant were a shadow of His priesthood to come, our marriages today constitute a holy union by which He reveals His second coming. This profound relationship between Himself and His Bride was made possible by His death and resurrection. It is revealed through the union of husband and wife today in the New Testament and serves as a shadow of that which is to come - the presentation of His glorious Church to Himself (v.27).

This sobering truth should awaken us the more to the esteeming riches that Divine Protocol presents. Shall we, with complete faith and obedience in going on to perfection, endeavor in His order that such riches might become ours?

This beautiful description of marriage resounds a message to husbands and wives that can breed surpassing love, peace, harmony and yes, protocol in every aspect of their lives. This order of God is the only order that will birth such attributes into a reality, not only between the man and woman, but also between Christ and the Church.

No other unison has ever been given to describe Christ and the Church. This profound truth should alert us to the intimate love that Christ has for us. We are to have this same affection toward one another. Such implication of order reveals the seriousness of this tender relationship. The very nature of its demands of both husband and wife are the same conditions that Christ demands of His Church - faith and obedience.

Is it any wonder that over 51% of marriages end in divorce? And how many of the remaining percentage are truly abounding in their marriages? This figure is not only true for the world, but also for the Church! Obviously, we have not been instructed in the way of Ephesians chapter 5 or we simply refuse to submit and conform to God's ways.

The women are instructed to submit to their husbands and husbands are admonished to love their wives. However, the world screams, "Woman, rebel against the man, and man love your own self". This same rebellion has found its way amongst those in the Church through the religion and traditions of men which have ignored the presence of rebellion, and instead, have fashioned it as an accepted way of Christian living.

Instead of accepting and submitting to the Word of God as pure children, institutions have been the norm which attempt to deal with spiritual issues via psychological means that plague the families who belong to God. Prayer is a beginning, but then the intellect of man takes over. I have often heard that the Word of God is good, but what is needed as well is a psychological profile to determine an individual's capabilities. We readily boast in the power of God, however, a more practical and reasonable approach is essential. Such a statement serves to reveal ones lack of faith and shallow relationship with the Lord if there was any to begin with.

Over the years, the Church has drifted away from trusting in the all sufficiency of their Father. Even as the children Israel grew weary of the ways of the Lord and His requirements time and time again, the Church has allowed an apostate attitude to overshadow it, and this through their unbelief.

Establishing protocol in the Church means establishing protocol in our marriages. If all the worship, knowledge and love that is expressed to others in our churches is not first being expressed to our spouse, then all such worship is vain and out of order. It is without true spiritual weight or conviction and those who do so are hypocrites.

Wives, submit yourselves unto your own husbands, as unto the Lord. ***Eph. 5:22***

Let us behold the blessed position that the wife has been given. She is instructed three times to submit herself to her husband as unto the Lord (v. 22,24,33). The wife is to be to her husband as the Church is to Christ. We are admonished to submit under the hand of God that He may lift us up in due time. What Christian has submitted to Christ in vain? None, no not one! Likewise, there is not a wife who could submit to her husband in vain if she does so as unto the Lord.

When a woman brings all of her energies into harmony with the protocol of God, she releases a powerful move of the Spirit of God within her home. An unselfish, submissive woman has the insight to know that God works through her to build His kingdom within her marriage. She has been given her part to fulfill which is no small matter.

Younger women who have husbands must realize that they can have either a positive or negative impact on them. The happiest young wives are not those who are demanding respect and attention, but rather those who are giving unto their husbands without eye service as unto the Lord, knowing that God will bless them.

It is imperative that we see through the eyes of the Spirit in order to understand such treasures of truth, lest through our own opinions of the flesh, we forfeit such profound insight.

I believe that there is a mystery to submission that the Body of Christ has failed to search for with deliberate fasting and prayer. We have been too hasty in comprehending this unique state with our own minds and wisdom which is foolishness in the sight of God. As a result, we are paralyzed from seeing through the eyes of our spirit.

Submission is a statement of trust, not a reaction of fear. Submission exemplifies character and integrity which breeds true strength. It is not to be confused with control or manipulation. This godly attribute belongs to those who are acquainted with liberty and freedom, not unbelievers who are held in bondage to sins and rebellion.

As believers, we can only obtain this grace when we submit to and place our trust in Christ. Even so, Christ could only justify us when He submitted Himself to His Father, even to the death of the cross. The whole working of submission is love! Christ gave Himself for us, that we would give ourselves for Him (2 Cor. 5:15). Salvation is a result of those who have given up their life that they might find it. Damnation will be experienced by those who refused to receive the Bread of Life. They chose rebellion rather than submission.

God, creative beyond expression, has not only blessed us inwardly with such a hope, but this working of His Spirit flows out of our lives into the world and the protocol of this truth finds itself being expressed to those closest to us - our husbands and wives.

Wives, you have been exalted to receive the love of God from your husband, even as the Church receives its love from Christ. You have been called of God to be washed, to be built up, adorned and loved, that you may be presented holy and without blemish before Him. Be still and let your husband be Christ to you, even as he allows Christ to be Lord to him.

HUSBANDS

Husbands, love your wives, even as Christ also loved the church, and gave himself for it. ***Eph.5:25***

Husbands, love your wives. This "love" in the Greek means "a direction of the will that expresses compassion". There is not any husband who can share the love of Christ with anyone else if he does not first share it with his own wife. Protocol!! If he prophesies, speaks with tongues of men and angels while giving his body to be burned to the poor, but has not first loved his wife, this man's labor has been to no avail. Such a man will stand in the presence of God and say, "Lord, look at what I accomplished", and God will reply, "These things will be considered and rewarded based on My protocol which first begins at home. Now tell Me about the love that you gave your wife".

As men, we could not be given a higher honor than to reveal the love of Christ to the world, and this first to our wives. Whether one is an apostle or an usher, God's Official Order that is Correct in the Dealings of His Kingdom begins with the bride, which is your wife, even as we are Christ's Bride.

The greatest speech that our Groom ever gave was "not mine will but thine will be done". The greatest demonstration of love that He ever displayed was laying down His life for the world. Is not this the gospel message that we as men and husbands uphold to be declared as the only Way, the only Truth and the only Life? Our answer to this will not be found in our lips, but in the fruit of our labors - our wives.

This love must be equated with Christ's love, not the world's. I have observed men in my generation attempt to love their wives with mere merchandise. They have built their marriage on the elusive appearances of success rather than the foundations of Christ. Spiritual pride, puffed up notions, and a total misconception of life has caused men to error in their thinking and values.

When we take a look at our men in the church, we see many of the same struggles. The only difference is that we know the solution, yet we are constantly seesawing between the two. As a man of God, you have to take action and act on the truth that you know. Passivity and simply assuming that the issues regarding your marriage will just take care of themselves reveals a man who is believing a lie and is fearful to simply face the truth. The kingdom of heaven suffers violence and you must be violent against the world, the devil and your flesh to capture the glory that God wants you to know as you pursue His Divine Order.

This fact of men contending against these forces which seek to destroy this revelation of Christ and the church is evident as we see the escalating rate of divorce within the confines of the Body of Christ. There are obvious insecurities among men in the church and the inability of many to instruct their wives in the wisdom and counsel of the Lord is growing to gross proportions that can no longer be hid. A great outpouring of God's mercy and conviction needs to fall upon the heads of our homes for a revival in our marriages to take place.

With sober minds and hearts, order must be established among the husbands in the Church. The sad reality of this plight is twofold. First, many of our churches are not teaching the young men with the authority of the scriptures supported with examples of real living from our leaders. Of course, this is not to say that all our leaders are not living what they preach. However, the reality of trouble in the ranks of leadership is real and it cannot be ignored any longer. This is having a profound effect upon the younger generation because they are the fruit of leadership's labors. One area of grave neglect in our churches is that real devoted time is not spent with men today. A great majority of leaders have distanced themselves from the flock to a place to where there is no true bonding. Our figures in positions of authority are seen more as lords and rulers that cannot be touched. While indeed God has appointed deacons and elders to help carry the weight that accompanies the needs of congregation, it is yet the head of that congregation which will set the tone of concern revealed in genuine mentoring for the young man. Due to this lack in leadership, many young men are ignorant of essential knowledge that must be imparted to them (Rom. 1:11).

Jesus even confronted the lawyers for deliberately leaving their disciples in the dark and to ensure they stayed there, took away the keys of knowledge. Those who appeared to show any form of determination were hindered from entering in. The system is alive and well today - just open your eyes.

> ***Woe unto you, lawyers! for ye have taken away the key of knowledge: ye entered not in yourselves, and them that were entering in ye hindered.*** ***Lu 11:52***

Second, the husbands themselves have not sought direction beyond that of men. They have not inquired of the Lord to be recipients of the wisdom which cometh from above without the aid of men. There is a saying that my father obtained from his mother (which was also in a popular song). It said, "Mama might have, Papa might have, but God bless the child that has its own". How true this is especially when it comes to the spiritual realities of life. While those who have a responsibility to their generation are, for one reason or another, not fulfilling it, the recipient is yet accountable to God for what they do as well as what they should have done. Blaming another man for the results of your marriage is not the method of God's kingdom. The younger man will have to endure some unnecessary hardship because the previous generation did not fulfill its role, yet every marriage has been given God's provisionary abilities to succeed through Christ Jesus regardless of the past. Though there is trouble in the land, there are always a remnant that have not bowed the knee. You simply must find them. You have the ultimate responsibility of taking care of your wife and presenting her clean before the Lord.

That he might sanctify and cleanse it with the washing of water by the word. ***Eph. 5:26***

Loving your wife does not consist of just taking her to church to hear the Word of God. Loving your wife means washing her with the Word yourself. You must not leave the intimate responsibility of sanctifying and cleansing her to another man. This purifying is a work of God through you to your wife, and the order of it begins with you - the husband.

Dare we try to cleanse our wives and we ourselves are found spotted? As Christ builds us up, the building of our wives will follow suit. Those who attempt to instruct their wives with the best of intentions, but are yet void of the Word of God in their own being, will indeed have the words but not the Spirit. This will only serve to frustrate our wives due to the lack of Divine Protocol and the submission to it in our lives.

Husbands, our goal is to present our wives spotless, blameless and without wrinkle or blemish unto the Lord. If we apply ourselves first and foremost to our wives, the fruit will indeed flourish. Deliberate attention and quality time is required to present our wives perfect unto the Lord. I would rather labor all of my life at building my wife into a spiritual house, than to execute energy on a congregation, seminary degree, mission field, or any such thing that would be void of fruit because my wife was left undone. It is not that all of ones life is needed to build their wife up, yet the issue of seeing to your wife is the most important one as far as God is concerned.

Husbands, who through patience and gentleness labor to give their wives the attention and spiritual insight necessary to build them up, are constructing a foundation for their marriage that will stand the testing storms that will come. Your wife will be your greatest witness for you or against you. She knows who you really are despite your elusive preaching and insightful knowledge. The gospel that she knows about is the one that her husband lives. God esteems the order of husbands to the wife so highly that, if left undone, even their prayers will go unanswered.

> ***Likewise, ye husbands, dwell with them according to knowledge, giving honour unto the wife, as the weaker vessel, and as being heirs together of the grace of life; that your prayers be not hindered.*** ***1 Pet. 3:7***

It is important for both husband and wife to realize that this love has nothing to do with the desires of the flesh but rather, the desire of the Spirit. Husbands who seek to please the carnal nature have never pleased their wives despite what it looks like. Wives who demand that their husbands emphasize their outward apparel are harboring motives that are impure, self centered and a stench to the Lord. As men and women of God, we must abstain from fleshly lusts which war against our souls (1 Pet. 2:11). Our affections must be on things above, not on things of the earth, for we are dead to sin, and our lives are hid with Christ in God (Col. 3:3). Therefore, we must mortify all such deeds that would hinder our marriages from experiencing relevant truth in our daily lives. We must put off the old husband and wife and put on the new husband and wife which are renewed in the knowledge of God's kingdom order (Col. 3:1-3,5,9,10).

> ***Nevertheless let every one of you in particular so love his wife even as himself; and the wife see that she reverence her husband.*** ***Eph. 5:33***

Without this order in our lives, we have no order. The Word of God will never pass away, and neither will His order. Regardless of what plans we have developed to carry out for God, if His plan for our spouses have been forsaken, then such plans are none of His. Those plans that are from the Lord will be fulfilled in accordance with His order. Taking the attitude that "God will work it out" is an attempt to cast off a burden that you must simply face until victory comes. I do understand that those marriages that are seemingly impossible (though not with God), have to be confronted and assessed on an individual basis. It is not my intent to apply this rule to every circumstance.

God loves your marriage. It is so special to Him that you would not believe it if He told you! He has established this holy sacrament after His own counsel, and it will only prosper and grow by His counsel. You will see just where this divine order will take you as you fulfill its call in your number one ministry - your marriage.

CHILDREN

Simply put, the order of children in this country is out of control. A large portion of Christians have literally dumped their responsibility from God into the laps of other people from the school teacher to teach them to the daycare to care for them. God's precious children have been sent to the basements of our churches to learn God's Word because many parents have not taught them. We rush them off to school to perhaps "gain a little peace and quiet" from the demands that are placed before us, while all the time not realizing the demoralizing impact that society places on them day after day.

Children are no longer disciplined as the Lord would have them to be. Many parents satisfy them at their slightest whim hoping to win their cooperation. Such unscriptual and weak tactics are producing unproductive, insecure and rebellious offspring that eventually will fail to make any contribution to God's kingdom in their generation.

The Phosophy of this world, namely, "they are only children" must be ostracized from the minds of believers that they may receive the truth of the matter from God's Word. They are much more than "children" in the sense of the word in which it is used. It denotes the same humanistic spirit as "after all, we're only human". Though these statements appear to be true, they are ill attempts to avoid the demands of protocol from God. Repentance is necessary that restoration may be experienced.

 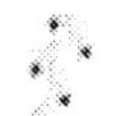

The main reason for such deterioration amid our children is due to the erosion among ourselves as parents who claim to honor the Lord. Not knowing the purpose for children awakens us to the fact that many parents are not aware of God's purpose for themselves. Whatever is lacking in children is usually lacking in their parents. As well, to the attributes that are vibrant and strong in the parents will undoubtedly surface in that child. The truth must no longer be ignored or belittled by a spirit of condonement that accepts vain ideas of Phosophy which are nothing more than tickets of unacceptable excuses.

The Wicked Norm

As the Body of Christ frantically attempts to get godly reins on this troublesome plight of its children, we must first cast out the "wicked norm" which has altered our thinking and hindered God's protocol.

This wicked norm has made the wrong appear to be right, and the right appear to be wrong. The Church has abandoned the high standards of God for the man made standards of this world. As a result, we base the rearing of our children on a wicked norm. While our children should be scholastically minded throughout certain intervals as youths, many are considered "normal" as TV junkies based on the position of the world. While God's perspective is to have productive children in our homes, the Church will quickly label lazy, inconsiderate and disrespectful youth as simply "going through a phase". God grants us power over the spirits that attempt to plague our children, but we refuse it and make room for strongholds that come through the channels of humanism, wrapped in a wisdom that is simply foolishness to God.

Until this "wicked norm" is rooted out from our thinking and our minds renewed with the order which is correct in the dealings of His kingdom, many will behold their own children captive to this evil world's rebellious spirit, and may experience betrayal by them as well.

> ***And the brother shall deliver up the brother to death, and the father the child: and the children shall rise up against their parents, and cause them to be put to death.*** **Mt 10:21**

While the Church has attempted to give their children a happy life by satisfying their self orientated desires through complying with the dictates of this world, the protocol of God has been forsaken.

Although we wholeheartedly desire that our children identify with God and receive a clear understanding of His kingdom, there remains a part of us that wants them to identify with the pleasures of this life and world. Are we to believe that God's standard for our children is any less for them than for us? Because they possess what appears to be an incapability to harm or receive harm, are they exempt from restraints or limitations? The adopted Phosophy from the world, "they're only children" (which has become a tradition to the Body of Christ), is the leaven which has caused us to no longer watch and pray, therefore leavening the potential of the seed of man's loins and the fruit of the woman's womb.

We must seek for God's standpoint which, without question, is the only standpoint that will prevail. It is this perspective that offers wisdom and insight to meet the needs of our children coupled with knowledge to effectively handle those needs correctly. In the present state of our society, those whom prevail over this surmounting rise of rebellion will be those who have sought and yielded to the standard of God. Only then will your home experience the protocol of God and your children bear the fruit of righteousness in their lives.

Too often, this has been a hope that is expected only when a child has gone astray. The Bible promises us that they do not have to experience this (Prov. 22:6). We must ask ourselves if we are in fact training them up in the Divine Protocol of God.

It is unfortunate that families must be divided during church service. Many of our children are so undisciplined that they have to be sent to children's church. The reason why sugar laden punch, cookies, videos and an occasional bible study are the norm is because our children are addicted to junk. Simply stated, they would really loose control if they did not have a junk food fix. Entertainment, in an effort to

control, is the method chosen to handle children who have not been trained in the ways of God.

> ***Train up a child in the way he should go: and when he is old, he will not depart from it.*** **Pro 22:6**

As fathers, we are to "train up" our children. The word "train" denotes a most definite learning. We interpret it to mean saying "no" four or five times or discuss the issue with our children for their approval. We play mind games and make promises to solicit their cooperation. This is definitely training - the children are training the parents!

The word "train" in the Hebrew is "chanak". It means "to imitate or discipline or to dedicate". This signifies the idea of a clear, concise objective in the mind of the trainer. There is a specific way in which he HAS determined his child will go. There are no gray areas or opinions about it and thus, he is resolute to train his seed "in the way he should go", not in the way that he wants to go, or even the way you or others want them to go.

That "way" varies from child to child in terms of specific purposes which God has ordained for their life. What is clearly understood for all children, however, is the way of obedience. We must train them in the way that God has made them to be in their personality and their gifting. We must not misinterpret this to mean for us to determine what our child will do, but rather cause our children to become aware of who they are and what God has purposed for them to be. It is this objective that we are to have in mind when we are training them for the glory of God.

Every mother "feels" what is right in her heart. There is a saying in the world which claims that since your own mother wiped your rear and can still smell milk on your breath, she supposingly knows what is best for your child. Everyone wants their approach to be the way your child should go. You must discern the correct approach which is revealed by having a relevant relationship with God through His Son Jesus Christ, while adhering to the specifics of His divine order.

These are some of the reasons why the church has produced homosexuals rather than heroes of the faith, wimps instead of warriors and cowards rather than conquerors. The father's role is to train up the child while the mother reinforces it. Those mothers who are without a husband can still allow a man of God to become a father figure for their child or children by laying down the rules with authority. The mother will then reiterate the rules when necessary.

Fathers, you must understand that your sons and daughters are more important to God than your job, your ministry and your vision. In fact, any true ministry or vision from God will include not just you, but especially your seed and their seed. God is after generations. God was not interested in Abraham for Abraham's sake alone. He was interested in Abraham for Christ. He needed a man who would think about others after he was gone and not just about himself while he was here on earth.

The very reason that God could reveal secrets to Abraham was that He knew Abraham would raise up his children in obedience to God's decrees and not withhold his only son from God.

> ***And the LORD said, Shall I hide from Abraham that thing which I do; Seeing that Abraham shall surely become a great and mighty nation and all the nations of the earth shall be blessed in him? For I know him, that he will command his children and his household after him, and they shall keep the way of the LORD, to do justice and judgment; that the LORD may bring upon Abraham that which he hath spoken of him. Gen. 18:17-19***

God knows what we will do with His children by what we do with ours. As fathers, we must not confuse or mix the standards of this world with the standards of God's kingdom. If one who has denied the faith by not providing food and shelter is worse than an infidel, tell me then, what is the state of a believer who does not provide the things of God to his family?

In order for God to obtain the fullness of His will from you, you must transfer yourself into your children that they may continue to express the glory of God in the earth. It is not possible in your lifetime for God to accomplish the fullness of His purpose in you. God is interested legacies and generations. What you are doing in your children today, you are doing in their children tomorrow.

Your training is a statement of fact to God and the devil. It proceeds past mere words. Your confession places you in a position to act, for it is faith without works which is dead, not faith without words. When our fathers focus on their children and see them as God does, they will behold an eternal soul whose destination depends on their ability to follow God's Official Order that is Correct in the Dealings of His Kingdom.

PIERCING THROUGH

Once we have pierced through the many interpretations of man's opinions in training our children, we must yet strive to grasp the mystery of this truth for ourselves. This is not a mystery solely in the kingdom of God, but one that is only revealed to those who possess the good ground that is necessary to understand it. Those who see the reward of this powerful scripture consists of hearts who have wholly accepted it.

The excuses which serve to take away the promise of our children not straying is easily believed by the hearts of those who have not fully accepted what the Word says about the rearing of godly children. What God has spoken, He has proven! His promises are His assurances that if we train up the child, He will see to it that they will not depart. The obvious implication is if they do depart, they were never really trained by the authority of God in the home. Herein lies the acid test of which many parents have failed, yet God's grace enables us as parents to experience beauty for ashes at the mercy that God displays when He redeems the time and grants grace for our children that they nor we deserve. When we confess our faults before the Lord, He then can make all things work together for the good. If we yet insist that we are not wrong, the working of God's good will not manifest.

There must be a readiness among us all to accept the fact that raising a child is an intensive work that does not last very long. It should not be viewed as a passive option void of struggle and conflict. To "train up" in the Hebrew means "to imitate, to teach, to dedicate, to consecrate, to inaugurate." This term occurs only five times in the entire Old Testament. It denotes an order of protocol that is of the highest and therefore, to behold its reality demands a depth of sacrifice that much of the Body of Christ has not been willing to give. Many of our Sunday school programs are conducted like miniature amusement parks with more emphasis on pleasure than in the Word of God. Sadly, this vital hour of every week is the only time that a large majority of children have an opportunity to hear the Word of God which is able to save their souls.

How many studies are necessary for us to realize that true training begins at home, not with the child, but with the parents? For too long, we have underestimated the intelligence of our babies and toddlers and continue to do so. Thus, when they emerge one morning as young adults, regardless of what we have preached, what rules we have "laid down", or how harsh our punishments have been (or for that matter how lenient), they will most certainly reflect us in attitude, in spirit and in deed.

To experience God's Official Order that is Correct in the Dealings of His Kingdom as it pertains to our children, His order must first be established in us. We must cease from the deception that we can sow one thing in our children while sowing another in ourselves. It has never been the words that children have responded to. Rather, it has been the deeds of their parents which have made the most impressionable impact on their lives. Our children will walk our walk, not our talk. Scripture boldly testifies to this truth:

> ***And he did evil in the sight of the Lord, and walked in the way of his father, and in the way of his mother, and in the way of Jeroboam the son of Nebat, who made Israel to sin.***
>
> ***1 Kings 22:52***

The Body of Christ must come to grips with the truth that our children manifest our true character, even as God's children manifest His true character - obedience! As we are "working out our salvation" as God's children, they are working out theirs as our children. Through this process, the foundation of obedience for the parent and then the child never changes. Therefore, the standard of Divine Protocol brings the harmony of an obedient family unit.

They Shall Walk Our Walk

And the Lord was with Jehoshaphat, because he walked in the first ways of his father David, and sought not unto Baalam.
2 Chron. 17:3

We have all heard a similar saying of "I don't care how you live before your children. When they get older, they will still do as they please". This is an unfortunate perception to have. It is one of instability and double mindedness. It also denotes an attitude of unbelief in the order that God has established in His kingdom. Not only is it worldly and unscriptual, but it is derived from a demonic source which stifles the parent from training their child in the way they should go. God has decreed that when they are old they will not depart from it. In contrast, it is the exact opposite of God's Divine Protocol, yet will certainly be the experience of those who believe it. The way that we walk before our children is a powerful exhibition of obedience, character and love. Even though it may seem subtle or appear to go unnoticed, it is the most powerful act of training that we will ever give our children. It will either affirm what we have spoken to be true, or it will deny our words the weight or credibility necessary to convict our children that we have spoken truth. Regardless of how challenging our own walk might be, as our children behold our sincere hearts and pure communion with the Lord, it is ever building in them an awareness of God and of His protocol.

As parents, we must allow the Lord to instruct our children through us. Even as we allow Him to "train us up", we likewise must yield our minds and wills that He may impart to us specific direction in the rearing of our children. We have failed to realize that training does not consist of yelling "yes" to this and "no" to that, while justifying our actions with common phrases such as, "because I said so", or "as long as you live under my roof you will abide by my rules". There are many other such quotes that have found their way into Christian homes and have resided for generations among us that must be rooted out of our minds.

It is unreasonable, as well as unscriptual, to expect change in our offspring when there has not been any change in whom they have sprung from! It behooves us to grasp the importance of a demonstrative life which impacts the minds of our child to conform to the life of God that they see in us. Without demonstration, our oration will have no illustration. This only brings frustration in the hearts of our children who are trying to visualize what we are talking about. How frustrating it would be to hear a movie and not see it, then be expected to explain what you did not see.

As we observe the last days readily advancing upon us, it is imperative that we, the Church, obtain Divine Protocol in our hearts and minds toward the souls that He has entrusted to us - the souls which take on our flesh and blood. Those whom He has blessed with the faces of our faces and smiles of our smiles. Most certainly, perilous times await those who will not submit to God's Official Order that is Correct in the Dealings of His Kingdom. It is far from the will of God for the structure of our children's characteristics to be diminished to the likes of the beggarly elements of this world. However, God will not do for us that which He demands we do for ourselves. Nor would He place any demands on us that He has not supplied the ability to accomplish and fulfill.

Shall we do away with our fleshly excuses and slothful minds and instead, renew our zeal to apprehend what Christ has granted us to experience, namely, authority and order in all the affairs of our children's lives? We have the ability to choose life or death.

As the consummation of our salvation draws nearer than when we first believed, we must purge, eradicate, ostracize and violently arrest every high thing that exalts itself against the knowledge of God. This is especially imperative regarding the demoralizing effect of TV which is piped into homes in the form of demonic cartoons, anti-family sitcoms and diets which offer no value toward character. These deceptions must be exposed and arrested. Let us remind ourselves that we must act in order to "bring into captivity every thought to the obedience of Christ,

and have a readiness to revenge all disobedience when your obedience is fulfilled" (2 Cor. 10:5,6). God awaits our move. What we sow He shall ensure that we reap, for God will not be mocked.

The Body of Christ will triumph in the end and our children will do great exploits beyond our comprehension. I pray that both your sons and my sons, your daughters as well as my daughters are walking side by side declaring the wonders of God to a dying world. This is divine vision, attainable only through Divine Protocol.

Relatives

Without an understanding of God's order with respect to those who are related to us by blood or marriage, we will undoubtedly become the victims of a continual whirlwind of besetting circumstances and setbacks. Americans have developed a distorted view of the purpose for relatives. I shall attempt, with all simplicity, to communicate a few essentials to the end that some might be established.

Without respect of persons, Jesus declared the protocol on this issue without reservation. It was a statement made after Israel as a nation rejected the Messiah as Lord and King. To make clear that their trust in their natural heritage meant nothing in the sight of God, (rather it was His choosing of them that made them the elect of the earth as a nation), Jesus used His own relationship with His family to reveal Divine Protocol in the sight of God as it pertains to relatives. We must not view this with exceptions toward anyone. Dare we bring anyone into comparison with the honor and respect that is due our Father in heaven?

> ***While he yet talked to the people, behold, his mother and his brethren stood without, desiring to speak with him. Then one said unto him, Behold, thy mother and thy brethren stand without, desiring to speak with thee. But he answered and said unto him that told him, Who is my mother? and who are my brethren? And he stretched forth his hand toward his disciples, and said, Behold my mother and my brethren! For whosoever shall do the will of my Father which is in heaven, the same is my brother, and sister, and mother.*** **Mt 12:46-50**

It is clear that Christ was not ignoring the existence of relationship among relatives, but rather placing them in order. We are admonished throughout the scriptures to honor our father and mother and to love and raise our children. It is within the scope of God's kingdom order that all relatives, whether brother, sister, mother, father, son, daughter, husband, wife and any others, are not manipulating, dictating, or instigating the rule over ones spirit which belongs solely to the Father. Only God, and that through His Son Jesus, can bring life and order in every facet of our existence regardless of who are family purports to be.

To their own detriment, many have assumed their salvation, identity and authority based on their natural descent rather than on the protocol of God's kingdom. Such ideas truly reveal the existence of deception and rebellion of the human heart. Let us be quick to remind ourselves that He is Lord of all and refuses to allow or disallow any of His workings in the earth to be subject to those known as relatives.

How many divine callings have been ignored, ministries forsaken, dreams unfulfilled and God given abilities found dormant due to a person who interferes through the means of relationships to oppose God's will for ones life. Instead, they see better to force their own will upon God's property. The question of who you yield to should be based on whose blood was shed for you, rather than whose natural blood flows through you. Besides, when you died, you were divorced from all that is contrary to God, to be married to all that is of God (Rom 7:4).

The ancestral ties of some families can indeed be very domineering to the extent that many people are void of their own wills to choose their individual lot in life. In order for God's children to move in the protocol of His kingdom, this unscriptual, as well as unspiritual concept, must be arrested, and God's child set free!

But as many as received him, to them gave he power to become the sons of God, even to them that believe on his name:

Which were born, not of blood, nor of the will of the flesh, nor of the will of man, but of God. ***Jo 1:12-13***

The children of God must no longer identify themselves as anyone except a child of God. Their identity and allegiance is, from beginning to end, to God. With such an understanding, one cannot be swayed by the control of natural yokes. God's Offical Order That is Correct in the Dealings of His Kingdom is not partial toward relatives. If we are called to lose our own lives, how can we be justified in disobeying God by making exceptions for our relatives? If Jesus did not make one for His own mother, what right do we have in making one for ours?

American Christians have yet to realize the magnitude of service that we are called to. We are prone to reconsider God's will over issues that would have received the death sentence had we lived under the Old Testament Law, which was outside the dispensation of grace. We will do ourselves much harm if we refuse to submit ourselves under the hand of God and instead, do so under the hand of our spouse, mother, father, child or even minister. Satan will use any means necessary to keep you from flowing in divine order. Yes, he will most certainly use those closest to you.

> ***Think not that I am come to send peace on earth: I came not to send peace, but a sword. For I am come to send a man at variance against his father, and the daughter against her mother, and the daughter in law against her mother in law. And a man's foes shall be they of his own household. He that loveth father or mother more than me is not worthy of me: and he that loveth son or daughter more than me is not worthy of me.*** **Mt 10:34-37**

Despite the disappointments that befall us in the natural conflict of our families, it is God's appointment to join us with His family. One will never give up a person for the Lord and not be restored many times over (Luke 18:29-30).

While many of us have experienced the cross of denying loved ones for the sake of the Gospel, others have experienced just the opposite - God knitting families together. My emphasis is to exhort the children of God to keep their spirits under the rule of the Holy Spirit, not under the control of another spirit be it human or spiritual (angel or demon). The distance we should keep from loved ones is reflected in the same distance that our spirits keep from each other. In other words, though we fellowship and worship together as one body, our spirits are not one with each other, but one with Him. Through Him, we are one and have fellowship with one another. We are never independent of His joining us together, for in Him all things are unified and enabled to produce fruit that edifies the Body in and for love.

> ***But speaking the truth in love, may grow up into him in all things, which is the head, [even] Christ: From whom the whole body fitly joined together and compacted by that which every joint supplieth, according to the effectual working in the measure of every part, maketh increase of the body unto the edifying of itself in love.*** ***Eph 4:15-16***

The human man is always attempting to build a tower above God's rightful place to rule over him. Satan is directly responsible for infusing the mind of man with such tantalizing hopes of self realization. He webs his victim in vices of deceit through any available channel. When he finds it difficult to use money, fame, or pleasure, he will pull out the "relative card" and play it until he realizes that as far as you are concerned, your relatives are those who hear the Word of God and do it! In conclusion, our relatives, whether in or out of peace, must be kept outside the sphere of God's rightful place as Lord and Ruler of your every move. Whatever we are commissioned to fulfil for our Lord will indeed be questioned by somebody. If we are not free from the ties of the family, and this by Divine Protocol, we stand to lose those things which we have wrought.

> ***Look to yourselves, that we lose not those things which we have wrought, but that we receive a full reward.*** ***2 Jo 8***

On Being Single

To believe that your life is incomplete without a spouse exhibits a lack of communion with the Father in the depths of your spiritual being. Looking for a spouse denotes ones lack of involvement with God's will for their lives. Marriages that originate due to sexual appetites that are burning hot will discover that in the end it would have been better to simply cool down.

Most would be surprised to discover that it is not the will of God which determines if you marry, or even who you marry. It all rests with that person's will. While the scripture does testify that "every man hath his proper gift of God, one after this manner, and another after that" (1 Cor. 7:7), it also clarifies this in a much clearer way.

For there are some eunuchs, which were so born from their mother's womb: and there are some eunuchs, which were made eunuchs of men: and there be eunuchs, which have made themselves eunuchs for the kingdom of heaven's sake. He that is able to receive it, let him receive it. ***Mt 19:12***

Sovereignly, God knows if you will marry and if it is best for you to marry. Yet it will be your decision to tie the knot, not God. He will simply join you to whom you have chosen to be joined to. God even knows who is best for us in our marriage, yet that does not mean that we know. The danger here is that we read things into our lives about God that are not true about us in actual attainment. If you have not developed your spirit to the degree of His leading, though His will is clear in His mind does not mean that it is clear in your mind. Those who do not have this leading must depend solely upon their emotions to guide them in crucial decisions to remain single or become married.

There are no secret formulas to determine if or who you should marry. The Word of God gives us our choices and also declares that remaining single is better.

So then he that giveth her in marriage doeth well; but he that giveth her not in marriage doeth better. ***1 Co. 7:38***

Simply because you marry does not guarantee success. This type of thinking cannot be found in scripture. The protocol necessary for it to be successful is found throughout the Word of God. Guarantees are provided on everything in our society from pizza to computers. Therefore, we subconsciously expect a guarantee in the areas of non-material things such as marriage, family and daily life. Food and electronics can be replaced but an original marriage, a thriving family and an overcoming life cannot. These things have to be lived out and whatever failure you experience, the consequences are certain to accompany you. You cannot exchange a marriage for another one.

Though divorce is seen as an easy option (even for those in the church), it is not the perfect will of God. I believe that most Christian divorces are simply unscriptual. There are unique cases that perhaps warrant additional discerning, but for the most part, the majority of marriages are set for failure from the time they say, "I do".

I recall counseling a man who was simply miserable in his marriage. He treated his wife with such disrespect that it really offended me. She would be just as nice, yet he would simply refuse her kindness. I offered an ear to see if he wanted to share what the problem was. As it turns out, when he was released out of jail, he had no place to go. He had just given his life to the Lord and then he met this very nice Christian woman. Under the burden of guilt, he was persuaded by her to marry so they would not be in sexual sin. However, as time went on and he began to grow and become acquainted with his newfound life, he realized that he was taken advantage of while he was weak and vulnerable and unable to make a sound decision. In essence, this lady had deceived him because he was not operating within the free course of his will. I counseled him to share this with her and ask her to apologize to him and to release his will (1 Cor. 7:37) to choose marriage because of love and not because of fear. He was clearly relieved.

Those marriages that qualify for scriptural divorce will find its way within the courts of adultery. I believe this to be both spiritual and physical. We understand the physical aspect clearly. When it comes to spiritual adultery, we will find it when Jesus dealt with the scribes for calling Him Beelzebub after He cast out a devil (Mt 12:24-32). He asserted clearly that all sins will be forgiven but the sin of blasphemy against the Holy Ghost. He was dealing with spiritual adultery. If a spouse consents to willfully blaspheme Christ with an understanding of his or her actions, the offended spouse has legal grounds to seek for divorce. If Christ has left, why should they be bound to stay (1 Cor. 7:15)? There are levels that lead to this within the church which would appear not to be blasphemy at the onset, yet as the tree continues to bear fruit, it is found to be corrupt in the end (v 33).

An example of early traits of this problem is found when a spouse begins to have spiritual communion with another person that falls into the arena of familiarity. In other words, the only reason why they come together is for spiritual interplay. Truth is not the foundation but instead, a spiritual voyage in the name of Christ void of scriptural support and order. This is has been the cause for many marriages ending in serious turmoil from within the walls of the church. There are people who are in church today for one reason; to prey on the ignorant. Many young men and women have been sexually assaulted from men right in the church through supposing a purifying process that involved becoming completely naked to be anointed with oil. Instead, they were aroused and violated.

There are people in the counseling profession with serious problems. The sole reason that they offer counseling is to get closer to those who can be taken advantage of. How many horror stories have we heard of the counselor having some form of imbalanced relationship with the counseled, either physically or spiritually? I could go on to describe how child molesters penetrate church leadership to simply gain their trust to work in the children's department. It was publicly exposed that sects and cults provide a step by step procedure on how to successfully infiltrate churches and establish such relationships. Some have even boasted how easily it can be done. In some cases, years elapse before what has happened is exposed. In others, the church family is never made aware of certain things that finally surface in the end.

While it appears that I am being an alarmist (of which I am called to do), I am simply exposing the devil! The church needs to face the fact that we are in trouble and need to seek God to be cleansed within our hearts that we may discern these things. I have been led to expound at length on this topic because many families have been plagued by these satanic schemes. Following Divine Protocol as revealed in God's Word by His spirit, will expose the corruption this is within the heart of man by nature, and the demonic undertones it takes on when such vessels yield themselves to their lust. Read your bible!

But chiefly them that walk after the flesh in the lust of uncleanness, and despise government. Presumptuous [are they], selfwilled, they are not afraid to speak evil of dignities.
2Pe 2:10

This know also, that in the last days perilous times shall come. For men shall be lovers of their own selves, covetous, boasters, proud, blasphemers, disobedient to parents, unthankful, unholy, Without natural affection, trucebreakers, false accusers, incontinent, fierce, despisers of those that are good, Traitors, heady, highminded, lovers of pleasures more than lovers of God; Having a form of godliness, but denying the power thereof: from such turn away. For of this sort are they which creep into houses, and lead captive silly women laden with sins, led away with divers lusts, Ever learning, and never able to come to the knowledge of the truth. Now as Jannes and Jambres withstood Moses, so do these also resist the truth: men of corrupt minds, reprobate concerning the faith. But they shall proceed no further: for their folly shall be manifest unto all [men], as theirs also was.
2Ti 3:1-9

How that they told you there should be mockers in the last time, who should walk after their own ungodly lusts. These be they who separate themselves, sensual, having not the Spirit.
Jude 1:18 -19

Only through a healthy fear of the Lord, a serious diet of His Word, and intimate worship and praise, all resting upon His mercy, will you make it through this narrow path called the Pilgrim's Journey.

Marriage is to be a one time event. This is evident in the number of times a man or woman can be a virgin; once. I speak of the perfect will of God that many of God's children have forsaken or simply were not aware of. They have settled for His permissive will. Though His permissive will is permissive it is nonetheless not perfect. Therefore it will not produce that perfect fruit that God desires in our lives and the permissive will does not accompany the abundant life that Jesus promised we could have. The permissibleness about God's will is not of Him, but of us. God's will is always perfect, but He "permits" us to choose our own way. This is what makes it a permissive will.

I can assure you that the success or failure of your single life with Christ will be reflected in every facet of your married life. What is success as a single Christian? It is many things but when it comes to marriage, you are successful when you do not have to be married. As long as you think you have to be married, you are revealing that your body and spirit have not been advancing the Kingdom of God. You are responding carnally.

> ***But I would have you without carefulness. He that is unmarried careth for the things that belong to the Lord, how he may please the Lord: But he that is married careth for the things that are of the world, how he may please [his] wife. There is difference [also] between a wife and a virgin. The unmarried woman careth for the things of the Lord, that she may be holy both in body and in spirit: but she that is married careth for the things of the world, how she may please [her] husband. And this I speak for your own profit; not that I may cast a snare upon you, but for that which is comely, and that ye may attend upon the Lord without distraction.*** **1Co 7:32-35**

I know this sounds dramatic to the carnal man. In fact, it seems outright foolish (1 Cor 2:14). Yet it is a solid principle that cannot be refuted. If you are single and are not serving the Lord both in body and spirit, nor will you serve Him in body and in spirit when you get married. Even those who are married are to be as though they were not when it comes to carrying out the will of God. We are not being called to neglect our responsibility as a husband or wife, however, the implication here is that God's Kingdom still comes first whether you are married or not. If your idea of marriage as a Christian is sexual indulgences and romantic excursions to tropical isles around the world, then wake up, take a bath, repent and get over it because there is a serious work to be done in God's kingdom!

> ***Art thou bound unto a wife? seek not to be loosed. Art thou loosed from a wife? seek not a wife. But and if thou marry, thou hast not sinned; and if a virgin marry, she hath not sinned. Nevertheless such shall have trouble in the flesh: but I spare you. But this I say, brethren, the time [is] short: it remaineth, that both they that have wives be as though they had none;***

And they that weep, as though they wept not; and they that rejoice, as though they rejoiced not; and they that buy, as though they possessed not. And they that use this world, as not abusing [it]: for the fashion of this world passeth away. **1Co 7:27-31**

The seriousness of advancing God's kingdom is so paramount that although you are married, happy, wealthy or single, act like you are not, even though you are. The worse thing a weak person can do is get married. If someone would marry you while you are weak, they are simply telling you they are weak. Two weaklings will not make each other strong.

These truths concerning those who are single in Christ should cause you to quickly submit your thinking of marriage in its many different ways completely to the Lord. You should thrust your affections upward and give yourself quality time in drawing nearer to God. This will serve to protect you from other singles who are lurking around the church looking for someone to have legal sex with. You will begin to see this form of appetite in their eyes and discern it by God's Spirit. In fact, they will be aware that there is no pull from your spirit and they will avoid you. You will experience a calm state over your body sexually because God is abiding inside of you. You are completely content. Of course, you will have those moments of desire. That comes with being human. It will simply pass because your spiritual man is walking in God's Official Order that is Correct in the Dealings of His Kingdom.

Seeking a spouse does not have any specific relation to the work of God's kingdom. We are told in 1 Cor. 7:28-29 that to marry is not a sin, but you will have trouble in the flesh. It goes on to say that due to the magnitude of God's order, you must live as though you had no husband or wife! Marriage was also listed as an excuse for not attending the partaking of bread in the kingdom of God (Luke 14:20). Therefore, we must truly be kingdom minded as we go about choosing to become one flesh with another soul. If your desire for marriage is not for the advancement of God's kingdom, then troubled waters await you.

When one is single, their focus is also single on pleasing the Lord. Their heart and spirit careth for the things that belong to the Lord (1 Cor. 7:32). They are enriched by leaps and bounds for they can serve

God without distractions. In developing a strong spirit man through seeking the Lord with singleness of heart, they in turn learn to trust the Lord with all things. Single Christians must not acquire the attitude that the world has portrayed - "I need someone to love and to be loved by". Rather, they must perceive the blessing they have in much freedom to serve God and be loved of Him while seeking His kingdom.

You have to shake loose the chains of your own fleshly reasons and judge righteous judgment. Most views of being single are, "I'm looking for a spouse" or "Are you available"? rather than, "Here I am, Lord. Use me". When you perceive the liberty for marriage in your life, you must be careful not to see the carnal aspect of what this person can do for you, but first, how you and this person can serve the Lord and advance His Kingdom as one. Once this protocol is established, the next order in God's kingdom is how I can serve my spouse as unto the Lord. Too many couples center their marriages around what their spouse is going to do for them. If self is the motive for entering into a marriage, self will be the motive for leaving it.

While single, God's Official Order that is Correct in the Dealings of His Kingdom, is to search Him out and find Him. Obtain the purpose for your life and pursue it. Going to church, trying to act spiritual, and looking cute will get you just that - a cute, spiritual act for a marriage. As you discover the height, depth and width of God's view of spiritual life, you will begin to realize that unless you have lived and walked strong in the Spirit with the Lord, you are forfeiting a rare richness to totally serve Him. All this for fleshly reasons that will grow old and stale and in the end, fail.

Many of our single bothers and sisters in the Church must iron out their thinking. If you are single unto the Lord, you are blessed! If you are trying to comprehend your state through your own intellect, you will see that it does not add up. You must view this spiritually in order to understand that if your marriage is the result of wholeheartedly serving Christ while you were single, it will survive as you both to serve Him wholeheartedly in your marriage. On the contrary, if it is the result of selfish ambition and carnal appetites, it will continue to be just that. Naturally, this rule applies to those who are single in the Lord, and not to those who come to know the Lord while married.

The single Christian must question themselves regarding their motives for marriage. If the core of its purpose stems from the flesh regardless of how noble, innocent, sincere or blissful it appears to be, these are selfish reasons that are void of God's order and cannot insure a lasting, productive marriage for the kingdom of God.

We must be delivered from our sensations that are after this world when choosing a person to become one with. It is God Who owns our lives, not we ourselves. Furthermore, it is God Who has regenerated our spiritual man that we may be led in making this second most important decision in life; marriage (the first being salvation). Does it not stand to reason that whoever will serve the Lord with you should have a personal understanding of this through their own relationship with the Lord? There is no other order for those who call upon the name of the Lord and expect to experience Divine Protocol in their marriage. With the Christian community experiencing the level of divorce in this generation, we can no longer ignore this truth which shall deliver us from failure and enable us to knowing the surpassing bliss of the marriage covenant that God has intended. The Barna Research Group made the following report based on interviews with 3,124 randomly selected adults in the United States, including 1,220 born-again Christians.

- 1 out of every 4 adults who has been married has experienced a divorce.

- Born-again Christians are slightly more likely than non-Christians to go through a divorce. Twenty-seven percent of Christians have seen their marriage break up, compared with 23 percent of non-Christians.

- Adults who describe themselves as Christians fundamentalists are more likely than others to get divorced: 30 percent have experienced divorce.

In conclusion, the flesh profiteth nothing for "it is the Spirit that quickeneth" (Jo 6:63). If you are single and serving the Lord, I admonish you warn you and plead with you not to de ceive yourself by reasoning marriage with any of your fleshly senses. This is a joining of lives of which the flesh indeed has a part, yet not the primary part. The results of compassion, sex, joy, pain, laughter and all other attributes of the flesh and the soul will solely be dependent upon the foundation of which they are built. These things can never serve as a foundation in and of themselves.

For other foundation can no man lay that is laid, which is Christ Jesus **1 Co. 3:11**

Indeed, marriage is an honorable thing, and "whoso findeth a wife findeth a good thing and obtaineth favor of the Lord" (Prov. 18:22). But know this; that the favor and honor does not come from the marriage in and of itself, nor from a wife or husband. Both are extensions of what you already possess in Christ. The order of God's Kingdom for His single children is to be all you are to be in Christ. This will ensure your marriage to be all that it can be in Christ. Focus on Jesus, for He is your reward and He will give you the desires of your heart when He truly possesses it Himself.

Chapter 4

Prayer

To Know God is To Know Prayer
No Prayer, No God

f Christians were to trace their experiences throughout the years to the time that they were born again, all would be found standing in the same line; the prayer line. It was the sinner's prayer, to God the Father and through the name of Jesus, by which we were born again of the Spirit. And it shall be in prayer through Christ that we shall be perpetually effective in every facet of our walk while on this earth.

I feel it necessary to qualify that even though all people pray to someone or something, as Christians, we understand that the only one true God answers prayer, and that through the man Christ Jesus (1 Tim. 2:5). I shall attempt to focus on the order of prayer as it pertains to God's kingdom. Coupled with the understanding that prayer is the communion of man's spirit with God's Spirit, we shall proceed to grasp its protocol from a divine perspective.

American Christians will have much to account for on Judgment Day. There will be very few natural reasons to excuse the responsibility given to us by God to pray. This nation has the one facet of wealth that esteems us higher than any other - FREEDOM! The freedom that we exercise in the small issues of our daily life be it choice of clothing, choice of employment, or choice of spouse are dreams that will never be realized by countless others in this world. As a whole, we have lost the purpose for such liberty. Will we cry out to obtain God's protocol for our existence in this country of which we represent Him? By God's grace we shall.

Education, intellect and "connections" have deceived some current as well as aspiring leaders into believing that the gospel is really nothing more than the business of "motivating" people. By acquiring an elite circle of influence, the latest automobile, tailored Italian suits and a set of Mont Blancs, many spiritually naive leaders step out in a brazen, foolish confidence, believing that they are equipped with the goods necessary to deliver "the message" to God's people. Such are not preachers, but rather self exalted speakers of carnal thoughts. Even as God used the donkey to rebuke the mad prophet, so does He use men to save others, though they themselves are castaways (1 Cor 9:27).

Although God is truly performing great works in our midst, satan's ultimate desire is to entice our leaders as well as all Christians into negotiating and reasoning the order of God's kingdom while "standing up" instead of receiving it on ones face before His throne. Shall we realize this one thing; that whatever we can do for the Lord and His kingdom does not stem from the rudiments of this world. Rather, it shall always be what the Holy Spirit can do through us as vessels - simple channels through which His sovereign power flows as He wills, not as we or the systems of men so desire to in the power of carnality that must be brought down. Whether dressed in overalls or double breasted suits, driving wagons or Lexus', only the power of the Holy Ghost can establish the kingdom of God in this earth. This is the protocol that has always been correct and that shall successfully see us through this pilgrimage.

Praylessness and the Pulpit

Much and many have suffered in our generation due to men and women who grace the realm of the pulpit, but have not made their abode in the higher realms of prayer. I am the first to repent of my own lack in pressing evermoreso into this arena by which God's mighty workings would manifest through us as He sees fit.

The devil in all his vehement and cold hatred toward God and His people assails us with more effort than any other single issue in detouring us from where the work of God only matters: the spiritual labor which moves angels and causes heaven resources to manifest upon the earth prayer. Let it be understood the resources that we as leaders have given much attention to: money and spirituality that is of men and after men, will not turn the tide of deception and destruction within this nation and the church. Rather, the resources that brings conviction and causes repentance of a godly order is what we need as a people and this can only be birthed by prayer.

Without prayer, the pulpit becomes a stage to merely rally people around religion and not around Christ. Around causes and pursuits that are vain and even entertaining thought they may be good and humanitarian. We confuse the heavenly mandate of calling men heavenward in their passions, to maintaining men to pursue objectives that are a bit higher than the heathen and thus even lower. For we seek the things of this world in the name of God and by the power of Christ' resurrection. We do double offense, making the Word of God of non-effect by our traditions and causing men to seek God for that which is least in His sight. Oh how this pains His heart that we refuse to receive of heavens best.

And why? Why have we keep the people of God from experiencing the liberty that is found is the holies of holies through prayer? Because we would keep the hearts of men for ourselves. We would control their passions and affections for the agenda of our own hearts. We, through covetousness, have yielded to our natural inclinations of power and have turned the house of God into a den of thieves. God forgive us! God cleanse us! God open our eyes and bring us ever so to a place of true repentance from such motives that can only be purified in self-less prayer coupled with brokenness wrought by the sole working of your Spirit, for we are doomed without your sovereign working to keep us pure in the work of the pulpit.

Kingdom building has deceived and confused many sincere leaders and laity alike. We must not mistake the millennium reign with the dispensation of grace. We will reign upon this earth when the Lord sits upon the throne of David for a thousand years. Therefore it is not our place to pray for the reigning upon the nations as we will during the millennium age. Rather it a season for us to pray for it's coming and to see people of this current age born into it through faith in Christ alone.

Those who are found to be hireling and not men of God are false teachers and apostles and are deceiving the blind into a ditch. They are having a field day right now but God is going to expose the lie and shake the foundations of His people so that truth may prevail. We have entered into objectives and relationships that are nothing more than business deals motivated by greed, yet dressed in the religious garbs of the self righteous and religious. Though not all, many of these agendas are a result of prayerlessness in the face of the success and the resources that have made themselves available to the masses. Let's face it. Church has always been big business and when millions are at stake, you can be sure that men have been bought in every generation and ours is not exception. The 30 pieces of silver and the kiss of betrayal has always put Jesus in the hands of the Pharisees and Scribes. But as then, so will be today, He will yet triumph through those whose hearts are right and pure before Him.

The pulpit must be covered in prayer, entered in prayer and left in prayer. It is the entranceway of God's uttered word to His people and to the world. It is His chosen conduit to reveal corporately His objectives, His will and His relevant expression of Himself in unspoken words of glory that ascends upon the subjects of His kingdom. Therefore the pulpit is the most coveted possession of men, satan and God. Men have died to acquire it's power. Died both spiritually and physically to possess the power that it offers. To wield the wand of mesmerizing power over those who spirits are subject to its influence has become the eternal objective of Lucifer to corrupt and control. He uses men whose hearts and minds, in the church, that have not been brought under the Lordship of Christ through continual prayer. Satan himself, will forfeit nations for a single pulpit because he realizes that a pulpit can save a nation. Not through the Whitehouse does he conquer nations, kings and leaders, but through the pulpit. Not through television does he sow seeds of immorality, divorce and godliness, but through the pulpit it's allowed to exist unchallenged by heavens fire. For if the pulpit lacks the authority of heaven and the free course to declare thus saith the Lord with all conviction and conformity of the vessel, all these things are allowed to prevail upon society. But one pulpit can utterly destroy the works of the devil in every sector of our society.

We must believe and be persuaded that in keeping the pulpit bathed in prayer, birthed by His spirit, not by the foolishness or the wisdom of men, no network, no political agenda and no agenda of men or of satan can deny the wind of God's Spirit right away within the hearts of His people and of unbelievers.

E.M. Bounds, the 18th century preacher and author writes a whole volume on the dimensions of prayer.

"We cannot declare too often or too strongly that prayer, involving all of its elements, is the one prime condition of the success of Christ's kingdom, and that all else is secondary and incidental. Prayerful preachers, prayerful men, and prayerful women only can press this gospel with aggressive power. Only they can put in it conquering forces. Preacher may be sent out by the thousands, their equipments be ever so complete, but unless they be men skilled in the trade of prayer, trained to its martial and exhaustive exercise, their going will be lacking in power and effectiveness. Moreover, except the men and women who are behind these preachers, who furnish their equipment, are men and women in whose characters prayer has become serious labor, their outlay will be a vain and ineffective effort.

...A Christian or a preacher may live a decent, religious life, without secret prayer, but decency and holiness are two widely different things. And the latter is attained only by secret prayer." (The complete Works of E.M. Bounds on Prayer by Baker Books. Page 410)

Shall we strive to establish Divine Protocol in prayer that we may place our hearts, our homes and our pulpits within the hand and plan of All Mighty God.

Three Misconceptions of Prayer

Thanking God for our limbs, salvation, waking us up this morning in our right minds and acknowledging that if we had 10,000 tongues we couldn't praise Him enough, are testimonies that are to be expected from babes in Christ and that not for long. God has purposed a rich reality for understanding His order for prayer.

By His grace, I shall deal with a few obstacles which I believe have hindered many Christians in their prayer life. Communication is a means that has been in use since man has existed. Through this created form of expressing thought, facts and opinions, we have prevailed to tremendous heights of accomplishments. It shall do us well, however, to understand that the communication of mind to mind is not the same as communication of Spirit to spirit. This misconception has caused needless error and lack of effectiveness in the work of the kingdom of God. If our minds are void of truly knowing what we ought to pray for, it should alarm us to realize how vain and utterly useless our natural abilities are.

Likewise the Spirit also helpeth our infirmities: for we know not what we should pray for as we ought: but the Spirit itself maketh intercession for us with groanings which cannot be uttered.
Ro. 8:26

"Traditions" are yet still receiving the high praises of many. It is imperative for us to qualify our methods of prayer. While some utilize this God ordained communion as a means to talk with their minds, others go to dangerous extremes and turn such a heavenly blessing into an opportunity to decree things out of their own hearts instead of by the unction of the Holy Spirit Who expresses His will to the Church within the earth.

But as it is written, Eye hath not seen, nor ear heard, neither have entered into the heart of man, the things which God hath prepared for them that love him. 1 Co. 2:9

Misconception #1 - Prayer is Not Praise

Many Christians have the time of their lives praising God! We tend to "have church" in praise alone and rightly so, for He has indeed done great things. Be this as it may, hours upon hours of praise is yet not prayer. In the Greek, praise means, "to make a boast" and in the Hebrew it signifies " a thank offering". We are told in Psalms 100:4 to enter into his courts with praise. Praise is an expression of what God has done, or what we perceive He will do. It is also an act of being in awe of Who He is. "Praise is comely for the upright" (Psalms 33:1).

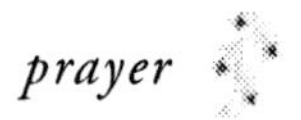

Praise prepares us to receive and entreats God to bestow His perfect will in your life. It creates an atmosphere of intimacy between God and His child and as a result, its purpose is paramount to insure effective communion in the spiritual realm. It allows the seeker time to become yielded and open in order to hear from the Lord and to position himself to apprehend what God has or is about to reveal.

In the Lord's prayer, the first order of prayer after addressing God as Father was to hallow Him. Other words for hallow include, "sanctify", "consecrate" and "to bless". This is a part of prayer but it is not the core of prayer. What praise is to prayer, foreplay is to sex. If a couple does not first experience the joys of simply touching and being naked before each other without rushing toward intercourse, their lovemaking will be dry, impersonal and fail to provide the intended atmosphere for effective and fulfilling worship. The woman is especially affected by this scenario. When we fail to praise God, this is exactly what we experience; dry, rushed and impersonal prayer.

Though hallowing the name of the Lord is a part of prayer, it should ensue before and after the very core of the praying process itself, not be confused with it. We close our prayer with, "For thine is the kingdom and the power and the glory," which are words descriptive of reverence. These are closing adorations that reveal a form of hallowing.

MISCONCEPTION #2 - PRAYER IS NOT AIMLESS PETITIONING

***But when ye pray, use not vain repetitions, as the heathen do: for they think that they shall be heard for their much thinking.* Mt 6:7**

As soon as our emotions have been "warmed up" in praise, many of us begin to shoot off countless desires or problems to God. We pull out a list of topics that we have decided with our mind to pray for instead of receiving from God what He has ordained to be prayed for before the foundations of the world. Bear in mind that petitioning is not wrong in and of itself. It is what we are petitioning that makes the difference. There is a definite protocol for approaching God in scripturally based petitions.

Despite our sincerity in our pursuit of God in prayer, aimless petitions become vain repetitions that we forcefully attempt to be heard from on high. Let it further be noted that usually those who are aimless in prayer are also aimless in their walk with God. How can they be any different, for one reflects the other? Our hearts are full of intentions that have not been nailed to the cross and rendered totally dead. This principle is reflected in the effectiveness of our prayer life.

To be aimless is to be carnal. It reveals dependence upon that person's mind or soul to direct their path in the ways of the Lord. In essence, it is fear of trusting His ways. Such fear is evidence that love has not been perfected in the understanding and in the heart.

***There is no fear in love; but perfect love casteth out fear: because fear hath torment. He that feareth is not made perfect in love.* 1Jo 4:18**

Torment is a powerful force and many of God's people are afraid of a variety of issues in this life ranging from God meeting their daily needs, wholeheartedly accepting the call to the ministry, or simply making the kingdom of God their single focus. Fear breeds torment. When we praise and pray out of fear, we are accusing God of not being faithful to keep His Word. Satan's ultimate, most useful tool that he has ever used is a question.

Adam faced a question before Eve was even approached by satan. The fact that Adam did not protest her offer to partake of the fruit and that he (Adam), was with her proves that he had already determined how to justify his actions; blame Eve. Satan questioned Eve on some basic issues and through fear being implanted in her mind, she answered by partaking of the forbidden fruit. Adam and Eve yielded to those questions and the torment of losing what that they already had was the result.

***And when the woman saw that the tree [was] good for food and that it [was] pleasant to the eyes and a tree to be desired to make [one] wise, she took of the fruit thereof and did eat and gave also unto her husband with her; and he did eat.* Ge 3:6**

Food, possessions and knowledge are the only issues that concern life. Satan's arguments will always be centered on one of these and Jesus showed us how to deal with them.

Mt 4:4-10 But he answered and said, It is written,

- Man shall not live by bread alone, (food)
- Thou shalt not tempt the Lord thy God. (knowledge)
- Thou shalt worship the Lord thy God and him only shalt thou serve. (possession)

Being aimless simply reveals issues in our hearts that we have not surrendered to God because of fear. As long as we are fearful and afraid, we will sin in our disbelief and never know the order of God that is certain. Therefore, cease from petitioning God on things that are borne out of what He has already given you; food, knowledge and possession. Adam and Eve had these things in abundance but they yielded to one question and lost it all. Never hold a conversation with satan on his terms. Your response should always start of with these words: IT IS WRITTEN! This will allow your prayers to become relevant and your praise a romantic interlude between two lovers who trust each other to death.

God's kingdom is so mighty, fear cannot abide for His doings are definite. His revelation to us does not need to be "processed" as does a mathematical equation. It simply needs to be transmitted to our intuition or our renewed spirit. To suggest much mental articulation by way of aimless petitioning is to reveal a religion not a relationship. This clearly demonstrates little or no order in the spiritual operations of God within the life of such a person and/or congregation. We become foolish by trying to perfect in the flesh what God has begun in the Spirit (Gal. 3:3). To maintain such a course of vain petitions and babbling is an attempt to touch the glory that belongs to God and God alone. In other words, unless God deals with us on our terms, we refuse to follow Him. Following Him out of obedience means He deserves the glory. The glory is the unseen and unexplainable. It allows God the right to simply do what He wants to do without having to reason with mere clay. This is why those who come to Him must believe that He is and that He is a rewarder of those who diligently seek Him (Heb. 11:6).

We refuse to operate in the realm of faith when it refuses to involve materialistic issues, or a quest for more spiritual rhema. Despite how much we already have, we yet refuse to produce with it. We really believe that if we just had that particular situation, it would make a difference. "If I can just go through one more course in seminary, I will be ready to go forth in ministry. If I can just pay off this mortgage, I will be free to evangelize without being concerned that I will lose my house. If I can just maintain my food stamps for another year, I will be able to take it from there". The list does not stop. Once you get ready to do what you think needs to be done, satan will have another five reasons why you have to maintain a life of prayer that centers around petitions and never moves into a spiritual domain of warfare for the advancement of the kingdom of God.

A person of this nature is likened unto those that the Bible describes as praying in the synagogues and in the corners of the streets that they may be seen of men (Mt 6:5). This reflects such whose concerns and desires have not yet been crucified to the cross. Their life is yet alive and as a result, they are under the compulsions of their soul rather than the yielding of their spirits to God for revelation. Such individuals can be found in the church just waiting for a chance to pray before God's people. They join the ministerial staff to have a chance to jaw jack. The pulpit is no place for such foolishness and our pastors need to be more discerning. People are anxious to lay hands on people when the bible says not to be quick to do so (1Ti. 5:22). Religious people are dangerous when it comes to prayer because they truly do not have the mind of Christ nor the discernment of God's Spirit.

Aimless Petitions are what man wants. Spiritual Prayer is what God has ordained.

Aimless Petitions are led by the emotions. Spiritual Prayers are led by the Spirit.

Never will one know the heartbeat of God through aimless petitions regardless of how noble they may seem to be. Those who are hindered in this area usually are unstable in the study of God's Word, therefore, their motives have gone without the fire of the Purifier. It is not the will of God for us to be aimless. If we are found to be so, we have failed to adjust to God's Official Order That is Correct in the Dealings of His Kingdom.

Misconception #3 - Prayer Is Not Part Time

There are churches in America that have morning, noon and evening prayer hours which is commendable. We all have some form of prayer life. Whether it is once a month or 7 times a day, it is a form of prayer life. For the most part, prayer has been confined to a particular time and structure. While understanding that we live in the sphere of time, it should not be the principal factor to consider when or if we pray. We all have heard the saying, "Timing is everything". Unfortunately, this phrase holds true for many of our prayer vigils in determining if we pray at all. Prayer is effective because of God. Prayer is not effective just because you pray. It holds no power in and of itself. Every facet of spiritual communion must involve the interceding work of the Holy Spirit in order for it to accomplish the will and mind of God. For this to be a relevant rule, we must not limit our praying to a certain time frame.

We have minimized God's rule in the affairs of our lives by clogging the lines of communication between God and our spirit. As soon as we arise from our praying position, our spirits become secondary to the mind rather than remaining alert and sober to the continual leading of the Holy Spirit. This is what it means to:

Pray without ceasing. **1Thess. 5:17**

Whenever Jesus was fellowshipping with His disciples or eating with the scribes and Pharisees, He was yet alert to the leading of His Father. Being sensitive to God is prayer, for prayer is receiving from the Lord His way and His will on a continual moment by moment basis. In order to know this in experience, we must exercise this in practice. The more you practice something, the more it becomes a normal part of you. No one ever became proficient at a skill doing it part time. When a person acquires a degree in a field of study, they did so by giving much time to it on a daily basis. It has been said to truly do well in a class, you should give at least two hours of study per day in that subject. If we are to gauge our commitment to God based on the time we spend in prayer, it would reveal the reason why we are successful or the reason why we are not. To believe that prayer is a convenience is to have a dangerous misconception which will only serve to keep you from the excellence of God's kingdom order.

Is there ever a time when we do not need to discern His presence, His purpose, His timing? Of course, your natural man objects to such spiritual mindedness, for it is yet battling for supremacy over God's rule. It knows that you have a specific time that you begin and end prayer. It will be more than happy to give you an hour of conscious communion with the Lord and be able to consume the rest of your day. However, as soon as you purpose to maintain your rule over it, your intellect will oppose you sharply. This is why you must practice prayer daily until it becomes such a part of you that your natural man has been put in its place. Once your spirit rises to its rightful place, you will not want to miss such Spirit led prayer. It is truly the source of your every move. You understand the danger in not yielding to God's Spirit and to avoid such consequences, prayer becomes an integrated part of your moment by moment existence.

Walking continually in the Spirit is paramount for victory over the works of the devil. Without this as a priority, Divine Protocol will be impossible. The fact that such a walk is a warfare is to be acknowledged. It is certainly a fight and a good one.

> ***Fight the good fight of faith, lay hold on eternal life, whereunto thou art also called and hast professed a good profession before many witnesses.*** ***1Ti 6:12***

Nevertheless, those who have purposed to do exploits in their life for the Lord realize that there simply is no other way to live. When God's Word becomes the final authority of your every move, the fight has been won. It will always remain a double standard (yours and God's), when there is yet a degree of flesh that holds a certain piece of ground and refuses to bring it under God's faithful rule. When full submission under His kingdom has become a reality in practice and undistracted attention is given in prayer, Divine Order will overtake you. Mysteries will be continually revealed. Love will be easy. The gifts will flow effortlessly. Direction will be clear. Patience will be a pleasure. Contentment will be the rule. Satan will be exposed and fearful of your presence. Peace will swallow up your understanding. Having a readiness to enter into God's kingdom will be your daily expectation. Through continual prayer, you will truly develop such a heavenly mind that you can be of earthly good for God's kingdom.

- Prayer is a continual realization of the things of God.
- Prayer is a continual revelation from the Spirit of God.
- Prayer is appropriating what God has revealed.
- Prayer is warfare against the enemies of God,
- Prayer is not subject to Rolex or Timex.
- Prayer is the ultimate way of knowing
- Divine Protocol in a time such as this.
- Discovering the Beauty of Being With God

Before an individual can ever expect God's protocol in their prayer life, the first order of business is to simply enjoy the beauty of just being with God. Nothing is more deceiving than believing that you have received something from God, while there has been no sincere adoration for Him. Adoration that exceeds the lifting up hands and bowing down before Him at church. In the midst of the traffic within the Body of Christ, we must remind ourselves that God's work is not accomplished in how much we do, but in how much He does. The only work that is of concern for us is to believe on Him.

Jesus answered and said unto them, This is the work of God, that ye believe on him whom he hath sent. ***Jo 6:29***

There is a beauty in being with God that is solely discovered within the confines of the secret place of the Most High, abiding under the shadow of the Almighty (Psalms 91:1). It is here that God reveals

Himself to us and we open ourselves to Him as a willing and living sacrifice. God is more concerned with receiving the admiration of His people and bestowing upon us His love and Spirit than our desire of struggling to obtain His will. Desiring His will moreso than desiring Him is to fall short of spiritual protocol. When you truly have Him, you not only have His will, but the way by which it will be fulfilled. If there is no purity for communion with Christ and the Father without attachments, then likewise, the will of God is desired with an impure heart.

The disciples who questioned Jesus on how to do the works of God were only desiring to obtain power to "multiply fish and bread" so to speak. They had absolutely no interest in Jesus or His Father on a spiritual level. They continued to badger Jesus to find out the "secret" to multiplying the fish and bread for self gratification. They attempted to intimidate Jesus by playing the Moses card. "Moses provided bread in the wilderness", they said. "What are you going to give us to prove that you are who you said you are"? Jesus cut through the rhetoric and brought them to the edge when He declared:

> ***Then Jesus said unto them, Verily, verily, I say unto you, Except ye eat the flesh of the Son of man and drink his blood, ye have no life in you. Whoso eateth my flesh and drinketh my blood, hath eternal life; and I will raise him up at the last day. For my flesh is meat indeed and my blood is drink indeed. He that eateth my flesh and drinketh my blood, dwelleth in me and I in him.*** ***Joh 6:53-56***

The Church today has become a sign and wonder seeking generation. We pack out auditoriums and coliseums waiting to be entertained. While I will readily admit that there has been great strides in pressing toward childlike intimacy, we yet must prepare ourselves to cast off those few weights and sins that still beset us from running this race with a keen awareness in the last hours of time. We are yet learning and never able to come to the knowledge of the truth. Ministries that are offering nothing but old wine year after year are encouraged to renew their love for Jesus and the Father. When our themes remain on the principles of the doctrines of Christ, we have refused to go on to perfection. These principles are to be laid only to be left. Therefore

<u>leaving</u> the principles of the doctrine of Christ, let us go on unto perfection; not laying again the foundation of repentance from dead works and of faith toward God,

> ***Of the doctrine of baptisms and of laying on of hands and of resurrection of the dead and of eternal judgment. And this will we do, if God permit.*** ***Heb 6:1-3***

> ***But, beloved, we are persuaded better things of you and things that accompany salvation, though we thus speak.*** ***Heb 6:9***

When we refuse to move on and build things that accompany salvation, we are unable to teach others, unable to understand the deep things of God and unable to digest meat and to discern good from evil (Heb 5:12-14). To have a stagnant faith and conditional motives in just being with God, is to ensure deception and bondage to men. When we avoid the beauty of just being with Him, we must camouflage our real motives with religious exercise. We must at least have the appearance of godliness even though we are denying its power (1 Tim. 3:5). These are called the commandments and traditions of men and they make void the law of God. Such religion will be here until the Lord returns. There is no need in trying to change it. Jesus said to let them alone for they be blind leaders of the blind.

The beauty of being with God exceeds the scope of meat and drink (Rom. 14:17). It is much more than doing a work for God outside the pure joy of being with Him.

> ***And he ordained twelve, that they should be with him and that he might send them forth to preach.*** ***Mark 3:14***

The Divine Protocol for our time and day of microwave religion and methods which offer quick fix remedies for our poor spiritual condition is to draw nigh unto God through Jesus Christ! We have stopped short of our searching and seeking of Jesus by searching and seeking for methods to multiply fish and bread. Jesus is the way to the divine presence of the Father and many of us have stopped at the door, when we are told to come boldly before His throne which surpasses the door.

Having therefore, brethren, boldness to enter into the holiest by the blood of Jesus, By a new and living way, which he hath consecrated for us, through the veil, that is to say, his flesh; And having a high priest over the house of God; Let us draw near with a true heart in full assurance of faith, having our hearts sprinkled from an evil conscience and our bodies washed with pure water. ***Heb. 10:21-22***

In such communion, there is an illumination in our spirits of Who God is. Our minds are incapable of knowing God in this way for "God is a Spirit and they that worship him must worship him in spirit and in truth" (Jo 4:24).

This depth of sensitivity is where we are made one with the Father in purpose, in will and in desire (Jo 17:21). Christians that are unfamiliar with this walk, are known to be critical of those who are. Any statement made to belittle the spiritual reality of another is to the detriment of the one who made it. It behooves us to realize the awesome God that we serve and to keep our logical opinions out of the lives of our brothers and sister who perhaps commune with the Lord in a depth unfamiliar to us. We are all aware of the existence of error in regards to spiritual things, however, judge righteous judgment!

But he that is spiritual judgeth all things, yet he himself is judged of no man. ***1Cor. 2:15***

The unqualified statement, "you're so heavenly minded that you're no earthly good" should be carefully considered by those who speak it, for they do so from their flesh and not by the leading of the Holy Spirit. Furthermore, observation of such a comment simply reveals their own conviction of not being spiritually minded as they should. I just wonder. If those who really believe such a statement would have thought of Jesus if they were living on earth during His ministry? Would they have railed with the others, "Crucify Him"?

It is impossible to be heavenly minded through the Spirit of the Lord and fail to be a jewel to this hurting earth. We are admonished to seek those things which are above, where Christ sits at the right hand of God. Our affections are to be set on things above, not on the things of the earth (Col. 3:1,2).

Those who are "good" for this earth are incapable of being vessels fit to execute the work of heaven, for the heavenly minded saint seeks a city whose builder and maker is God (Heb. 11:10,16). The kingdom of God does not come with mental observation - it is within you. It cannot be regulated by the scope of your mental ability. It cannot be controlled by guidelines that have been set by the flesh. To insult what one does not understand in regards to the moving of God is to greatly err and to reveal that one does not understand the scripture nor the power of God.

Great men and women of God in times past have proven to us that protocol in ministry far surpasses any form of explanation of the flesh. May we realize that just being with the Son and the Father, while being infused with the Holy Spirit's life and power, is the most single determining factor of our success in this great spiritual battle against satan's kingdom? It is a violent warfare to endure in order to take possession of truly surrendering to God and becoming intimate with Him. This is what it means to be known of Him, for those who did not "know" Him were known as the workers of iniquity.

And from the days of Jo the Baptist until now; the kingdom of heaven suffereth violence and the violent take it by force.
Mt11:12

Pressing into the presence of God is no light task. You pay for it with your life and when obtained, you wrestle to keep the "Beauty of Being With God" a reality (Mt13:44-46).

From the richness of such fellowship, one is inclined to "will and do of his good pleasure" (Ph. 2:13). There is no need to be anxious for anything. Fear and doubt cannot be found in the secret place. Daniel was not any different than other men living in his time. He simply possessed the secrets of God because he dwelled with God in secret.

But there is a God in heaven that revealeth secrets, But as for me, this secret is not revealed to me for any wisdom that I have more than any living. ***Dan. 2:28a,30a***

We must ask God to be merciful and instruct us to know Him, for we cannot instruct ourselves. Being with God must be given by God, for "a man can receive nothing, except it be given him from heaven" (Jo 3:27). As we, in faith and honesty draw nigh unto God, He shall draw nigh unto us.

To experience Divine Protocol, God's Official Order That is Correct in the Dealings of His Kingdom, is to experience "The Beauty of Being With Him". This is the highest order of all life. As fish enjoy the water and birds enjoy the air, so man enjoys the highest order of his being when he is with Him from Whom he was made. For those who trust in themselves to be at peace and yet God is not possessing their being, the delusionary power of ego has worked its effect. Only the mercy of God can open your eyes. I pray that you yield yourself to His love and be set free to know the beauty of being with Him.

Beauty must be defined on spiritual terms (1 Cor.2:13) in order to understand the implications given.

Beauty means a tranquil heart, a rested soul.

An awareness of a place unseen yet known.

Beauty is touching God with the real you.

And being touched by He Who made all things.

It's being "once blind" but now you see.

Not natural, but spiritual reality.

Such beauty is unseen to many and known by a very few.

God desires such intimate beauty to be experienced by me and by you. You must comprehend this beauty with that Person Who is within you whom you cannot see. It is your spirit man, made in the likeness of God. Prayer is where you discover it. It is a personal encounter and what you experience cannot be the experience of another. Each must experience it for themselves. This encounter is part of the filling that is given to those who "hunger and thirst after righteousness" (Mt 5:6). As well, it is a part of that peace and joy which is only found in the Holy Ghost.

To the determined few who discover and experience it, this beauty is ever increasing, never dull, leads to exuberant praise and opens profound doors. Of course, the door remains open to all for it is simply a matter of choosing whether or not to pay the price to enter therein. This abode of spiritual intimacy with Christ and the Father must involve the central theme of ones existence in order to understand and experience it as reality. Many Christians have the notion that being with God is somehow only set aside for those in the ministry. Regardless of a person's calling, we all are to share in the intimacy of being with God. To know Him is a prerequisite to seeing Him. Knowing Him is abiding daily in His presence. If one does not desire His presence now, will they desire it then? Jesus will say to many religious folk, "I never knew you: depart from me, ye that work iniquity" (Mt 7:23).

There are church going, tongue talking, religious bound folk, who are void of relationship with God through Jesus Christ our Lord.

Allow me to conclude with one thought:

The beauty of a diamond is never realized until it is yours.

Even so, the beauty of being with God until you are His.

God's Order of Prayer

There are countless books written on the subject of prayer that provide a variety of insights. To be certain, my intentions are not to tell you or anyone how to pray. I believe that it is impossible to show someone how to pray. It is like trying to instruct a husband how to love his wife. Jesus could only give His disciples a outline structure of what to pray as set forth in the Lord's Prayer. He provided examples and set the protocol of insuring that you would be heard by the Father. The very act of praying itself is an intimate interlude between two spirits. While there is corporate prayer, the effectiveness of it can only be weighed by the effectiveness of individual prayer. These are things that God alone must impart to an individual through a relationship built upon the single foundation of an unfeigned love for God and God alone.

As Christians, we have laid the foundation of praise, time, focus and being with God. Once these have taken their rightful place, where does prayer finally come in? Beautiful question!

You see, your prayer will manifest through fellowship with God. In conversing with you, God reveals in your spirit what your purpose is in the Body of Christ. It is your purpose that will be synonymous with your prayer. Even though our purpose is paramount in prayer, it should not be sought after with the same passion that you seek after God Himself. This is a dangerous area that we must be cautious of. Our enemy, satan, will do much harm in deceiving us from keeping our prayer life centered on the Person of Jesus Christ and sweet singleness of communion with the Father. We shall find ourselves unable to rest and busy about much work which will drive us to Christ with the same agenda as Martha who was cumbered about much work (Luke 10:40). Martha was so out of sync with sitting at the feet of the Master that she almost became a hindrance to Mary who had chosen to do that which was best. As we see, Jesus would not allow Martha's agenda to interfere with the highest order of prayer: being with Him.

Therefore, our first priority is not to bombard the courts of heaven with the words of our minds, but to listen with a quiet spirit through which God's will evolves to those who love Him and are the called according to His purpose (Rom 8:28).

Listening To God

And Moses said unto them, Stand still and I will hear what the Lord will command concerning you. ***Num. 9:8***

Prayer does not mean to talk. Prayer is the process of giving and receiving between God's Spirit and man's spirit. As a leader, Moses demonstrated one thing very well; he listened. If we are incapable of hearing God's voice, what can we say to Him that He would want to hear except, "Help!" Traditional religion has muffled the ears of many saints from hearing the most profound voice ever spoken. His voice is so close that your natural ears cannot hear it. His revelation is so vast, that the mind cannot contain it. What He speaks is so true that the intellect refuses to believe it.

To listen to God should be a most sought after delight. Our vacations should be opportunities to listen to God. Our first question in the morning should be, "What are you saying, God"? Prayer is an attitude. If you have a bad one, your prayer life will be in shambles. But if you have a godly one, expect wonderful things from the Creator of all.

From the time we receive salvation, God's main objective is to bring us under His complete rule as willing servants. His purpose for chastisement is that we might be partakers of His holiness and that we might yield the peaceable fruit of righteousness (Heb. 12:10,11). Both of these characteristics reflect one who has learned to be still and listen to the Spirit of the Lord. The purpose of trials is to develop a listening ear. Successful seekers and knockers are patient listeners. They are also full of faith. It takes faith to forsake the way of fleshly strength, be still and hearken to a voice that can only be discerned.

So then faith cometh by hearing and hearing by the word of God.
Ro. 10:17

If we spent more time after sincere praise and worship in perceiving God rather than rushing off to a "faith clinic", we would obtain the faith and revelation that God alone reveals. Again, our intellect wants to rule even in prayer. It is full of requests and petitions that far exceed the protocol of seeking God. We are told to make our requests known unto God (Ph. 4:6), yet when petitions become the center of our prayer life, they become repetitious. Such prayer only serves to reveal a focus on our own selves rather than on God.

Faith comes by hearing and hearing, or the ability to hear, comes by the Word of God. One can hear the Word of God day in and day out, yet if they are void of the quickening of God's Spirit, that which they have heard is incapable of imparting faith. This is why the study of God's Word must be an intense part of ones life if they are to know God's Official Order that is Correct in the Dealings of His Kingdom. This form of study should not be confused as religious pursuits of mere knowledge. It must remain a pure delight in wanting to simply know

Him. Should you have written a biography on yourself and one were to approach you presumptuously assuming they knew you just because they read the book, this would cause them to be seen as a fool in your eyes. How much more do we insult Christ when we assume our actions simply because we have knowledge of the scriptures based on ego and not a result of Him revealing them to us?

> ***Then opened he their understanding, that they might understand the scriptures...,*** ***Lu 24:45***

Before one can expect to demonstrate faith, they must first demonstrate the discipline of listening to the voice of the Lord. The purpose for faith is to do the will of God. Without God's will, one will be without God's faith. The order of prayer reveals that we must first listen, then perceive and discern the leading of God. Once this is accomplished, all else will follow suit regarding the Divine Protocol of prayer.

Let us be careful not to confuse listening with being passive. We are never to become inactive in our conscience waiting for some "outer force" to take over our wills or bodies. This is satan's method of operation. He wants his subjects completely under his reign without any freedom whatsoever. This is bondage to the works of the flesh and the devil. There are "movements" today that are based on this principle that have caused much harm and confusion to many of God's people. Such movements are in direct conflict to the scriptures and to the nature of God. Though God is supernatural, He is not weird or out of order in His operations within the manifestation of His Spirit.

Genuine evidence that God has been amongst a people is repentance. If there is not a turning away from wicked ways prior to seeking God for His presence, then there is a mere desire for strange fire and that is exactly what will manifest. As well, when God has visited His people, those who were not seeking repentance will be yet heavily convicted. When dealing with supernatural issues, there is no way to know the real from the fake but by the Spirit of the Lord. To attempt to judge by mere logic will not provide you with a confidence to know that you have discerned correctly. We are told not to believe every spirit but to try them to see whether or not they are from God.

Beloved, believe not every spirit, but try the spirits whether they are of God: because many false prophets are gone out into the world. **1Jo 4:1**

There is very little encouragement given toward this rule in our generation of Christianity and this fact should serve as evidence that satan's ministers are appearing as angels of light and deceiving the simple minded with signs and wonders that are not orchestrated by the Holy Spirit. While there should be a genuine desire to expect God to visit us, we should yet be submissive in allowing God the right in choosing how He will reveal Himself. When there is an insistent attitude toward God doing anything for us, our pursuits turn to witchcraft and sorcery that opens doors for satan to present a host of counterfeits which will be taken for the real workings of God. When the saint of God continues this avenue of prayer, they will be taken deeper and deeper into deception until they no longer believe God's Word, which has the final authority. They become speculative in their reasoning and become boastful in their experiences. There is no true desire for God moreso than for spiritualism that evokes sensationalism which feeds the flesh while allowing the spirit to become entangled in satan's grip of deception.

During this series of deceptive events and spiral towards deception, God's Spirit is always warning His child that they are in error and heading the wrong way. The Spirit's warning, however, is not loud and aggressive as we would expect. God warns His children through the intuition of their spirits that are pressed upon with love and gentleness. There has to be a desire to receive His direction in order for there to be an ability to perceive it. God's leading is internal, from within, whereas satan's leading is external, from without. To the mature Christian, God generally does not touch your flesh, your emotions, or your mind without first manifesting Himself in your spirit. Therefore, as a foundation, to judge acts of the spirit world which proceed from outside of your spirit such as emotionalism, word of knowledge, prophecy and the like as emanating from God is improper. Keep in mind that I am speaking specifically as a foundation. God does not operate in progressive a way in this fashion. Through His sovereignty, God does superrule. Yet to the mature, He maintains a co-rule, meaning God wants us to work with Him on a higher level of protocol. God will warn His children gently should one become dependent upon outer methods of discerning His will and way. This warning is to cause you to yield until He first moves upon your spiritual man.

While there are many examples of Jesus healing thousands of people and performing signs and wonders in His earthly ministry, we can readily see the results of those who had experiences to occur in their spirit first rather than just their natural person. One cannot dispute that many did come to believe on Christ because of the miracles and healings He performed. Yet scripture prophetically reveals the corresponding results of the two. Those who returned and worshipped Him was made whole. What happened to those who simply took the signs and wonders and continued on without honoring Christ? The point is that if God chooses to manifest Himself with miracles, He does so to captivate ones attention and ultimately, a commitment of worship from the recipient of this miracle. For those who choose not to receive the mercy of <u>advance</u> evidence, judgment would be more tolerable for Sodom and Gomorrah than for them. The sign and the wonder prior to God working within that individual will serve as a sign against them. To whom much is given, much is required. It is certain that Jesus did turn the water to wine and revealed His glory, yet the result was that His disciples believed on Him (Jo 2:11).

Imagine how all of Jerusalem could, with one voice, desire Him to be crucified Who had done such marvelous works among them. Even Pilate desired to set Him free, for he perceived that the Scribes and Pharisees had plotted His crucifixion because of envy, though we understand that it was to fulfill the scriptures. As we press to fulfill God's purpose for our lives while on the earth, we must press to solely believe on Him, for this is the work of God; not performing or living to see a sign and a wonder. The following scriptures testify that all such miracles that are wrought by God through Jesus Christ are to invoke belief in Him, not for the miracles.

Much people of the Jews therefore knew that he was there: and they came <u>not</u> for Jesus' sake only, but that they might see Lazarus also, whom he had raised from the dead. **Jo 12:9**

Now when he was in Jerusalem at the passover, in the feast [day], many believed in his name, when they saw the miracles which he did. Jo 2:23

Jesus answered them and said, Verily, verily, I say unto you, Ye seek me, not because ye saw the miracles, but because ye did eat of the loaves and were filled. Jo 6:26

And many of the people believed on him and said, When Christ cometh, will he do more miracles than these which this [man] hath done? Jo 7:31

Therefore said some of the Pharisees, This man is not of God, because he keepeth not the sabbath day. Others said, How can a man that is a sinner do such miracles? And there was a division among them. Joh 9:16

Then gathered the chief priests and the Pharisees a council and said, What do we? for this man doeth many miracles. Jo 11:47

But though he had done so many miracles before them, yet they believed not on him: Jo 12:37

Ye men of Israel, hear these words; Jesus of Nazareth, a man approved of God among you by miracles and wonders and signs, which God did by him in the midst of you, as ye yourselves also know: Ac 2:22

If I do not the works of my Father, believe me not. But if I do, though ye believe not me, believe the works: that ye may know and believe, that the Father [is] in me and I in him. Jo 10:37-38

Listening to God involves a free will choice to humble ourselves under His authority. Such choice cannot be taken away by any force whether in heaven, hell, or on the earth. Even those who are in bondage are in such a state due to their choice. Listening to God involves giving up the right to listen to reasoning of the flesh. Regardless of how noble, how intelligent, or how much peace it might appear to bring, God must be given the sole right to communicate all things through our intuition. We need not fear being too excessive in yielding ourselves to God. It is not that we no longer use the facilities of our minds but rather, we are simply allowing our minds to be instructed through the Spirit of Christ. The mind must be renewed according to the laws of God's kingdom and not that which is passing away. Once we endure the painful process of relinquishing mental dependency, such ways become first nature and not second nature. This is what it means to be "led" by the Spirit. Listening to God can take years to develop due to the props that we build to rely upon the flesh. Divine Protocol, God's Official Order That is Correct in the Dealings of His Kingdom, is a lifestyle for those who captivate the priority of communion with God through first developing a hearing ear.

Prayer Warriors are easily recognized and heard because what they say and pray reveals just who they have been listening to. Their spiritually enriching words are true nourishment to ones soul. In my estimation, listening is ninety percent of the battle, for all else is a result of knowing what God requires, then appropriating it back to Him.

Appropriating Prayer Back To God

Once a Christian has obtained a listening ear and can attest that they are perceiving the will of God which will manifest in the fruit of the Spirit as well as an understanding of the scriptures that are relevant for their generation, an inevitable shifting of gears takes place and that individual begins to speak with God. This understanding of the scriptures has a particular line of focus. While there are a variety of truths which such vessels become aware of that pertain to God's kingdom, this specific focus will be found pointing to God's holiness, Christ's authenticity as Lord and the Holy Spirit's role as the agent of God's workings within the earth. These godly and prophetic traits will produce soberness, humility and a boldness in Christ.

Soberness is needed because holiness ensues watchfulness, prayer, fastings and brokenness which provides strength in the spiritual man while the natural man is kept under control. Without soberness, one will become drunk on some form of outer life. Those who have battled the forces of darkness and refused their desires that they may obtain this secret place of worship and understanding, will keep their position by keeping their soul possessed with soberness.

Humility is necessary in order to understand the need to rely upon the power of God which is demonstrated through the Person of the Holy Spirit. The closer we come to God in communion, the more we realize how frail we are in ourselves. True spirituality can be measured by a humility that is genuine and not self produced. Thus, it has no value in resisting the flesh (Col. 2:22).

Boldness in Christ to remain true and steadfast in defending the faith against impostors and the falling away of which the scriptures declares in the last days shall come to pass (2 Thes. 2:3), must accompany the Christian who communes with God. A boldness of the spirit is necessary to affirm to the world that Jesus Christ is the only Way, the only Truth and the only Life. This boldness in Christ will be imperative as we behold those from amongst us deny the Lord Who bought them (2 Pet. 2:21). They will turn from the narrow way toward the doctrine of devils (1 Tim 4:1) and commandments of men which indeed have a form of godliness, but by their fruits deny Him Who considered it not robbery to be equal with God (2 Tim 3:5; Ph 2:6).

I would affirm just one more factor concerning boldness in Christ. As we behold the unification of a one world order in our generation, we must not presume that our departure, through the much acclaimed rapture, shall be prior to some form of persecution. As we look back upon church history, it clearly manifests that every generation suffered at the hands of established religion.

Our theologians have done well to dispel any question of enduring the tribulation period as one in which we go through. I wholeheartedly hope and desire that our departure shall be on a sunny day without any conflict or peril from those who oppose Christ as Lord, yet I dare not say that God's children should be caught off guard by a well argued doctrine of which no man can yet ensure its accuracy.

The scriptures declare that no man knows the day nor hour of His appearing (Mat. 25:13). Nonetheless, many read into this and declare that they know the "season". My desire is not to argue "pre", "mid", or "post" tribulation, but to declare the need to be found ready whether you are in a palace or in a dungeon; whether you are free or taken before the courts because you refuse to denounce your Jesus. Perhaps it will not be to the severity of such trials. Maybe we will lose certain rights in the work place that would clearly call for us to "bow the knee" to systems designed to force conformity to humanism or forfeit the ability to work. Lastly, the church, or those who say they are but are found eating at Jezebel's table, become lukewarm in their standard and a tolerance for the clear and concise Word of God is found wanting. Holiness and the idea that God would send one to hell for not believing that Jesus is the Only Begotten Son of God will be grounds to be reprimanded. Worldliness and being friends with those in it have already become an overlooked reality in the lives of many who "profess" Jesus. The music industry of the church today is full of secularism and compromise. Satan is alive and well and without a boldness for Christ, it is a matter of time before every soul yields to the flattery of men and the well orchestrated temptations of the devil.

Even today, 50% of seminary graduates admit they have a degree of concern with the Immaculate Conception. Therefore, for those in the pulpits who possess such an adamant rejection of Jesus coming in the flesh as God, holiness, soberness and boldness in Christ will not declare the clarion call that distinguishes a praying people who delight in appropriating single hearted prayer back to God.

These are characteristic pillars that will be the mark of those whose passion is Christ and whose home is not of this world. They are truly looking for a city whose Builder and Maker is God. They realize that perfection will not occur until the consummation of all things unto Himself comes to pass (Heb. 11:39-40). Our confidence is found impregnable. Our peace and assurance that He hears us is solid and is found operating exploits in the earth to bring those who are lost into the marvelous kingdom of God.

And this is the confidence that we have in him, that, if we ask any thing according to his will, he heareth us. 1 Jo 5:14

Through listening, we have obtained His will in every facet of our lives. We can have this confidence that whatever we are praying for has been heard by God. Even though we know in part and prophesy in part (1Cor.13:9), that which we do know we are to appropriate in prayer. We are responsible to produce spiritually with whatever we have received from heaven. The excuses revealed in the "bidden to the feast parable" (land, wife etc.), will not satisfy God when fruit is demanded. We should not fall short due to unbelief when God has spoken. The one drawback that Moses had after listening to the Lord was his lack of trust in himself to believe God.

And Moses answered and said, But, behold, they will not believe me, nor hearken unto my voice: for they will say, The Lord hath not appeared unto thee.

And Moses said unto the Lord, O my Lord, I am not eloquent, neither heretofore, nor since thou hast spoken unto thy servant: but I am slow of speech and of a slow tongue.

And he said, O my Lord, send, I pray thee, by the hand of him whom thou wilt send. *Exodus 4:1,10,13*

This form of doubt kindled the anger of the Lord against Moses. Moses determined to say to God what God had not said to Moses. We must pursue the will of God with confidence in the Spirit through Christ. In so doing, we shall receive of God the power to accomplish His will. Our confidence should not be in ourselves or upon the intellect of men. Rather, our confidence must be upon the Spirit of God within our renewed spirit. It is then we can readily declare, "I can do all things through Christ which strengtheneth me" (Ph. 4:13).

This is where many people of God are becoming confused with motivation, self awareness, positive thinking and their self esteem. Such is a movement of religious humanism that has crept into the church and has its roots deeply entrenched in satan's kingdom. While it appears to be merely lifting up a person's confidence about themselves, it is really causing them to become less aware of their real person; the spiritual man. It purports to provide the lift that is needed to "take control" of ones life and overcome any obstacle that would hinder their progress. Everything and everyone is good based on your vehement decision to induce yourself to believe this. Despite what is obvious, by being positive, you can make it what it is not. The Tower of Babel is being erected in the heart against accountability toward God and ones fellow man. It becomes "life according to me". Such a life can end in the darkness of hell whose theme song is, "I did it my way".

For the Christian who appropriates this form of prayer to God, it becomes a web of serious confusion. For every area of their life, they have a positive affirmation for it instead of the power of truth for deliverance. To replace emotional turmoil as a child or an adult, they outrun their hurt by taking classes on "freeing the person within". For the man whose father did not father him, he positively affirms with all his might that he can be the father to his child that his father was not to him. He chants this 101 times a day and smiles through the pain.

The kingdom of God is not about you or I trying to convince ourselves that we have what we so desperately need and desire. God's kingdom has delivered all of its subjects from their past with His death and has made all kingdom heirs new with His resurrection.

> ***Know ye not, that so many of us as were baptized into Jesus Christ were baptized into his death? Therefore we are buried with him by baptism into death: that like as Christ was raised up from the dead by the glory of the Father, even so we also should walk in newness of life. For if we have been planted together in the likeness of his death, we shall be also [in the likeness] of [his] resurrection: Knowing this, that our old man is crucified with [him], that the body of sin might be destroyed, that henceforth we should not serve sin.*** **Ro 6:3-6**

> ***Therefore if any man [be] in Christ, [he is] a new creature: old things are passed away; behold, all things are become new.*** **2Co 5:17**

Therefore, as we are appropriating prayer back to God, we must not replace scriptural protocol with humanistic Phosophies. This we will do if we have not first listened to God. What better way to listen to God daily than to immerse yourself with His Word? There is no other way for the child of God to bring their being under His rule than by having an unquenchable appetite for His Word. Without His Word being hid in your heart, kept before your eyes and ruling your mind, you will spend countless hours in prayer praying out of sync with God's kingdom. You are wasting your time. You will pray what you have your mind on, what you set before your eyes and what your heart is really believing. God is no respecter of persons. He has determined that His Official Order That is Correct in the Dealings of His Kingdom in prayer will be based on His Word as revealed by His Spirit.

When we line up with Christ as Lord, we are then able to line up with His Word in spirit. Outside of Christ, the Word has no life. This protocol brings true boldness and courage as we speak to God one on One.

Those who pray courageously are adding faith to what God has said with the faith that God has given. Those who respond in fear have failed to listen and understand the will of God. Even though one can have all the necessary attributes to serve successfully, they will indeed fail if they allow their intellect or natural mind to take over once God has spoken.

How many of us are wrestling with what we perceive so strongly in our spirit, yet will not appropriate it? How many times has someone confirmed what God had already revealed to you and yet His will remains undone? When this is the case, each time that you return to prayer, you will encounter this same issue staring you in your face because you have failed to carry out what God has spoken. Until you do, you cannot progress any further.

Prayer is progressive because it reveals what God is doing. He is performing His will. He does not halt His progress for anyone. It shall be accomplished with or without us. When we take upon ourselves to inquire of the Lord to be still and listen to Him, we also become liable to partake in heaven's treasures. God is aware of every gift given and every truth revealed for one day, both must be accounted for.

But he that knew not and did commit things worthy of stripes, shall be beaten with few stripes. For unto whomsoever much is given, of him shall be much required: and to whom men have committed much, of him they will ask the more. Luke 12:48

Those who carry top positions in the Armed Forces carry the knowledge of crucial information. If used, such information could drastically have a corresponding effect. This information is classified as "Top Secret", a term that many of us have seen at one time or another. Those who possess such classified information have an equal responsibility to the knowledge that they possess. If this is found to be true on a natural level, how exceedingly greater is this responsibility on a spiritual one? Even the smallest of spiritual revelation surpasses the effects of natural possibilities. Negligence, on a natural occurrence, will cost natural lives, yet negligence on a spiritual level will cost souls. Though soldiers can be replaced as a result of natural negligence as far as unbelievers are concerned, the soul is forever gone as far as God is concerned. A soul can be lost and the natural person still alive; evenso the natural man destroyed and yet the soul saved. (Heb 9:27). The point is your spiritual position upon death is far more important than your natural one. Jesus said, "do not fear him who can destroy the body, but Him who destroy both the body and the soul" (Mt. 10:28).

Effective prayer does not exist in the lives of uncommitted saints. I am speaking of effectiveness to the point of bringing a relevant change in the earth for the kingdom of God's sake. This change is only wrought through having the mind of Christ which is the result of effective prayer. One is unable to discern the heart of God when their heart's desires are paramount, rather than the advancement of God's kingdom. Western Christianity is losing its battle for souls. Churches in America are on a moral decline and are in need not only of revival, but a return to the first principles of the doctrines of Christ. These facts and many more, are a result of not articulating to God what God has articulated to us. And why? Because we are not listening! We are admonished to "seek ye first the kingdom of God and his righteousness; and all these things shall be added unto you" (Mt 6:33).

Our seeking is to rest on His faithfulness to meet our needs, not on the motives that all things will be ours.

 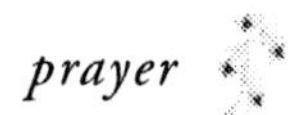

O generation of vipers, how can ye, being evil, speak good things? for out of the abundance of the heart the mouth speaketh. A good man out of the good treasure of the heart bringeth forth good things: and an evil man out of the evil treasure bringeth forth evil things. **Mt 12:34-35**

This holds true in what we say to people as well as in what we utter unto the Lord. We will utter whatever is harbored in our hearts. Ears that have not heard in prayer can be determined by the mouths that cannot appropriate to God in prayer.

In like manner, it is a sin to fall short of wrestling with God in working out what you know He has revealed to you to accomplish. Despite ones sensitivity and reverence to the Lord, the negligence to act upon His leading is without excuse and bears consequences. Christians who are caught in this syndrome have run to the opposite extreme which reveals a person who considers themselves more than they consider God. Is there really any difference between the one who thinks they can do it without God and the one who thinks God can do it without their working faith? In both instances, they are found wanting, for their eyes reflect the same chief concern - themselves.

Indeed, boldness is required to appropriate that which is unseen, unheard and illogical in the natural realm. But such is God's way.

While we look not at the things which are seen, but at the things which are not seen: for the things which are seen [are] temporal; but the things which are not seen [are] eternal. **2 Co 4:18**

But God hath revealed them unto us by his Spirit: for the Spirit searcheth all things, yea, the deep things of God. **1 Co. 2:10**

Those who prevail in appropriating the will of God will most certainly prevail in understanding Divine Protocol and the order that it represents - spiritual.

The prayers of a righteous man availeth much, not because of who he is, but because of Who's he is. This provides God an assurance that we will pray His mind concerning every area of our life as it pertains to the advancement of His kingdom.

To confuse the labor of appropriating with the pastime of speech is a disclosure of ones ignorance of spiritual issues, for this labor represents the very existence for the Church in the earth today. Christians must be loosed from the notions that prayer is nothing more than rattling to God from the impulses of their soul or their unrenewed mind. It is here where we draw the living waters, the seeds of life and the surge of power to endure in a perverse generation while shining forth as lights to those who grope in darkness. To appropriate is to speak what God has ordained to be. It is to decree the mind of God in the earth. The power of a decree does not rest upon the act of it in and of itself, but upon whose authority it possesses.

Thus saith the Lord, the Holy One of Israel and his Maker, Ask me of things to come concerning my sons and concerning the work of my hands command ye me. ***Isa 45:11***

God's Official Order that is Correct in the Dealings of His Kingdom in appropriating to God is first of all to have asked God what He wants to hear. If we have not conformed our lives to the service of God's kingdom, if our desires have not been nailed to the cross, if we are yet uncertain about doing all that He requires of us, then we are yet unable to appropriate correctly to God concerning His kingdom work in this earth. The only prayer that is heard of God by those in such a state is, "Help me, Lord" and if declared with sincerity, help He will.

Let the Church be purified of its facades. Shall we speedily repent of traditions that make the things of God of none effect in our lives? May our prayer altars serve to liberate saints to cry out the heartbeat of our Father and not the lusts of themselves! It is imperative in this hour that we cease from our own efforts of the flesh and be still in order to know Him as the Warrior that He is.

The LORD [is] a man of war: the LORD [is] his name.
Ex 15:3

How long must He tolerate our inexcusable behavior, our continual excuses and our repetitious sins of the flesh? When shall we cease to show contempt to God Who is a Consuming Fire?

Shall not America be judged for its harlotry? Who amongst God's children will be found dabbling in its pleasures and caught in its vices of deception and rebellion? We must live in America (this world), yet not after it. We give more honor to this country than the country whose builder and maker is God.

Ye adulterers and adulteresses, know ye not that the friendship of the world is enmity with God? whosoever therefore will be a friend of the world is the enemy of God. ***Jas 4:4***

Wherefore if ye be dead with Christ from the rudiments of the world, why, as though living in the world, are ye subject to ordinances, (Touch not; taste not; handle not; Which all are to perish with the using;) after the commandments and doctrines of men? Which things have indeed a shew of wisdom in will worship and humility and neglecting of the body; not in any honour to the satisfying of the flesh. ***Col. 2:20-23***

God's people need to get their homes back to the order of prayer! How many more crimes, killings and financial failures must we witness in order to understand the times that we are in? We can tell when rain is about to descend, yet we are blind to the signs of the times! Hypocrites!

Those who hold the truth in unrighteousness, those who hold it in arrogance, even those who think that they are the sole possessors of it, had better sober up to the truth! God's kingdom business is much too vast to waste on individuals who maintain this prideful attitude.

There are those who have been appointed by men to be God's leaders for Him and such show the shallowness of their appointment by their prayers and preaching. God is raising up a breed of wa riors in this hour who understand that His ways change; not Him. His ways and operations in the earth manifest in differently to reveal that He is still the same today, yesterday and forever.

There is a relevant word for this hour that shall set many free. There is a prayer for this hour that is pertinent and it must be revealed by God. Popularity, prestige, having a following, money, education, or labor for the Lord cannot and does not qualify one to be a recipient of what God is saying to His people today. His sovereignty alone decides it.

Shall we humble ourselves from our lofty heights and allow God's order to be established? American preachers and saints must be careful, for we should not esteem ourselves more highly than any of God's people and vessels in the earth. God has a word, a revelation, yes, a prayer to be prayed. May we listen, for it comes from a place only known to the pure in heart?

Chapter 5

The Body of Christ

You and I are one
It is we, not me.

ay we rub our foreheads and our eyes to clear away our prejudice views and conceptions of how we see ourselves and each other as the Body of Christ. We have become so knowledgeable that we have intellectualized this profound mystery. We have tied it down and dissected it like a frog nailed to wood. Our search for knowledge has only led us to be found wanting for the purpose of our pursuits in Christianity. We retreat to the mountains, to Jerusalem, to tranquil parts of the earth in search of our place within this community of souls who have found redemption through Jesus Christ our Lord.

Such pursuits are worthy of their efforts and likewise, some are not. I would venture to be as bold as to say that the majority of the Body of Christ is looking unto itself for its source, its leading, its wisdom, its teaching, its healing and especially, its identity.

Never has such knowledge of God's Word been revealed to the Body of Christ as it is today. Teaching courses are available regarding every imaginable facet of the Bible. Commentaries as thick as the Yellow Pages line the walls of the preacher's study and seminary libraries around the country and yet there still appears to be an immense hunger for the Word of God throughout the Body of Christ.

It appears that instruction is going forth in great proportions in the North, East, South and West. God has raised up teachers capable of expounding on Greek and Hebrew while making truth known by His

Spirit that have indeed edified the Body of Christ tremendously. Even so, many are yet uncertain about their purpose. Unfortunately, it appears that such revelations have become the objects of worship instead of remaining a mere word that points to the Christ of these truths; namely, Jesus. This fanfare must cease. Spiritual exercise without passion for God is man-made religion whose praise and glory is to the likes of men and grievous to the heart of our Father.

How easily we deceive ourselves into attempting to predict God's ways, God's direction and even God's order! "We have been saved for years", we say. "I know how, when and where God is going to move!" We have become so busy as the Body of Christ to where we have lost our perception and place as the Body of Christ.

Divine Protocol must become our supreme method for the Church with Christ as our single focus. God's Official Order That is Correct in the Dealings of His Kingdom must be diligently sought after first on an individual basis, then corporately. We shall know our purpose within the Body as we seek Him for it rather than seeking seek. Yes, we are some seeking people. But whom do we seek? The hand, the foot, or the ear and the mouth? We must quickly realize that God has placed many parts within the Body but only one rules - The Head!

Let us not be satisfied at where we presently are, for it will most certainly rob us of where we need to be. We all are aware that God is blessing His Body and we certainly have come a long way! Praise be to God for His undeserved goodness. But dare we justify ourselves with the good that He has done? Dare we ignore what He totally requires because we have fulfilled a portion of it? Dare we fall short of God's revelation for the Body of Christ today!?

Not as though I had already attained, either were already perfect: but I follow after, if that I may apprehend that for which also I am apprehended of Christ Jesus. Brethren, I count not myself to have apprehended: but this one thing I do, forgetting those things which are behind and reaching forth unto those things which are before, I press toward the mark for the prize of the high calling of God in Christ Jesus. **Ph 3:12-14**

Even the Apostle Paul, who is esteemed highly, recognized that he had not fully apprehended what Christ had apprehended of him. He also realized the danger of assuming such a state, for to do so would constitute a need for him to no longer rely upon Christ and thus, press toward the mark of the high calling. Instead, he might have reminded himself of the works that he had done and become comfortable and complacent with himself, while never realizing that God had moved on in a new direction.

God has always had a heavenly order for the Body of Christ and He always will. It is through submission that we come to know it and through submission, we shall continue to know it. Divine Protocol does exist within the Body of Christ, for God is the God of order and the God of purpose. This order and purpose merges to bring us to relevant expression of God's will for you, for me and for us within the Body.

The Purpose For the Church

The purpose for the Church is evident to most Christians as being the "light of the world" (Mt 5:14) and the "salt of the earth" (v.13). In unison, we sing praises unto the Lord and with outstretched arms, we exalt His name.

We observe Christian television, radio and ministries upholding the banner of salvation for the millions of lost souls. Through these means each day, we are fulfilling the Great Commission to:

> ***Go ye therefore and teach all nations, baptizing them in the name of the Father and of the Son and of the Holy Ghost: Teaching them to observe all things whatsoever I have commanded you: and, lo, I am with you alway, even unto the end of the world. Amen.*** ***Matt 28:19,20***

The purpose for the Church is as multifold as those who make up the Church. There is not any one interpretation for its purpose that will suffice each individual member. Granted, there is a corporate scope of purpose and yet it hinges on a personal acceptance and understanding of ones own revelation of God's purpose for them in the Church which coincides with scriptural support and spiritual integrity.

Many of us are satisfied with the relationship we experience amongst the saints, while simultaneously untouched by the reality of a communion with God intimately and independent of others. How many are members of a congregation yet not of the Body of Christ? How many are sealed with the Holy Ghost and yet uncertain of Who they believe and why?

Thousands of Christians are not experiencing the personal, vibrant, spiritual awareness of life that has been promised and given to everyone who believes on Christ, Who, without respect of persons, grants gifts that are to be used in accordance with spiritual protocol.

> ***But the anointing which ye have received of him abideth in you and ye need not that any man teach you: but as the same anointing teacheth you of all things and is truth and is no lie and even as it hath taught you, ye shall abide in him. 1 Jo 2:27***

> ***And they shall not teach every man his neigbour and every man his brother, saying, Know the Lord: for all shall know me, from the least to the greatest. Heb 8:11***

The place of God's vessel of ministry must not be confused with the place of God Himself. Even though we can recognize the obvious differences, we yet are but flesh and thus subject to the error of believing or trusting who or what we see, feel and understand, rather than in God Whom we must approach in faith believing that He is.

The sowing and watering of God's Word, mysteries skillfully unfolded, interpretations of tongues, signs and wonders, even a word of knowledge that hits the bull's-eye, only avails to the extent of a sincere spirit to Spirit communion between creation and Creator. All else is fleshly and a master work of deceit from the devil. Even when such moves of the Spirit are genuine, they must remain untouched by the flesh in order to work God's righteousness.

The purpose of the Church is directly related to God's quickening power upon the subjects of the Church. Though the scriptures attest to truth, in and of themselves, they are unable to usher Divine Protocol into the spirits and minds of God's people without the Author of those scriptures working within both the mind and the spirit of the believer.

> ***Then opened he their understanding, that they might understand the scriptures.*** ***Luke 24:45***

The Apostle Paul was a murderer of God's heritage, totally supporting his views based on the law and was convinced to the point of murdering that he was right. One day, while going to do havoc upon God's people, Christ quickened Paul through a mighty confrontation which brought him to a realization that he was wrong. Paul certainly knew the word, but was ignorant of the truth. Once Christ showed him his error and opened his eyes to the truth, those same scriptures became the very foundation to prove that Jesus was the Messiah. He further expresses that through this encounter, he knew his purpose within the Body of Christ to a point that he would suffer much for the kingdom of God as foretold by the Lord to Ananias (Acts 9:16).

> ***But I certify you, brethren, that the gospel which was preached of me is not after man. For I neither received it of man, neither was I taught it, but by the revelation of Jesus Christ.*** ***Gal 1:11, 12***

It was Peter who had received his purpose in the Body of Christ, when he was told to feed the sheepfold. Yet he became concerned with Jo's purpose in the Body. Peter was concerned with what would become of another man's purpose, rather than focusing on what Jesus had instructed him to do. Further in the scriptures, we see that Peter was again concerned about the thoughts of men and this time he received an open rebuke and caused division among the brethren (Gal. 2:11-13).

> ***Peter seeing him sayeth to Jesus, Lord and what shall this man do?*** ***Jo 21:21***

It is imperative in this last millennium to mind our own purpose and to be sure of it. God is ever willing to reveal to us His purpose and will for our lives. However, when we are more interested in what God has prepared for others, it simply reflects the lack of spiritual maturity and hidden motives of our own heart. It reveals our insecurities and the need we have to realign ourselves with Divine Protocol. Never are we to seek God with a nosy spirit as it pertains to another. His reply will be the same to us as it was to Peter:

> ***Jesus saith unto him, If I will that he tarry till I come, what is that to thee? follow thou me.*** ***Jo 21:22***

The purpose for the Church is found in Christ, not the Church. He is the Shepherd. He is the voice that is heard and followed by His sheep. No man can enter into this sheepfold but by Him. All that do are thieves and robbers. There is no other way into God's kingdom than through Jesus Christ. It is here that one becomes a part of His Body.

There is "one mediator between God and men, the man Christ Jesus" (1 Tim. 2:5), thus only one way to know God and His purpose for you in the Church.

As we withdraw ourselves from the gathering of the Body, we shall find the secret dwelling of Christ in our hearts yearning to commune with us for and by Himself. When we place the Body before Christ, we are yielding to the sin of the scribes and Pharisees. We become spiritual adulterers, "having a form of godliness but denying the power thereof" (2 Tim. 3:5). May it be far from us to seek after His treasures, His wisdom, His power and not seek after Him. Such ways are common among the religious in both times past and times present. They truly believe that God is void of knowing their motives. In their own foolishness, they have determined that through the searching of the scriptures they will find life, while yet refusing to come to Him Whom the scriptures testifies of (Jo 5:39). Who would be as absurd as Lucifer in believing that he could overthrow God Almighty? Likewise, we can fall into the same pit by approaching the Consuming Fire with guile.

> ***Jesus answered them and said, Verily, verily, I say unto you, Ye seek me, not because ye saw the miracles, but because ye did eat of the loaves and were filled. Then said they unto him, What shall we do, that we might work the works of God?***

Jesus answered and said unto them, This is the work of God, that ye believe on him whom he hath sent. Jo 6:26,28-29

The sole purpose and work for believers in the Church is to believe on Him. We have become entangled and preoccupied with ourselves, with each other and with opinions and judgments. Our prejudices, ranging from racial to denominational, validate the present state of apostasy in America. The desire for revival in this country must be changed to the desire for revival in ourselves. The weights and sins that so easily beset us take place with our permission. The altar calls that attract the same flock for the same reason week after week reveal a lack of genuine, godly sorrow. It shows that Christians desire prayer with conditions. We want to know God's purpose without commitment, sacrifice, or suffering. This quick fix religion is booming and will be the reason for the falling away of many who call upon the name of the Lord. It is a billion dollar industry, selling false hope for contributions to support the democratic rule of man. Many have placed a classified ad in the chambers of their hearts that read:

WANTED:

TEACHERS TO SCRATCH ITCHING EARS
(2 Tim. 4:3)

The divine purpose for believers in the Church is born out of prayer; listening and appropriating. The prayer life of one who is living sacrificially on a daily basis is the prevailing prayer which attracts the heart of God. The prayer of one who has not refused the cross from working deep inside of their hearts, character and mind and has refused to surrender their being to God's kingdom and the advancement of it, is prayer that has yet to obtain God's attention.

The Church must return to Her first love. The knowledge of God's Official Order that is Correct in the Dealings of His Kingdom will not be found from within this book, from your pastor, from seminary, from a weekend conference or even from your Bible alone. It will only be discovered while on your face before Almighty God, prepared to obey His leading and solely do His will.

We shall come to the measure of the fullness of Christ when we begin to measure ourselves by Christ and not by His Church. Shall we not gather together all the issues that pertain to us as a people and allow them to be settled by Christ? May we not be deceived into the many entrapments that will only serve to distract us from that which is true and the work that we have been called to accomplish.

My little children, of whom I travail in birth again until Christ be formed in you. ***Gal. 4:19***

Motives and Methods

It takes the light of God's Holy Spirit to reveal the intents of the heart of man to one another, as well as the heart of the man to himself. The depth of ones soul harbors ideas, opinions, motives and methods that must be purified in order for God's order and purpose to be established through us, the Church.

In order to gain an understanding of what must take place, the mind of man must submit to the mind of God. We must acknowledge ourselves as unable, inadequate and wanting in order to ascertain the insight of God. We must not, in any way, mix the wisdom of God with the wisdom of men. Man's most noble insights and the best of mental persuasions are yet found to be foolishness to God (1 Cor. 3:19). The motives and methods of God demonstrated through His character of holiness and the power of His Spirit cannot be combined with those of the flesh. In their own blinded conceits, men have insisted on delighting themselves with "good" ideas to express and explain the Father and His Son, Jesus, without realizing that only God's knowings will prevail. We are so vulnerable to our soul (for it resides closely to our spirits), that unless continual watching and praying exists, we are certain to allow our soul to offer methods which contain prideful motives and carnal methods.

The issue at hand is to allow kingdom methods and godly motives to be the thrust behind kingdom service. Easier said than done, for to see Divine Protocol in front of us, it must be so within and about us. Purification must be allowed to inhabit within the confines of our being.

Motives

It behooves us to know the purpose in all of our dealings with God. It should not come as a surprise to discover that many individuals are not altogether clear as to why they attend church, respond to an altar call, or portray themselves as saved. While there is an awareness that these things are desired and needed, the motives can be found leaping from a basis of fear, pride, or simply, religious zeal.

I am sure that you have heard the saying, "I don't know why, but I just feel...". Anytime a person's reasoning stems from their emotions, it is not the perfect will of God. While there are times when God does touch us to obtain our attention, He guides us by His Spirit within our spirit, in order to keep our attention. Speculation is not an attribute to be found lingering in the kingdom of God. Motives are always traced to a source and that source will reveal the root source of ones activity - whether they are inspired through sincere fellowship with God which leads to divine direction, or whether they are yielded to fear, pride or wisdom that cometh not from above.

> ***Who is a wise man and endued with knowledge among you? let him show out of a good conversation his works with meekness of wisdom. But if ye have bitter envying and strife in your hearts, glory not and lie not against the truth. This wisdom descendeth not from above, but is earthly, sensual, devilish. For where envying and strife is, there is confusion and every evil work. But the wisdom that is from above is first pure, then peaceable, gentle and easy to be entreated, full of mercy and good fruits, without partiality and without hypocrisy. And the fruit of righteousness is sown in peace of them that make peace.*** ***Jas 3: 13-18***

It is from our mouths that true motives of the heart are revealed. We must not deceive ourselves or be deceived by others into being assured of our salvation due to the works of mere flesh. God's Official Order That is Correct in the Dealings of His Kingdom is an order of righteousness, holiness and truth. Those who fulfill His programs must understand the purpose that they have been chosen of Him. There were many kings that reigned throughout the dispensation of human government and likewise, there were many failures in those kingdoms due to the motives of the heart purged from its deep harbored wickedness.

One king in particular whose life we have pierced into frequently is King David. He experienced victory and defeat many times over. Despite the many brushes with death, he yet trusted in God. However, when we observe his failures, we can see that they were a direct result of his motives. Is this the core reason with any great servant that we unveil within the Word of God? Unquestionably, yes.

Consider the first man to have had the breath of life breathed into his nostrils. Was it his love for his wife that caused him to partake of the forbidden fruit, or was it his motive that he justified himself by accusing God of creating her? Adam had his own motive for adhering to Eve. If Adam had purposed in his heart to obey God, Eve would not have persuaded him. Regardless of how much he loved Eve, how lonely he thought he might have been without her and all of the emotional attachments which were dictating his decisions, it was his own motive that opened the door to the temptation to sin against God. This very act destroyed Divine Protocol in its purest form.

How does one regulate their motives? Where do you obtain and maintain the reason for searching, serving and worshipping God Almighty? Amidst the commotion of a troubled world and the striving of the saints, God has provided a way that is divinely simple. However, from a divine paradigm, simplicity can be complicated for the natural man to accept. The intellect of man searches too high for it. His will is aggressively ambitious about the pursuits of obtaining and acquiring the rudiments of this world. Wealth, fame and the ever present temptation of knowledge, has the soul of man steeped in his own vain glory. Dare he descend into the valley of nothingness to find the vast of everything discovered in the simplicity of Jesus Christ, the Holy One of Israel?

This way is so very foolish to man, that he has to become a fool in worldly wisdom in order to know it. He must endure the pain of losing his props and watch in agony the rejection of men and occasionally, the Body of Christ. This is why becoming a child is the only means to walk with God. A child does not require an explanation; they simply do what Father requires because they have an innocence that is revealed in their mind. It never questions or doubts their loving Father's will and way that He has ordained to for them.

And said, Verily I say unto you, Except ye be converted and become as a little child, ye shall not enter into the kingdom of heaven. **Mt 18:3**

To become a child in heart is to realize that you are totally dependent upon your Father. It is a state of being that finds delight in nothing more than being in the presence of Abba. You perform the work of the kingdom as a yielded, undistracted vessel whose heart is aflame with pleasing Him with the work that has been placed in your hands.

But Jesus answered them, My Father worketh hitherto and I work. ***Jo 5:17***

Such work is only revealed to the pure in heart whose motives are unfeigned and have been tried by the fire of God. It is likened unto a son who beholds his father painting and in turn, he decides to paint. Or perhaps he works on the car just as his father does. Such laboring is not built upon any other reason other than the pure enjoyment of the relationship, for during the painting or repairing, the son delights not in doing things, but in the mere fact of being in the presence of his father.

Many wonderful works are being wrought in the Church today. If we were to step back and ask God just how many of them were of His sheepfold, His answer would not be, "Those of this denomination, those who look spiritual, those who are healing folk, casting out devils, prophesying, speaking in tongues, attending seminary, or constructing massive buildings".

Many will say to me in that day, Lord, Lord, have we not prophesied in thy name? and in thy name have cast out devils? and in thy name done many wonderful works? And then will I profess unto them, I never knew you: depart from me, ye that work iniquity. **Mt 7:22-23**

The labors of an individual will directly reflect their motives. Though keen discernment is necessary, the spiritually mature Christian will perceive it. This is precisely why many of God's children are deceived. Without growth, one is unable to know the works of insincere men from those whose works reflect the true labors of God. Those whose motives are founded upon themselves are such who feed the people the gospel of self. "What God can do for you! What God will do for you! What God must do for you! What God for you. What God you. God you. You".

Financial gain has brought a snare to many Christians. Divine Protocol, as it pertains to prosperity, is in much need of being clearly defined. The Church must be built upon the Rock of Christ, not the rubble of uncertain riches. This is where those who are sincere and those whose diets consists of guile, hypocrisy and the flesh are separated. Unless we guard our hearts against the gospel of self, we are certain to be deceived into funding projects that are not in God's will to fund. While it is clear that many sincere Christians are feeding self centered pursuits unawaringly, it is yet inexcusable! The exhortation to grow up, to mature, to seek the Lord for ones self is clearly defined throughout the Word. If being deceived is a direct result of ones refusal to ask for knowledge, such is the deception of the blind. Many children are painting the wrong picture and fixing the wrong car. If you are performing a duty outside of His presence, then it is not after the counsel of His will. Either consciously or unconsciously, people have allowed their motives to reside beneath the standard of God's requirement; the total denial of self. While it is certain that this is a process, it is imperative that one stays progressive in their process.

The Gospel of Christ causes men to realize their sin and the fact that there is no way out except through repentance and total dependency upon Christ. This gives them access to His kingdom and the rest necessary to give up those motives that are rooted in fear and condemnation. The motive of persons found upright before God is simply to obtain a witness in spirit and conscience that God is pleased. It is the awareness of God's presence that assures His pleasure toward us. This confirms that our motives are striving in the right spirit for the right purposes.

As children, we must desire the sincere milk of the Word that ushers in a continual flow of wisdom. In turn, this establishes Divine Protocol for our existence and performance in the kingdom of God with motives proven purified by the swords dividing power of both soul and spirit.

METHODS

Certainly, the motive for performance will determine just how it is done. Carnal motives seek carnal means. This type of strength is obtained from all that is seen, understood and self rewarding. Good and noble they may seem, yet incapable of reflecting Divine Protocol.

Numerous are the methods found in the Church today. Methods for acquiring finances, getting people to attend a meeting, adding new members to the church and the like all require means and methods to accomplish it. God is a God of methods. We see many methods in the Word of God given to accomplish a certain task. From having Noah to build an ark as a method of salvation for his home, to turning Lot's wife into a pillar of salt as a method of chastisement for her disobedience, God's methods are beyond the calculation of any form of reasoning and can only be grasped by those who are living an active spiritual life, not a religious, carnal one.

Methods are a means to accomplish a desired goal. Never should we become too involved in the method if we have not first determined what result we are looking for. If God has given a task to be accomplished, He will also give the method that goes with it. The method always comes later, so you will definitely have to exercise patience as you await His instructions. In fact, you should have the same kind of prayerful attitude in asking God to reveal the how of what He desires to accomplish through you. Many times finding out what God wants is easier than finding out how He wants it done. How much more should we inquire of the Lord "HOW would you have me accomplish this great work oh, Lord? HOW"?

Marketing is a method used to share a message or a product. Throughout the history of the Bible, God has utilized varies methods to "market" His Word and will. There are countless examples found in

His Word that reveal His approach to marketing and I am confident that we all would agree His marketing never rested upon the ability or the consent of man. When God marketed, He used an unqualified person in an unexpected way to accomplish His unexpected will. To know and experience the relevant move of God, you and I must align our marketing abilities with a divine order for all of the available technology to be effective as God would have it, rather than as man would have it.

I believe that the Church should utilize every means possible to accomplish God's will, however, this becomes dangerous when we place our security in the method rather than in God. We are prone to rely upon the appearance and acceptability by the people to determine whether or not such a method is acceptable. It is very easy to justify the ways and means that are available when they seem to offer a solution to what we believe is the will of God. Surrounded by the indescribable advanced technology of our era, many methods convey an appearance of obvious effectiveness to comply with our need. After all, God made technology, airplanes, cellular phones, microwaves, televisions and radios, so why should a particular method not be used to achieve God's will? To be certain, the method in and of itself is really not the issue. Rather, the issue lies with choosing our method, or choosing God's method.

Gideon's army was reduced from 32,000 to 300 men to defeat the enemies of the Lord. 70,000 soldiers of David's army was slain because he dared to trust in a 1.3 million member force. Marching the army of Israel around the walls of Jericho did not seem to be a strategic move that would mark the caliber of a warrior such as Joshua. Elijah's demand of the widow woman would be considered absurd to the minds of many people today. Many are the testimonies of the methods that brought victory in the lives of God's men and women.

Why is the Lord particular concerning the methods utilized to accomplish His purpose?

And the Lord said unto Gideon, The people that are with thee are too many for me to give the Midianites into their hands, lest Israel vaunt themselves against me, saying, Mine own hand hath saved me. ***Jud 7:2***

The strength of man's soul and the deceitfulness of his own heart is never ending in its pursuit to out perform God. The desire to rule is the core of all sin. Trust in God will not be a choice that is made by the soul of man. It will be the leap of faith from his spirit to obey God's will. That same leap of faith must also be taken to acquire the method that God has chosen for His will to be done.

The purpose for faith has been limited to healings, houses, cars and carnal methods to ensure the work of heaven to manifest. While believing God for our needs to be met and our bodies healed, we must also exercise our faith in performing His will - His way. I submit to you the vast purpose for faith - to perform the will of God the way He has ordained from the foundations of the earth! Many of the healings and material things that we need have not become a reality for the simple fact we are not interested in doing God's will, God's way. If we acquired the car and obtained the house while receiving that much needed healing, we would probably drive where we should not be going, cooking what we should not be eating and doing what we should not be doing. God said these things will be added, after we have sought first His kingdom.

You see, a true vessel of faith projects an aura of authority that is not self generated. Their insight, discernment and anointing will always reveal whose methods they have chosen. It will reveal that such methods are of God and not of themselves. God's methods will be supported by God's ability, while man's methods will have only man's ability. As we approach the next millennium, there must be a sincere effort to guard our minds in choosing our methods. Many works will suffer because the methods chosen were not of God.

Why should we expect Divine Protocol in our life and ministry when we have succumbed to methods that are less than divinely ordered? Again, the "how" is not the focus, for God can choose to operate in any fashion that He pleases. Rather, it is knowing the very specific way that He desires to perform His will that causes success.

> ***A horse is a vain thing for safety: neither shall he deliver any by his great strength.*** **Ps 33:17**

The means which many of our ministers have taken have not been the choice of the Father. Lack of confidence, purpose, faith, clarity of speech and most of all, power in proclaiming His sacred Word attest to this fact. The entrapments that have hindered God's servants range from relationships that are not ordered by the Lord, to preaching or teaching on subjects that one has not been quickened to express. Our methods will always be dictated to by our motives. If the motive of the heart is twisted, the method we choose will reveal self interest and preservation.

When human flesh takes to the pulpit to express the things of God, whatever proceeds forward is everything that is in the heart of that vessel. There is much mixture in the declaration of God and His kingdom. Even though we will always perfect this message, there is a standard of excellence and maturity that God demands before we utter His Word before His people. When preaching on holiness, holiness should be a reality to the preacher. When declaring forgiveness, you must ask yourself, "is your heart holding a grudge against someone"?

> ***And thinkest thou this, O man, that judgest them which do such things and doest the same, that thou shalt escape the judgment of God?*** **Ro 2:3**

> ***But I keep under my body and bring [it] into subjection: lest that by any means, when I have preached to others, I myself should be a castaway.*** **1 Co 9:27**

God is preparing the next generation of preachers to be selfless and humbling the present generation of leaders to selflessness. When the sermons of a generation are for the most part, "Let's go over to the Promise Land" or "This is the year of jubilee," it merely reveals that we are still getting ready. The next generation will demonstrate that the crossing of the Jordan has taken place and they will show the head of

Goliath in their hands, rather than a sling to take him down. Present day generation has prepared the coming generation in many ways, while God has divinely imparted certain understandings and abilities sovereignly.

Seminary is the study of God as taught by men. Whether or not they are anointed to teach should not determine if this method of schooling is for you. Far too many teachers are not anointed and totally rely upon intellect to teach the things of God. Bible history has nothing to do with what God wants of you today. While it helps in bringing out a particular point, it is nonetheless futile in assisting the messenger to understand what God is doing today, this very minute. One should never elect or be elected to attend seminary. It should be as divinely appointed as any other aspect of your life and ministry. It should never be esteemed as the obvious direction that a chosen minister should take. The one common place of study that we all are to attend, whether preacher or laymen, is "The School of Feet" - yes, at the feet of Jesus!

Until we have experienced the defeat of ourselves at the feet of Jesus, our methods will continue to rob us of an endless supply of divine living. The abundance of resources are without end when we are drawing on the supply of God methods. We will encounter a spiritual restlessness, unable to be satisfied when we jump from one project to another attempting to perform what we think is God's will. This will most certainly open the door to a competitive spirit with others and such a one will remain in the realm of generalities regarding God's kingdom instead of those which are relevant for our times.

Every denomination within the Body of Christ has selected certain methods to obtain their desired results for their particular ministry. Prophetically speaking, our leaders must pray and seek the face of God in proving that their choices are not of themselves, but of the Lord. In doing so, it will only bring us in tune with that still small voice of God. Only brokenness brings true dependency upon God. For those who refuse to submit, our heavenly Father will break them. If we reject His breaking and continue to rebel, our works will end in failure even though they might appear to be successful all along. This is the reality of Divine Protocol, God Official Order that is Correct in the Dealings of His Kingdom.

At this point I must, in earnest sincerity, speak my heart concerning the young man of God as it pertains to the methods he has chosen to fulfill his ministry. He is a vessel chosen during one of the most exciting as well as complex times in the history of the Church. Transitions of many kinds are taking place simultaneously within Christendom, while he is being pruned and perfected by God in his own personal life. Issues of morality, false doctrine, leadership roles among men and women and the breakdown of the family within the church, contribute to a whirlwind of processes that are not easy to face.

While sincerely desiring to ascertain God's perfect will, young men are being faced with denying man's will as well as their own. Deciphering between the Word of God used to counsel them that is of the flesh and that which is truly of the Lord usually takes the experience of many failures to come to a place of knowing the difference. My point is that many young men have settled for methods that reveal fear rather than those that reveal faith.

Fear has caused young men to submit to ministries that have served to intimidate them to submission, rather than love them to submission. Fear has caused reactionary ministry rather than responsitory laboring based on love and power through the agent of the Holy Spirit. The young man has dealt with his insecurities by putting on an image of strength through apparel, popular acquaintances and/or academic achievement rather than nailing them to the cross. In most cases, this has been a learned way of coping by watching current leadership operate, or by not being mentored and discipled as to the correct ways of spiritual maturity.

The young man has the been the prized object to conquer by some of our leaders today even as he has been in all generations. Javelins of many kinds have been hurled at his call, his zeal for God and for the threat that he poses to the insecure Sauls that have always attacked the Davids whose heart is after God. All this and more, has caused methods to be acquired by the young warrior that must be forsaken if he intends to experience how God has prepared him to close out the next millennium with power as he follows Divine Protocol.

The anointing that is on the young man of today is one of a warrior contending for the faith in a specific way for these last days. He is relentless in his pursuit to bring joy to the Master's heart and yet the methods of others distract him from pursuing the path that God has chosen for him.

Amid the transition, many of God's leaders find a great challenge in trying to contain the zeal and the perception that the young warrior possesses of God's kingdom. Oftentimes, their reaction is to qualify how God has anointed him by trying to fit to size this wisdom and insight so that it will fit their own. This leads to placing upon him weapons that he has not proved. The reaction is that of any warrior; he refuses to operate the will of God in your prescribed way.

If there is not a godly understanding sought between young and old, the young warrior will eventually leave and start this process over at another ministry, or he will stay to tolerate the situation until he can politically position himself to make the best of the circumstance. If the young warrior is mature enough, he will use spiritual wisdom coupled with godly methods and allow God to work through this and teach him a valuable lesson. When completed, God will determine the outcome that will bring peace within his spirit rather than fear. Even when you must face rejection, all is well for God is always in control.

Under no circumstance is that leader to be touched by either your words or deed. You must recognize him as God's anointed vessel. Even when they are not God's anointed, vengeance yet belongs to God. Forgive them who despitefully use you and pray for your enemies. This is Divine Protocol when dealing with situations that would cause conflict and sow seeds of bitterness in your spirit for years to come. You must not let it take root in your heart, mind, or soul whatsoever. It is a trap of the devil to keep you in bondage and legally unable to strive for the masteries.

The ruddy boy David was dressed in the armor of Saul to face Goliath, however, he replied, "I cannot go with thee; for I have not proved them" (1 Samuel 17: 39). At this, David removed the armor of man in exchange for the armor of God. This truth exposes that God's methods are not the same as man's and this must be respected by all.

Saul's way of facing the enemy was for Saul and David's for David. Both were a result of God's method for one and His method for another. God's chastisement will be experienced by God's leaders and His young warriors who are touching each other beyond their due authority. Many young men are being encouraged to be still and acknowledge leadership. While there is a definite place for this principle, it has nonetheless been greatly abused in many circles. The result has been that many young men have not developed a dependence solely upon the Lord. There is a counsel that only the Lord can and will give to each individual that is a direct result of a personal relationship with Him. It is the whole thrust behind the New Covenant relationship which cannot be manipulated or interfered with in any capacity by any agent other than Jesus Christ and the Father.

On the same token, many young men have refused their pastor's counsel for reasons that center around themselves. Though this is wrong, refusal does not necessarily mean rejection. I can refuse to agree with your decision, but it does not mean I reject you because of it. The wisdom of Divine Protocol is to set the proper order at the conception of relationships to determine if they are joined by flesh or by the Spirit of God. While no two situations are the same as to why these issues take place, we must, through prayer and discernment, know the motive of the leader as well as the motive of the follower. Without this principle, methods will manifest to reveal that agendas clash and what ensues is the process of coming to a final conclusion which can take months and even years to achieve. One even takes the risk of losing God's original purpose for their life and ministry at the expense of not adhering to God Official Order that is Correct in the Dealings of His Kingdom.

Beautifully illustrated is the relationship and effectiveness of unity between the leader, Moses and the young warrior, Joshua:

> ***Then came Amalek and fought with Israel in Rephidim. And Moses said unto Joshua, Choose us out men and go out, fight with Amalek: tomorrow I will stand on the top of the hill with the rod of God in mine hand. So Joshua did as Mosses said unto him and fought with Amalek: and Moses, Aaron and Hur went to the top of the hill.***

And it came to pass, when Moses held up his hand, that Israel prevailed: and when he let down his hand, Amalek prevailed. But Moses' hands were heavy; and they took a stone and put it under him and he sat thereon; and Aaron and Hur stayed up his hands, the one on the one side and the other on the other side; and his hands were steady until the going down of the sun. And Joshua discomfited Amalek and his people with the edge of the sword. ***Ex 17:8-13***

Among the many truths found in this scenario of unity and order, a few are outstanding:

• As a leader, Moses was the delegated authority recognized by God.

• As elders, Aaron and Hur were the delegated support recognized by God.

• As arms of war, the young men were the delegated hand recognized by God.

Let us quickly attest to the fact that one could not have succeeded without the other. Regardless of our age, as men of God, we must not rely upon methods that are acceptable to us but instead, those that are approved by God.

When we observe the consequences of neglected leadership, it is imperative that the young black man be given priority attention amongst black leaders as it relates to Divine Protocol. The fact that 23% percent of all Negro men are in prison, on probation, or on parole on any given day is clear evidence of the need for aggressive measures to be taken to recapture the young generation whose time for leadership is upon them. For Caucasians, the figure is only 6.2%. Though Negroes account for 15% of all monthly drug usage (they account for 37% of drug possession arrests), once caught, they are more likely to do time than are Caucasians (Newsweek, April 1993, p.30).

There must be a more deliberate plan of action for young men called to ministry within the ranks of Christianity, regardless of their nationality. Leadership efforts and mentoring must include much more than carrying a preacher's briefcase, or learning the dress codes that provides an appeareance of success, while networking to insure a prosperious evangelistic career. We have yielded to the ways of the heathen in determining our acceptance of God.

> ***And walked in the statutes of the heathen, whom the LORD cast out from before the children of Israel, and of the kings of Israel, which they had made.*** **2Ki 17:8**

Even as satan killed all the Jewish infant boys in an attempt to kill Jesus, he now attempts to abort the young man's ministry by disqualifying their mission through being ill prepared for the next millennium by the standards of men rather than the commandments of the Lord.

> ***Who shall ascend into the hill of the LORD? or who shall stand in his holy place? He that hath clean hands, and a pure heart; who hath not lifted up his soul unto vanity, nor sworn deceitfully.*** **Ps 24:3, 4**

By causing motives and methods to become entangled in the complicated process of relationships which result from traditional systems that compete with God's relevant agenda, satan has greatly hindered the progress of the dynamic and fearless ministry of the young man that God has ordained for our generation.

Due to these traditional methods, I truly believe that the harvesting of the young man is long overdue. I believe that many of our young, bold drug pushers are to be gospel preachers. Many who have opted for becoming lawyers, doctors and professionals had a deep urge to become evangelists, pastors and prophets. Yet without the encouraging voice of the leaders, how could there be an answer? It will be the young who reach out to the lost souls of the young, yea, they shall even reach the old! Church leadership must play its role in developing church leadership.

The church that provides the liberty for the young man of God to simply apprehend God in the fashion He has ordered will be a blessed church indeed. While not forsaking the need to adhere to accountability principles, let us be reminded that we are accountable to the young even as they are accountable to us. The young warrior simply expects leadership to lead and to provide the resources necessary to develop the gifts that God has bestowed. The greatest resources any leader can provide is the spiritual and emotional support necessary to ensure strong spirits and an unwavering faith in God. This is shown by proactive leadership based on security and love, not reactionary leadership based on fear and insecurity.

We have funds for just about every church project, but where is the provision for God's young warriors to shine as lights and herald the truth to their generation? To believe that we waste our building fund dollars to support such a work is to be in confusion regarding who the building really is. There should be a fund to enable young men to work in a capacity of ministry so that he may be without distraction in serving the Lord. This is not to say that he should not work; I simply am referring to the fact that there are millions of dollars of resources within the Church today and very little has gone toward preparing the next generation for effective ministry for the next millennium. It is to be expected that my judgment is limited, for I have not seen the efforts of every church. However, the point is that we must see a lot more deliberate attention and action given to this area. The protocol of the hour is to finance those ministries who can reach this generation. They are an essential part to filling your building up as well as building your building up.

My observation concerning the young man of today is without guile toward our leaders whatsoever. I am careful to speak the truth and to do so with respect and protocol, yet be it far from me not to speak what God hath required lest the blood be on my own hands.

In conclusion, we must perceive God's methods and by faith, implement them. Never should we elect for the "intelligent" choice, for to do so will guarantee that we miss the divine choice. The choice of flesh will only hinder the ways of both God and His people. Be this as it may, in His omnipotence, He will bring forth good in the countless circumstances that are experienced by those whose hearts are upright before Him. For those who search after God with all their hearts, soul, mind and strength, He takes every experience and is glorified by it. He will give them beauty for ashes and in the end, they will soar the skies of eagles and perform great exploits for their God!

Our leaders today have toiled very hard in building God's kingdom for our generation. They have sacrificed beyond the call of duty to usher God's people into His will. The burdens that they carry and continue to carry will never be understood by the majority of the saints. The past 20-25 years have involved a number of transitions that our leaders have had to deal with, while providing the support of leadership for communities as well as God's sheep.

They have suffered at the expense of their families, their jobs and sometimes their own mistakes. Some have taken on too much on the side of love, not entrusting God to do what they could not do. As a result, many have died before their time. It was too much for their bodies to handle. Likewise, many of their marriages and children have suffered to advance the kingdom of God within the earth. Great accomplishments have been realized by Christian leadership today and our country would not have avoided the moral decay to its present extent had not God anointed and appointed those who led the church toward its reunion with Jesus Christ. Thank God for our leaders who have taken the helm to build, expand and enlarge the borders of Christendom in every sphere of our society.

As we prepare to enter into the next millennium, it will be imperative that our current leadership be so ever discerning as to enlisting and preparing new leadership. As I observe corporate America, the sports league and every organization making strides toward recruitment for the next generation, I see the Church very lethargic in being aggressive in taking claim on its young generation, especially the young man. As the vision increases, so must the laborers. Many of our leaders have had to work so hard on this battlefield that they never learned to delegate some of their work to others. Out of survival, they have learned to do what needed to be done with or without assistance. This has to change if our leaders want to see their labors remain. For leadership to wait five years to mentor new leadership because they see themselves slowing down, is both too long to wait and the wrong reason to move. For leadership to wait until they become sick is poor preparation for the future.

When you plan to expand your building, you should also plan to delegate leadership. If God has called you to invest money into building, He has also sent you the help you will need in leadership. If you have the building vision without the leadership vision, then your vision is of the flesh. The vineyard that God has planned to enlarge is either yours or His. If it belongs to Him, there are laborers on their way to do what you cannot do. They are on their way to bless and not curse. They are the blessing. Before God can bless His leaders financially, He occasionally blesses them with the gifts necessary to justify the money or else, we would not have the spiritual accuracy necessary to target those funds correctly.

Allow me to address a transition principle in God's kingdom that is totally different than any other organization known to man. It is a protocol that is not natural and it almost seems to be unfair. Yet it is God's way of appointment to leadership in all dispensations of His kingdom. As we adhere to God's official order that is correct in the dealings of His kingdom in the scope of transition, it will bring a joy, a blessing and a rest. As with any aspect of life, it will bring its challenges as well. Regardless of where we are as leaders, God is our ultimate reward. Let us handle our works soberly for they always belong to Him. I realize this is a large block of scripture, yet I would ask that you read and reread it to truly discern how important this is in this hour.

For the kingdom of heaven is like unto a man [that is] an householder, which went out early in the morning to hire labourers into his vineyard. And when he had agreed with the labourers for a penny a day, he sent them into his vineyard. And he went out about the third hour and saw others standing idle in the marketplace and said unto them; Go ye also into the vineyard and whatsoever is right I will give you. And they went their way. Again he went out about the sixth and ninth hour and did likewise. And about the eleventh hour he went out and found others standing idle and saith unto them, Why stand ye here all the day idle? They say unto him, Because no man hath hired us. He saith unto them, Go ye also into the vineyard; and whatsoever is right, [that] shall ye receive.

So when even was come, the lord of the vineyard saith unto his steward, Call the labourers and give them [their] hire, beginning from the last unto the first. And when they came that [were hired] about the eleventh hour, they received every man a penny. But when the first came, they supposed that they should have received more; and they likewise received every man a penny. And when they had received [it], they murmured against the goodman of the house, Saying, These last have wrought [but] one hour and thou hast made them equal unto us, which have borne the burden and heat of the day. But he answered one of them and said, Friend, I do thee no wrong: didst not thou agree with me for a penny? Take [that] thine [is] and go thy way: I will give unto this last, even as unto thee. Is it not lawful for me to do what I will with mine own? Is thine eye evil, because I am good? **Mt 20:1-15**

As you review this block of scripture, several points become very clear. God's kingdom involves workers that have been hired by the householder Who is Christ at different intervals. They are all paid by God and He will continue to hire other laborers to join in with the present laborers until the last hours of time. Some of them will receive just as much as those who started many hours before. There will be a temptation on those who have borne the heat of the day to despise these last hour workers by not allowing them the freedom to labor along side them, sometimes in a far greater capacity of power and knowledge.

The temptation that our leaders (who have toiled tremendously), will face is to allow their eye to become evil because others will enter into their labors, reaping where they have not sown and/or receiving honor from God's people that exceed the honor that they have received. To a degree, I see this happening today in every denomination. Although we are striving toward perfection, our leaders must not yield to this spirit for one second or else it will utterly destroy their labors or cause God simply to remove them altogether for their good and to avert the trouble that it would bring.

The righteous perisheth and no man layeth [it] to heart: and merciful men [are] taken away, none considering that the righteous is taken away from the evil [to come]. **Isa 57:1**

Unless God's anointed leadership yields to God's movement and positioning of certain gifts that He is raising up, He will physically remove anyone who does not sanctify Him as God before His people and deliberately hold His will in contempt.

***And the LORD spake unto Moses and Aaron, Because ye believed me not, to sanctify me in the eyes of the children of Israel, therefore ye shall not bring this congregation into the land which I have given them.* Nu 20:12**

***Remember therefore from whence thou art fallen and repent and do the first works; or else I will come unto thee quickly and will remove thy candlestick out of his place, except thou repent.* Re 2:5**

Though this is not His perfect will, He will nonetheless exercise His right as the landowner to give it to whom He chooses. Death is not always the method that God will use. Sometimes He will simply remove His Spirit from working in the midst of such a work and it will fade away or struggle to maintain on its own strength.

None of our fields belong to us. We have been enlisted to work them. Although we will receive our rewards, they do not belong to us. God has the right to put whom He has chosen where He elects to put them. If the fruit of His anointing is upon a vessel, it is for the benefit of that leader. Had Saul embraced David, what would have been the end of his days?

There is a Phosophy that is dangerously cutting in on the labors of some of our leaders and although it sounds fair, it is nonetheless unscriptual. This Phosophy declares that unless you start at the bottom of a ministry to prove yourself, you cannot expect to carry out a leadership role. The idea is to cause people to adhere to certain criteria that has been set up to insure quality control. Of course, I will be the first to affirm that every leader should maintain some form of leadership accountability and standard of proving a person's ability, however, when there is a legalistic rule that does not allow for God's Spirit to move and direct, such systems will only serve to hinder the progression of God's kingdom among the people. There has to be a Divine Protocol in proving laborers, not a paganistic system of control.

In the book of Acts, leadership was appointed by prayer and fasting rather than systems of natural observations and credits. Who can earn the right to be anointed and empowered to fulfill the work of God? Those who are truly appointed by God have not chosen themselves, let alone having been chosen by another person.

> ***Beginning from the baptism of Jo, unto that same day that he was taken up from us, must one be ordained to be a witness with us of his resurrection. And they appointed two, Joseph called Barsabas, who was surnamed Justus and Matthias. And they prayed and said, Thou, Lord, which knowest the hearts of all [men], shew whether of these two thou hast chosen, That he may take part of this ministry and apostleship, from which Judas by transgression fell, that he might go to his own place.***
> **Ac 1:22-25**

> ***Wherefore, brethren, look ye out among you seven men of honest report, full of the Holy Ghost and wisdom, whom we may appoint over this business.*** **Ac 6:3**

> ***As they ministered to the Lord and fasted, the Holy Ghost said, Separate me Barnabas and Saul for the work whereunto I have called them.*** **Ac 13:2**

In these few scriptures, we observe that God does not overlook the natural element of qualification and faithfulness. Nor does He allow men to make the final decision on who performs various roles in His kingdom. In order that Divine Protocol might be a reality in our churches in these last days, we must discern who God appoints in our churches and places over the works that we have built in sweat, blood, prayers and fastings. As leaders, we cannot come to the most crucial point in our ministries and take lightly the appointment of those who will become pillars of the church. Faithfulness to God cannot be weighed by sheer tithes, offerings and church attendance. Most definitely, they are a part by which we weigh faithfulness, but only a part. Through such means, deceivers have crept into churches and brought havoc to the fold. There are impostors who make it their career to infiltrate ministries for the sole purpose of making a living. Their vision is to be important and to get on staff, yet they offer no spiritual value for that leader or the church. They possess carnal ideas void of spiritual insight to God's relevant will for the advancement of the ministry that God has called you to. Such can be a heavy weight toward advancing your present work and future plans for the next millennium. They entangle themselves by building soul ties with leadership that causes the leader to feel obligated to them. They realize they have no real spiritual value, but they make themselves appear valuable through appealing to the natural needs and or weaknesses of the leader. As a result, they can end up with more control over the ministry than the leader thinks they have.

Such control can be compared to witchcraft in some situations and ultimately, that leadership will never have those who are truly sent by God to work the ministry. Those who are in the flesh and work within the courts of leadership are always fearful of the Daniels and Esthers coming on the scene. They immediately react to those who come in the Spirit of the Lord to uphold that leader and work with a spiritual discernment that can usher his labors to a new level. Obviously, they are fearful of losing their position or being showed up for what they really are - dead weight!

For those leaders who have allowed such insecure individuals to become settled in your ministry, if you intend to move on to the next level, repent before God, apologize to them and remove them from any office that they are not producing in. You are not beholding to anyone that expects you to show them favor in a field that does not even belong to you. In fact, until you remove them, God will not send you the ones truly appointed by Him. They may be sitting right under your ministry and you cannot even discern them.

There are examples throughout God's Word which reveal that many times, God will not move until He first removes. For Him to move by His Spirit, He removes that which is of the flesh, or simply is not a part of His plan and purpose. God does not have to explain Himself and many times He doesn't. If we insist upon people, He will let us have them along with the problems they will bring.

With Abram, it was his nephew Lot. With Gideon, it was 31,700 who had to be removed in order for just 300 to destroy the Midianites and Amalekites, a band of desert nomads who repeatedly raided the country. With Joshua and Caleb it would have called for all of Israel in order for them to enter into the Promised Land had not Moses interceded on behalf of Israel. God would have removed everyone and taken those who believed. Jesus had to remove observers before he healed Jairus' daughter taking only Peter, James and Jo with Him.

There are people in your life that are costing you your ministry and until you remove them, the divine will of God will not come to pass. Never believe that you have to have that person there or you just would not make it. Many times, we, as leaders select individuals based on our own insecurity rather than our security. It is time to get over what you are afraid of and allow skilled people to come and labor for your benefit.

If God has anointed you to be where you are, do not worry; no one can replace you. Separation is a reality when pursuing God's kingdom. It is a price that many people do not want to pay. Yet God will allow circumstances that will cause those people to leave you. When that happens, please allow it to be completed. Do not attempt to reconcile a relationship that God is breaking off. The breaking of a relationship does not necessarily mean the breaking off of fellowship. What is seen as a breaking in one way is merely a realigning in another way. Sometimes we simply put the wrong gifts in the wrong capacity. There are those in certain positions who realize they should not be there and perhaps are afraid of admitting this. In any event, be prepared for the changing of the guards to become a strong reality as we behold the days of tomorrow become the days of today.

Those who are spiritual will not try to prove themselves in carnal ways. You must discern them. They will not be intimidated by leadership games in an attempt to win positions. They will show their willingness for submitted labor through unfeigned support and a life-style of prayer which emanates from their being. Others will discern such individuals to be of great benefit and in His own way, God will bear witness to those who have been called of Him to labor within the field of your ministry.

While it is somewhat easy to assume that the burden of proof is upon those who have been sent to your ministry, this same principle is applied to leaders by those who have the spiritual abilities that your church needs. Often, those who are spiritually mature come across as high minded or self confident. While it would appear that they carry themselves this way, it is really their seriousness about what they know they have been called to do. Jesus did not attempt to persuade anyone of Who He was. He simply performed God's will and allowed His works to speak for Him.

The last days workers of God's vineyard will not come expecting a lot of talk and explanations of who they are to the point of the law. They will come with God's anointing to carry out their part in your ministry and you will be blessed. They will even expect certain conditions so that God's work can be carried out. These conditions will not be of a carnal sort but through spiritual discernment which they understand. They realize if certain things are not done a certain way, God's work will not succeed. God will never have a laborer to implement a work without bearing witness with the spirit of that leader as well. Though the leader might not understand it, God will yet speak to the under shepherd regarding the genuineness of a particular direction.

When God takes a church to a new level, He sends gifts as evidence of His calling to that level. The pastor can only pastor. There are specialists who are more skilled than the pastor to carry out duties that the pastor should not carry out. As we enter this next millennium, I pray our leaders discern the need for true prophets and evangelists as well as other offices of spiritual gifts and helps.

While such men and women exist today, there will be certain characteristics that accompany those of the last hour workers. They will have a zero tolerance level for sin amongst leadership. They will deal with spiritual issues on their knees in serious fasting and prayer. They will expect God to do miracles to confirm His Word with signs and wonders following. Maturity will be a demand and not a request. They will come across as short tempered to those in the flesh. However, they have an understanding that Christ's return is soon and there is no time to waste over issues that are designed to distract and delay God's will.

Though they will be loyal to leadership and respect those in authority, they will not be controlled by leadership or play the political games that many have been entrapped by. They will live a life of sincere consecration and will align themselves with those who are spiritual and moving with God in a relevant way.

As I close this particular section, I do so realizing that I have not scratched the surface on the topic of Divine Protocol in the ranks of leadership. It is a topic that deserves a whole chapter in and of itself, if not a complete book. I simply believe it was the will of God for me to address these simple but important principles as we head toward the next millennium for the Body of Christ. While some information shared here might not be perfect in knowledge or in its presentation, my prayer is that the content as a whole is understood to accomplish one purpose: God's leaders receiving the godly appointed help they will need for the next millennium while avoiding those who have sent themselves or those who have been sent by the devil. Through adhering to God's Official Order That is Correct in the Dealings of His Kingdom, leadership will move toward the perfect will of God in a relevant way for this generation and the next.

The Message and Its Messengers

The relevance of God's message to the world through His Son Jesus Christ is undisputed. The messenger of God must, with all diligence, fulfil the highest commission that could ever be granted to a human being.

> ***And say to (your name), Take heed to the ministry which thou hast received in the Lord, that thou fulfil it.*** **Col. 4:17**

Priorities amid God's messengers must reflect three things:

1) The pursuit of God.

2) The pursuit of God.

3) The pursuit of God.

Due to the suffering conditions in most third world countries, this very act is done with few distractions for those inhabitants. The reason is obvious; their very survival depends on hearing from God. In America, however, we are pursued by everything that appeals to the lust of the flesh, the lust of the eyes and the pride of life. If we are unconcerned with Divine Protocol, whatever is designed by God to be a blessing will inevitably turn to be a great hindrance to fulfilling the Great Commission.

The Message

Jesus said unto him, Thou shalt love the Lord thy God with all thy heart and with all thy soul and with all thy mind. This is the first and great commandment. And the second is like unto it, Thou shalt love thy neighbor as thyself. On these two commandments hang all the law and the prophets. Mt 22:37-40

Should not our message reflect this central theme? We must ask ourselves, "from where did I receive this message that I preach"? Indeed, the appearance of preaching and teaching is easily duplicated, but the spirit of it cannot be. The same anointing that was upon our Lord and Savior, Jesus Christ in Luke 4:18 is upon His true servants and messengers of today. The height of His intent is not for us to be rich, to be healthy, or to be eloquent, but to be presentable to God the Father.

And now I am no more in the world, but these are in the world and I come to thee. Holy Father, keep through thine own name those whom thou hast given me, that they may be one, as we are. Jo 17:11

Oftentimes, the key message of the kingdom of God is replaced with the elementary aspects of God's kingdom program. As a result, the highest purposes are abandoned or seldom realized. Wealth, health, knowledge, love and every godly attribute and characteristic finds its proper place when ones focus is deliberately on obtaining the redemption of their souls and beholding the face of the Lord Jesus Christ.

One can perceive the true message of the Lord, for it is heavenward and full of hope, faith and love. God sends a word to challenge us to change for His glory, for His delight and for His will. The message sent from heaven is never to be tampered with, altered or edited (Rev. 22:19). His Word is sharper than any two edged sword, dividing asunder everything that is contrary to Him (Heb. 4:12-13).

The instruction of God's Word is to better understand His message, not to become vain in pursuits that end in error. The Spirit of the Lord holds His message and uses man to utter it. Man can do nothing without the Lord in expressing the mystery of God's kingdom. The flesh profits nothing and it will never glory in the work of God. Due to the rebellious nature that man yields to, he must continually insist that his good is but dung.

> ***But what things were gain to me, those I counted loss for Christ. Yea doubtless and I count all things but loss for the excellency of the knowledge of Christ Jesus my Lord: for whom I have suffered the loss of all things and do count them but dung, that I may win Christ and be found in him, not having mine own righteousness, which is of the law, but that which is through the faith of Christ, the righteousness which is of God by faith: That I may know him and the power of his resurrection and the fellowship of his sufferings, being made conformable unto his death; If by any means I might attain unto the resurrection of the dead.***
>
> ***Ph. 3:7-11***

To shorten this passage would take away the full intent of the Holy Spirit's purpose in pointing out the never ending temptation of the human heart to establish its own righteousness and even its own gospel. It reveals that the only way to avoid the identical sin of Adam and Eve is to count all your goodness as worthless. Our aim in declaring His message must not be the message in and of itself. The impact of any message will be found in having a relevant relationship with the originator of the message. Without this protocol, we will certainly lose our focus of Christ Who is the Head and be found declaring a word that does not have any relevance for the hour.

We will toil in developing sermons that are scriptural and full of definitions and interpretations, while all the time still void of power. Such preaching has a form of godliness, yet the lack of demonstration of power only reveals that it originated with man. It will take much human argument and energy to express what we have found in this sacred Word that we want to express. Who can predict the wind? Likewise, no one can predict the moving of the Spirit of the Lord. Only He knows what needs to be declared, to whom it will be declared and how it should be delivered.

What we consider to be gain, we must count as loss. Gifts which we possess as natural abilities such as singing, writing, speaking and even those which we have acquired through education, will lead us to adopt our own form of righteousness if we fail to rely totally upon Christ as we operate the abilities that He has given. It will rob of us of the joy of knowing Him and the power of His resurrection and we will consider the fellowship of His suffering as a thing to despise. As a result, our message will not be to attain to the resurrection of the dead, but to conform to the ways of humanism and therefore to the ways of the world.

But beloved, I am persuaded of better things concerning you and myself. I believe that for the messengers of God to render themselves helpless is the only safeguard against altering the message of the Lord. Those who yield to this subtle tactic of satan, already have or will err from the faith and be found shipwreck upon the shores of many deceitful and hurtful lusts.

The message that is correct in the dealings of His kingdom must remain in the hand of God, untouched by our hands, received in the Spirit and uttered without respect of persons or fear of men. For if we seek to please men, we should not be a servant of Christ (Gal. 1:10).

We must ask ourselves, both individually as well as corporately, "Why are many of our pulpits without conviction, without holiness, without power?" Without the message of the Lord, many more will be found void of power and of a clear word from the Lord to His people today.

For whosoever shall call upon the name of the Lord shall be saved. How then shall they call on him in whom they have not believed? and how shall they believe in him of whom they have not heard? and how shall they hear without a preacher?
Ro. 10:13-14

Throughout the ages of time, God has set the mold of human people to carry the oracles of His heart. Such a commission has been given to mankind. Only once did God use an animal to speak His message and that was to rebuke the mad prophet.

As we trace God's Word from Genesis to Revelation, we will see that the standard of Divine Protocol for the messengers of God has never changed and has always maintained a core passion for God and then His kingdom:

And I will raise me up a faithful priest, that shall do according to that which is in mine heart and in my mind: **1 Sam. 2:35a**

Therefore, seeing we have this ministry, as we have received mercy, we faint not; But have renounced the hidden things of dishonesty, not walking in craftiness, nor handling the word of God deceitfully; but by manifestation of the truth commending ourselves to every man's conscience in the sight of God.
2 Co. 4:1, 2

As mentioned previously, the priority among God's servants must always be the pursuit of God. However, times have changed and the last days have brought on many agendas that compete with the pursuit of God and the advancement of His kingdom. Many ministers have developed comfortable life-styles that do not provide room in their life for sacrifice. Careers and jobs are justified by an array of carnal excuses that simply reveal that the Word of God, amongst those who declare themselves ministers of righteousness, has fallen upon hearts that are not single in serving the Lord. While indeed we are always being brought toward the end of ourselves, there is yet a contempt toward sacrificial living that God has always demanded of His servants. Whether it would be poverty, rejection, or the sword that would bring glory to God, we find a religious way to avoid what is clearly a part of Christendom.

> ***But in all [things] approving ourselves as the ministers of God, in much patience, in afflictions, in necessities, in distresses, In stripes, in imprisonments, in tumults, in labours, in watchings, in fastings; By pureness, by knowledge, by longsuffering, by kindness, by the Holy Ghost, by love unfeigned, By the word of truth, by the power of God, by the armour of righteousness on the right hand and on the left, By honor and dishonor, by evil report and good report: as deceivers and [yet] true; As unknown and [yet] well known; as dying and, behold, we live; as chastened and not killed; As sorrowful, yet alway rejoicing; as poor, yet making many rich; as having nothing and [yet] possessing all things.***
> **2 Co 6:4-10**

Every man and woman of God will be tempted to succumb to the worship of the devil through compromising the truth when faced with paying the price of suffering that comes with it. While one does not worship him as lord directly, there is yet a relationship developed when satan arrests the affections, fervor and purpose of anyone from serving God. Satan is a ruthless, spiritual legalist who knows how to discredit spiritual labor better than you and I. Without a full adhering to the whole counsel of God, error is certain and therefore, a compromising gospel will follow, powerless to convict or persuade the hearers.

Indeed, as messengers, we want the highest anointing and we desire to walk in the depths of revelation knowledge. To experience Divine Protocol in ministry should be every messenger's desire. Yet, we show our ignorance of kingdom order as well as contempt when we insist of God's conditions based on our own righteousness by which we will serve Him. Such a state of rebellion exemplifies arrogance and pride which must be purged from the hearts of God's messengers by the holy fire of God!

> ***Talk no more so exceeding proudly; let not arrogancy come out of your mouth: for the Lord is a God of knowledge and by him actions are weighed.*** ***1 Sam. 2:3***

Competitiveness, financial gain, popularity and other enemies of sincerity and truth run rampant among God's servants. They have even caused many of God's servants to become entangled with soulical traps that hinder the pure unadulterated Word of God from coming forth. Men begin falling over one another as well as women stepping out of their place as women. Indeed, God has used and is still using His women in the scope of His kingdom. Nonetheless, they are not men! This is not a chauvinistic statement - it is simply the truth. Even as women in society are demanding equality, so also are many within God's kingdom. We fail to realize that equality is not what a woman should be as compared to a man, nor is it what a man should be as compared to another man. Rather, let us be content with who God created us to be. We cannot become anyone else.

Both men and women messengers alike are guilty of desiring equality of some kind. At this point, we must submit ourselves to God and resist the devil's schemes. If God has called you to teach or to preach, your fruit will reveal the genuineness of the call. If God has approved us, we need not seek the approval of man. God will always send a witness from among His people. When we are seeking it out, however, we will pursue the wrong people and in the end, it will not satisfy.

***Cease ye from man, whose breath is in his nostrils: for wherein is he to be accounted of?* Isa. 2:22**

It is imperative that we relinquish the business that belongs to God and tend to the business that He has given us. Whatever you think a person should or should not be doing as a minister whether young or old, man or woman, boy or girl, should not concern us beyond the scope of our relationship with them. Even when there is a relationship established, they are yet free moral agents who reserve the right to take any path they believe God has called them to. While we judge each other from the outside, God knows the very core of our thoughts.

***Who art thou that judgest another man's servant? to his own master he standeth or falleth. Yea, he shall be holden up: for God is able to make him stand.* Ro. 14:4**

It amazes me how quickly people are to tell you what is or is not of God as it pertains to ministry. You will have some who say, "It is time" and just as many who say, "Wait on the Lord". Some will be sincere, while most will be religious. Some right and most wrong.

If you have not heard from God yourself, you will not know what the Lord is saying and how He is leading you. Even if a person speaks a word of knowledge to you, it still will not be yours until you get it from the Lord for yourself through your spirit! It will remain just a word until you press into God's kingdom and fulfill all righteousness for the reality of the promise to come to pass.

God desires His messengers to have the most beautiful relationship among each other that organizations of the world would seek to imitate. Edifying each other would ignite such glorious fellowship that the desire for self would fade away. Esteeming each other better than ourselves is not a choice, it is a command. A command that is contrary to that of self. You and I must be fulfill one or the other, for we cannot serve both God and man.

Since we are messengers who are called to walk in and reveal God's official order that is correct in the dealings of His kingdom, we must purge ourselves from all that offends His work from being effective though our lives. Though we are advancing, we yet have much ground to cover. Shall we purpose in our hearts to turn from ourselves and press into God? And the Church said, "Amen"!

Purge Yourself

Nevertheless the foundation of God standeth sure, having this seal, The Lord knoweth them that are his. And, Let every one that nameth the name of Christ depart from iniquity. But in a great house there are not only vessels of gold and silver, but also of wood and of earth; and some to honour and some to dishonour.
2 Ti. 2:19,20

The wood and earth within the character of God's servant must be removed, for it represents the carnal and earthly nature. The messenger of God cannot operate with traits of dishonor and expect the work and the ways of the Lord to operate in their lives that will bring rewards of effective service. The wood and earth are manifestations of habits in our life that we have not brought to the cross of Christ. It could have been our childhood where we learned to be prejudice of other nationalities, or the traditions of our churches which taught us to justify iniquity in the life of a Christian as normal as well as scriptural. Society and its ideologies have caused many of God's servants to form views and opinions that blind us from seeing the truth. Perhaps it is your zeal for your denominational traditions more so than for God and His kingdom that provokes you to reject His protocol.

What is your wood or earth, your dirt, your log in the eye, that is hindering you from being all that God made you to be? What God has given you, is the gold and silver that will manifest His glory through your life. We are that house or temple which contain vessels of honor.

These are recognized as the gifts, both natural and spiritual, that will bring joy and fulfillment to the Lord when we purge ourselves from that which has no value. All the while, we are developing the silver and gold within us which shall prove us worthy to be used of Him. These treasures are the real you that God has made, the real you that He wants to use and the real you that satan fears. It's fear on satan's part because he realizes that the success of his kingdom is determined by the failure of you becoming enlightened about who you really are in Christ Jesus. This is the greatest threat that you can become to satan and the greatest asset you can become to God.

As a messenger for the gospel of Jesus Christ, God has given you jewels that are to be utilized in order to fulfil the mandate on your life. The purpose is revealed in the gold and silver, not in the dirt. When we focus on the dirt, we confuse our own intent and the intent of others with God's original purpose for making us. Only when we purge ourselves, will we have the sensitivity to perceive the intent for our existence and begin to nurture it. The vastness of God's gold and silver in you is so great that you will need another lifetime called "Eternity" in order to experience it.

If you will purge the dirt and keep on purging it, the vessels of honor will emerge and the Master will use you within the eternal plan of His kingdom. He will sanctify you, set you apart and you shall accomplish great achievements for the Lord.

Man and Woman - Is There a Head?

I have somewhat gone into length regarding the responsibility of the messenger because the New Covenant is brought to us through the foundational vessel of the man of God. God does use the woman, but He does so through the delegated authority of those men who are harmoniously walking with God without respect of persons. Allow me to say that I do believe we have anointed women that are used of the Lord even as Esther, Deborah, Mary and others who were used to carry a distinct message for their generation. Women called of God who move in the spirit of understanding and know their place move forward in the spirit of a true handmaiden of the Lord. Yet those who pursue ministry as women without regard to the scriptural protocol for the man, should seriously weigh their motives. God has built His Church upon men in the five fold ministry while divinely ordering certain missions to be fulfilled by the vessel of a woman in the scope of His overall plan and purpose for the Church. Ignoring this scriptural truth will only breed resentment and rebellion against God's appointed authority and ultimately, against God. This is that spirit of feminism whose root is found in independence of man, rather than wo-man, dependent on man in accordance with God's design.

The role of the man is clearly articulated in scripture as the head of the wife even as Christ is the head of the Church (Eph. 5:23) and that the woman is the weaker vessel (1 Peter 3:1-7) and that by God's wisdom. This weakness should not be viewed as a negative. Instead, it should be viewed as a descriptive character of her purpose as compared to the man.

One reason why the issue of man and woman is in the forefront of our lives is due to the lack of strong men in our generation. Many woman have had to develop an aggressive character to make up for this obvious lack and serious need. The answer will not be found in becoming who you are not; rather, it will be discovered in being exactly who you already are; A WOMAN! A BEAUTIFUL, FEARFULLY MADE WOMAN!

There is no indication in the New Testament that our sexual identity has been canceled. Instead, the New Testament uses several examples of man and woman to show our place with one another in Christ and Christ's place with us and His place with God. I do recognize a particular scripture that is used to uphold that there is neither man nor woman which is found in Galatians 3:28. Though emphasis is solely upon verse 28, it should be viewed by the verse before it and the verse after it as well.

> ***For as many of you as have been baptized into Christ have put on Christ. There is neither Jew nor Greek, there is neither bond nor free, there is neither male nor female: for ye are all one in Christ Jesus. And if ye [be] Christ's, then are ye Abraham's seed and heirs according to the promise.*** ***Ga 3:27-29***

When we see the verse in this light, we realize that Paul was not doing away with our sexual identity but was declaring that in Christ, we are heirs. Not in being a Jew. Not in being a Greek. Not in being a slave or being free. Being White or being Black. Being a woman or being a man. None of these things mattered when it came to being an heir of God through Christ. When I became saved, did I lose my ethnic identity? Does a Latino cease to be a Latino? None of our natural born traits change. I am yet a man designed to fulfill God's purpose as a man. The woman is yet a woman, designed to fulfill the will of God's designed as a woman. Therefore, this scripture should not be used to uphold the reason why a woman would be called to share the same distinct purpose as a man.

Miriam is an excellent example of a woman who was considered the first prophetess under the ministry of Moses. She held the highest post ever held by a woman, but her pride led her to exceed her boundaries when she attempted to usurp the authority of Moses publicly by confronting him concerning his Ethiopian wife.

And Miriam and Aaron spake against Moses because of the Ethiopian woman whom he had married: for he had married an Ethiopian woman. And they said, Hath the LORD indeed spoken only by Moses? hath he not spoken also by us? And the LORD heard [it]. **Nu 12:1-2**

Through yielding to pride, she was immediately out of protocol. As a result, God rebuked her publicly by touching her with leprosy. We hear nothing else of Miriam from that point on in the history of Israel as it pertains to being used in ways previous to this act of rebellion. She did have a place in ministry, but when she became heady and high-minded, she not only lost her post, but she was judged. Had Moses not interceded for her, the leprosy would have remained more than 7 days and she would have eventually died.

God's judgment upon Miriam was not because she was a woman, but because she yielded to wanting more authority that was determined for her to have. Though Aaron was also responsible for confronting Moses as well, the fact that Miriam was judged rather than him, perhaps reveals that she brought this confrontation on. This confrontation follows right after Moses is instructed of God to appoint 70 elders to receive an anointing to judge Israel that rested upon Moses (Numbers 11:15-17). This burden was so great that Moses asked God to die. It is then that Miriam takes the position that she does and is thus dealt with by God.

There are certain temptations that men face that women do not and likewise, women face that men do not. When it comes to being deceived, it was not the man; it was the woman.

And Adam was not deceived, but the woman being deceived was in the transgression. ***1Ti 2:14***

As a woman moves forth in ministry under God's delegated leadership, she will face the temptation of wanting more than what God has ordained, even as Eve did. She will believe that the place and purpose that God has provided her within the Body of Christ is not sufficient as revealed in God's articulated capacity (His Word) for the woman. This is what Eve believed and her presence, being as powerful as it was, caused Adam to yield to what he knew was wrong. It is not that man does not fall into this error, but the woman is more susceptible to usurp authority than the man. As the man is tempted to believe that God is withholding from him that which is good, so the woman is tempted to believe that man is withholding from her that which is good.

God has never ordained a woman to have the position of the head and this is the exact capacity that both Eve and Miriam decided to operate in. As far as a woman walking in the position of a pastor, bishop or any other main office of authority within the ranks of the Body of Christ, I will only say that God's Word never addresses positions such as these specifically for the woman. They always begin with the male figure being addressed. Understanding that God will pour out His Spirit upon all flesh and that He reserves the right to use whom He chooses, if it is truly of God, there will be an awesome awareness of sensitivity in reverencing the delegated male authority in her life. If she has none or has merely an image of one, this is not Divine Protocol according to scripture. If a man does acknowledge a woman under his leadership, he must understand that he will be accountable for confirming her fruit to justify her post. Her fruit will be her husband and her children and the impact she first has upon other women along with how she has entreated the saints prior to this unique placement in God's vineyard (Titus 2:3-5; 1 Tim 5:2-16). It should not be her intellectual poise or a gift to speak. Gifts do not replace anointings or justify appointings within the hierarchy of God's kingdom.

Unless we understand the protocol of the man and woman as revealed in scripture, order will be greatly confused in the lives of many of God's people and the consequences must be faced.

Without a dogmatic spirit of any kind, I simply desire to share what the Bible clearly lays forth regarding this issue. There is no need to be defensive or offensive, but simply sharing the scriptures in love, is my sole responsibility and desire before God and His people.

What follows here in 1 Corinthians, of which I leave the verses numbered, further reveals the order of God's mind as it pertains to God, Christ, man and woman.

1Co 11:3 But I would have you know, that the head of every man is Christ; and the head of the woman [is] the man; and the head of Christ [is] God. 4 Every man praying or prophesying, having [his] head covered, dishonoureth his head. 5 But every woman that prayeth or prophesieth with [her] head uncovered dishonoureth her head: for that is even all one as if she were shaven. 6 For if the woman be not covered, let her also be shorn: but if it be a shame for a woman to be shorn or shaven, let her be covered. 7 For a man indeed ought not to cover [his] head, forasmuch as he is the image and glory of God: but the woman is the glory of the man. 8 For the man is not of the woman; but the woman of the man. 9 Neither was the man created for the woman; but the woman for the man. 10 For this cause ought the woman to have power on [her] head because of the angels. 11 Nevertheless neither is the man without the woman, neither the woman without the man, in the Lord. 12 For as the woman [is] of the man, even so [is] the man also by the woman; but all things of God. 13 Judge in yourselves: is it comely that a woman pray unto God uncovered? 14 Doth not even nature itself teach you, that, if a man have long hair, it is a shame unto him? 15 But if a woman have long hair, it is a glory to her: for [her] hair is given her for a covering. 16 But if any man seem to be contentious, we have no such custom, neither the churches of God.

Matthew Henry interprets the above scripture as follows. "Paul writes this in the midst of an attempted uprising of women who were prophetesses in Corinth desirous to make the claim of superiority over the man. Through cutting their hair, they publicly declared themselves a position that did not belong to them, but to the other sex. This would be an equal statement from her that a sex change was desired".

In considering this statement made regarding sex change, it brings my attention to the reality of lesbianism within the church and the spirit of how it operates. When a woman is operating within a certain capacity of ministry and she takes on the personification of a man, there is a problem directly associated with this spirit. When the feminism of a woman is no longer present, this is a natural manifestation of a carnal misplacement of desires within. When desires surface to a certain level, it reveals itself by wanting to walk, talk and operate in the capacity of what it wants to be. When a man yields to desiring a man, one of them acts like the woman. When a woman yields to desiring a woman, one of them acts like the man. Therefore, when you see a woman's body preaching like a man, talking like a man and treating men like women, you have a person who is carrying out a warped, deceived and demonic role that has flourished to dangerous levels. Such people have no power over flesh and fleshly life-styles are permitted around their ministries (Rom 1:32). When a woman only has women around her, void of any men operating in the capacity of ministry, this too testifies of an imbalance that has abandoned the natural order that God has ordained. Though men are in abundance when accompanying one another in ministry, this is expected as revealed in scripture.

God's anointing never abolishes the natural order of His creation. Though He used the donkey to rebuke the mad prophet and the rocks would have cried out, when finished, the donkey went back to donkeying and the rocks back to being quiet. When dealing with human agents, He does not change the personality of a man to a beast or to a woman. Then why would He change that of the woman to the man? I speak as a fool to make plain the truth.

It was laid upon Paul to take 14 verses to ignite some order in Corinth. He closes his thought with one statement of which now I understand why; "if any one wants to keep contending with this issue, we have no other way of looking at it" (paraphrased). I want to take aim at several verses and highlight them so that we may clearly understand Divine Protocol with regard to man and woman in the Body of Christ.

Verse 3 establishes a foundational point. The head of Christ is God, the head of man is Christ and the head of the woman is man. There is no way you can have two heads on one body. If you insist, you will create a freak and the only result will be division. The head determines the direction of the body and the ordained order has been determined that Christ will be directed by God, the man will be directed by Christ and the woman will be directed by the man. In stating "directed", it is not my intent to do away with God's relationship with leading each individual by His Spirit, but to clearly establish that God does have delegated authority in the earth for everyone.

The reason that God has appointed man as head is due to the fact that the man is the image and glory of God; the representative of that glorious dominion and head ship which God has over the world. It is the man who is set at the head of this lower creation and therein bears the resemblance of God (Matthew Henry's Commentary - Volume 3, New Testament, pg. 1047).

Verses 4-7 uses hair as a sign of covering to show the distinction of man and woman. The Eastern culture believed it to be a signification of shame or subjection for persons to be veiled or covered. It was interpreted as weakness to be submitted. Therefore, to avoid this stereotype, some women would cut their hair to be viewed as liberated. A woman's hair automatically grows long, while a man remains much shorter by nature. Though his hair will eventually grow, it is uncomely for him to let it do so for he aligns himself with the position of a woman. As well, for a woman to shave her hair is rendered to be ashamed. This was meant to shave her hair completely off or relatively close to the scalp. The woman is the glory of the man. She is his representative. As well, she is God's representative, but it is at second hand. Second hand does not mean second rate. She has her place after the creation of man. She is the image of God, inasmuch as she is the image of the man. God's order cannot be tailored fit for individual purposes, lest leadership loses its divine order; God over Christ, Christ over man, man over woman.

Verse 8 states the reason for woman's creation. She was created for the man. Remember that satan's method is to always pervert the original intent for God's creation. God will always operate within the prescribed order of His creation. As it pertains to the fulfillment of the Great Commission, this order remains steadfast and intact. The ministering of the mystery of salvation works within the protocol of God's Word. Therefore, it is understood that the woman is to help and assist within the scope of God's kingdom. If she is married, she is to first of all help her husband. Should her husband be called to the ministry, it is order for his wife to help him. The duties that she carries out will be directed by him as he is directed by Christ and Christ by God. There are variables that will be encountered from ministry to ministry. The issue is that the woman remains subject to her husband. If he is a pastor, she also maintains a respect and honor for those men who are called of God under his leadership.

Verse 9 reveals who was made for who. The woman was made for the man. It is here that a spirit of resentment is stirred against the man to an extent that some men are tempted to recoil and refuse to walk in the truth of who they are in Christ Jesus. The reason for this is multifold in and of itself. Yet to really understand the reason for disorder, you must first understand the times in which you live.

I could elaborate of how the object of satan's attack is the man, the man, the man. While he attacks him with pornography, alcohol, cigarettes and an array of sexual forces, the woman, out of her rightful desire to be led, has begun to lead herself. The end does not justify the means in God's kingdom. The solution is to pray that God would restore the foundation of society (man) to his rightful place.

More and more women are stepping forward in ministry today while fewer men are answering the call. This fact alone should cause there to be a concern within the Body of Christ, for a shift such as this that has never taken place before in the history of the Church. While understanding that God is pouring out His Spirit upon all flesh, He will yet do so within the guidelines of divine order. Those who take it lightly will be faced with consequences in churches across this nation of a rise in feminism and a spirit of Jezebel that is due to abandoning God's order as it pertains to the place that God has ordained for the man and woman. The same principle applies to the man when he steps out of his place and proposes to be God. The human nature wants to go "up" a level and that "up" level for the woman is to operate in a man's capacity, as the "up" level for the man is to operate in Christ's capacity. This is rebellion indeed.

I have seen men of God in need of help in ministry and he places his wife as an assistant pastor. This is not scriptural. God will provide another man who has a call on his life and would be faithful to that pastor and to his wife. We begin to get in the issues of anointings and gifts. Does your gift automatically determine that your wife is also gifted with a spiritual endowment? Absolutely not. The issue here is that the wife should always, by all means, help her husband, yet her help should maintain within the guidelines of her gifting and her gifting within the guidelines of scriptural order. Just because she can speak does not mean she has been anointed to preach. This is spiritual warfare. Far be it for a man to place his wife in a position which carries the mandate of a heavenly call to first be separated as a voice, as well as to endure the making process to be qualified to defy demons and heal the sick, while declaring the heavenly message of salvation. There must be Divine Protocol: God's Official Order that is Correct in the Dealings of His Kingdom within the courts of our ministries if we intend to be prepared to confront the realities of end time ministry.

To suppose that a wife is just as anointed as her husband in ministry cannot be substantiated in scriptures by either word or example. Years of faithfulness or church growth does not and should not dictate this decision. God alone anoints and appoints within the predetermined order of His Word according to the purposes of Himself.

Sarah, the wife of Abraham, was the mother of many nations. She is used as an example of how women are to relate to their husbands. She also reveals the danger of what happens when she is yielded to for direction that should be inquired of God by the man. Clearly, God uses our wives to support a decision as led by the Lord, yet He will confirm this as well to the head of the home.

> ***And God said unto Abraham, Let it not be grievous in thy sight because of the lad and because of thy bondwoman; in all that Sarah hath said unto thee, hearken unto her voice; for in Isaac shall thy seed be called.*** ***Ge 21:12***

Though Sarah suggested that Hagar be instrumental to bear a child, it was Abraham who accepted it. Both wives and women have some great ideas sometimes about God's promises to men and husbands. While quickly affirming that God confirms His Word many times through our wives, that does not mean we are to get in bed with every idea. It simply means to wait and let God speak to the head as well, or else when you make the mess, they will be showing it out the door just like Sarah showed Hagar out of hers.

For after this manner in the old time the holy women also, who trusted in God, adorned themselves, being in subjection unto their own husbands: Even as Sara obeyed Abraham, calling him lord: whose daughters ye are, as long as ye do well and are not afraid with any amazement. ***1Pe 3:5-6***

Verse 11-12 reveals that the woman was made for the man. Therefore, the man is not without need of the woman. It strikes a powerful balance in causing men to realize their place and to not abuse their role as head of the woman. In fact, the woman is to receive such honor for her position that she enjoys being a woman. You will find this is not the rule but the exception in our generation and without knowing how to cope with this dilemma, many women are "taking charge of their life" by attempting to become what they were not designed to be; the head. Often, this desire for the "head" position is not a deliberate one, yet it becomes deliberate when the woman usurps the authority of her husband or pastor by trying to do what she thinks he should be doing. Even confronting the man in the spirit of judgment about what he should be doing is the same as usurping his authority. Although the woman can be correct in her assessment, she is incorrect in her method. Only God can confront the man. It would be wise to pray and love him with your conduct, with your support and with your affection. This will go a whole lot further than confrontation out of frustration with sharp words.

Paul takes a natural approach to this in verses 14-15 by simply putting before us that for a man to have long hair reveals his lack of understanding of his role. Some men who are taking a complete bald approach, are declaring they are trying something new to identify with. The only reason why any of God's men shaved their head was because they had taken a vow (Acts 18:18; 21:23-24). While society has made it to appear in style and chic for men, it actually is a symbol of weakness and an improper concept of male identity. In essence, many men are attempting to replace his responsibility of being a godly man in character to looking like a worldly man in image who appears to be in control. The temperament of a man's body will determine who he really serves. His fruit will likewise reveal who he really is as he grows throughout certain intervals of his life.

As mentioned previously, Paul closes this with no room for a continual discussion on the issue. It appears that there was a reason for him to take such a stand on concluding it. Obviously, there were those who did not want to receive this truth. Instead, they pressed the issue to a contentious level. Paul's final word was, "we have no such custom, neither the churches of God" v (16).

As I conclude this observation, I do so with a sensitive heart toward the woman who sincerely desires to please God and not be hindered from fulfilling His purpose. I realize that many men today have become spiritually lethargic and simply lazy in seeking God and as a result, many women are suffering one way or another. Perhaps you feel hindered from pressing into God's kingdom, especially if you are married to a man who is saved but is simply not seeking God. Your answer will be found in knowing Christ for Christ; not knowing Christ in or through a work. Do not allow satan to distract you from scriptural order because of your emotions. Your answer is Christ alone.

It could be that your marriage is blessed and you simply discern a call to public ministry that would coincide with scriptural protocol as a woman. Again, such a call from God will also be in agreement with your husband. God will not overrule His delegated authority in your life. Mary knew she was called to give birth to the Son of God. Joseph knew that he had not touched Mary, therefore, as far as he was concerned, she had committed adultery. He had determined to put her away privately but God spoke from Heaven through the vessel of an angel... "to take unto thee Mary thy wife: for that which is conceived in her is of the Holy Ghost" (Matt 1:20). If God showed Joseph while he "thought" on these things, God will show your husband as he thinks on the issue of ministry for his wife. If what you have in you is conceived by the Holy Ghost, what is man that he should be considered? God will ensure that it comes forth. Just remember, Mary kept her place and allowed God to confirm to Joseph that Whom she borne was truly of the Holy Ghost, for God had respect unto Joseph. Likewise, he has respect unto your husband.

Too often, most women who believe they have a call to the ministry received such a call from another woman. They also received such aspirations through entertaining imaginations that needed to be cast down. It does not mean you cannot receive the call of God through the vessel of the woman of God. However, the majority of the time there are many unqualified individuals blurting from their emotions what they believe to be from God, while they themselves are out of order and experiencing the consequences of it in their own lives. There is a large amount of divorced women in ministry which speaks loudly at the caution we must display regarding this issue. It is not that a divorcee, whether man or woman, cannot serve in ministry, yet, it is a fact that cannot nonetheless be overlooked. Older women are admonished to teach the younger women to be sober, to love their husbands and to love their children (Tit 2:3-4). If a woman is giving advice to another woman and has not fulfilled this scripture, they truly should be quiet and get things right in their own lives. As well, the effectiveness of a man's ministry should be measured by the effectiveness of his family (1 Tim 3:1-5).

When you begin to look at the role of the man and the woman, you will begin to see that the conduct of a person at home is really who they are. The nature of man will not get in bed with another man (unless that man's nature has been perverted). When a woman takes on the role a man, the man is going to get out of the bed. Though she is a woman in her body, she has become a man in her role. Though she is wearing a dress in the natural, she is putting on pants in her identity. Although many men cannot explain what is going on, they just know one thing; it is abnormal. As a result, they leave and the woman feels free to pursue her life of ministry, not realizing that her ministry just walked out the door!

Your ministry is to help your husband by winning him over without the Word by how you live your life in front of him for Christ, not in front of a church trying to serve Christ's Bride. You are committing spiritual adultery by giving to others what you should be giving your husband; love, longsuffering, patience, kindness, meekness and passionate affection. Rest from looking beyond your home for fulfillment. Your fulfillment is within you, namely, Jesus Christ. Now give some of it to that man, for he really needs your help.

Without playing on the words of scripture and having respects of persons, have not the scriptures spoken plainly concerning this issue? Amen.

The Affairs of This Life

No man that warreth entangleth himself with the affairs of this life; that he may please him who hath chosen him to be a soldier.
2 Ti. 2:4

There are certain liberties given to the people of God that are not given to His messengers. The affairs of this life range from our wife and children to the purchasing of goods that afford us conveniences. Paul realized his right to have a wife, a job, or even an offering, yet he sacrificed these rights in order that nothing would hinder his call to preach or be found abusing his power in the gospel.

Have we not power to lead about a sister, a wife, as well as other apostles and as the brethren of the Lord and Cephas?

But I have used none of these things: neither have I written these things, that it should be so done unto me: for it were better for me to die, than that any man should make my glorying void.

What is my reward then? Verily that, when I preach the gospel, I may make the gospel of Christ without charge, that I abuse not my power in the gospel. For though I be free from all men, yet have I made myself servant unto all, that I may gain the more.
1 Co. 9:5, 15, 18, 19

What an example of not being entangled in the legalistic affairs of this life! We deceive ourselves if we find contentment in just abstaining from obvious sins, without realizing that we make our legal rights sin when we place them as priority over the Lord. It is more commonly known as self righteousness.

American Christians have developed a real attitude with servants who live and die for God. The Church itself has also been known to raise an eyebrow or two when ones sole desire is for the Lord. They cannot seem to accept a man and his family being content with serving the Lord while enduring the hardships that come with being a servant of Christ. In fact, we have gone to great lengths to prove that it is not God's will that we suffer. The Bible, in countless verses and examples, emphatically declares that you will suffer in some form or fashion for a variety of reasons ranging from being discipled, to being rejected for testifying of the truth. If everyone accepts your word and you have no conflict and trials in your life, then you have believed a gospel that has no cross and a gospel without a cross is a gospel without salvation!

> ***Saying, The Son of man must suffer many things and be rejected of the elders and chief priests and scribes and be slain and be raised the third day.*** **Lu 9:22**

> ***For I will shew him how great things he must suffer for my name's sake.*** **Ac 9:16**

> ***And if children, then heirs; heirs of God and joint-heirs with Christ; if so be that we suffer with [him], that we may be also glorified together.*** **Ro 8:17**

> ***For unto you it is given in the behalf of*** **Christ*****, not only to believe on him, but also to suffer for his sake;*** **Ph 1:29**

> ***I know both how to be abased and I know how to abound: every where and in all things I am instructed both to be full and to be hungry, both to abound and to suffer need.*** **Ph 4:12**

Concerning married couples, many men seek the approval of their wives in serving the Lord. Some have been threatened with divorce for desiring to set out to accomplish the will of God. "That woman" will not be an excuse on Judgment Day. It will not be good enough. Was it good enough for Adam? As Job refused to yield to it, so should you.

> ***Then said his wife unto him, Dost thou still retain thine integrity? curse God and die. But he said unto her, Thou speakest as one of the foolish women speaketh. What? shall we receive good at the hand of God and not evil? In all this Job did not sin with his lips.*** ***Job 2:9, 10***

Dealing with a situation such as this must be executed in prayer and serious contention against the devil. Without fail, when the wife is unwilling for her husband to press forward in fulfilling the call of God, it is because of fear. Fear of not having. Fearing of losing the house. Fear of the children not being provided for. Fear of not having enough money to get her hair done. Fear of this. Fear of that. Her mind is like a pinball that is ricocheting from one concern to the other. The problem lies in your neglect to wash her with the water of the Word. You would be surprised at how many preachers do not see to their wives spiritual needs. The problem is not that your wife is necessarily against you pursuing the ministry, though sometimes it is and this should be made clear before you married (unless of course it happened after you were saved in your marriage). More so, it is the fact that she has not been persuaded through your pursuit of God and your spiritual management of her that you are for real. When God is truly being sought after and prayer fills the life of a person, hearts are changed and desires conform to God's will. If a woman loves the Lord and the man whom she has married, the problem is not with her; it is with her husband.

If God is going to be with you in the field of your ministry, why would He abandon you in your own tent? A house divided against itself cannot stand and when you go forth to preach, the devil does not recognize what you are saying. Rather he is recognizing what you are living. If he has your tent, he has your whole ministry. Most of the time, the wife just needs a serious bath and affirmation from her husband that God Is and that her needs are as important to you as getting a word for the people.

When you have been marked by God, it does not mean that you are to walk off the job, sell the farm, kiss the wife and children goodbye once you have dropped them off with your mother and hit the road. Having a call on your life means that if God speaks to you, you are willing and able to move! Jobs, homes and securities of any kind are leeches that will destroy your life if you are too entangled with them to the point that you cannot fulfil your purpose as it pertains to the will of God.

The pursuers of excellence are never found "majoring" in "minors". The man of God must keep himself free to seek God and then to obey all of His instruction. Your occupation that provides for your responsibilities must not be chosen by how much money you can make, but rather how much freedom it allows for you to keep moving with the Master. You have to trust God for your job, home and everything that concerns your life. Your wife must pray and not be deceived with the world's conception of happiness, which, outside of the will of God, is no happiness at all.

This is *The Order of God's Kingdom*. Any other order must be rejected, for it falls short of lawful striving.

> ***And if a man also strive for masteries, yet is he not crowned, except he strive lawfully.*** ***2 Ti. 2:5***

Men and women of God who are called and chosen must press until the doors of glory open up to receive them. The rewards of serving the Lord surpass our comprehension. Let us not draw back, but believe that God is and that He is a rewarder of those who are used to establish Divine Protocol in His kingdom which shall soon overtake this world!

Chapter 6

Divine Worship

There is a Worship of the Flesh
God Seeks Those Who Do So in Spirit

King David, in all of his works and labors, was ultimately always striving toward worship. While shepherding the sheep, he was worshipping. In his protection of the sheep against the lion and the bear, he was expressing a form of worship. When going to battle against Goliath, he was declaring that God's people worship the only true and living God, for no uncircumcised Phistine would defy the living God before David. He was cloaked with a spiritual zeal and fervor and went forward without hesitation to honor God in the worship of warfare. Goliath was slain by a pebble that had been endued with the hand of God sent from the hand of a boy who understood the protocol of Divine Worship!

David was a man of passion. He was not reserved in his worship of God, nor was he ever ashamed. He danced before the Lord with all his strength, cloaked solely in a loin cloth. His wife, Michal, despised this worship simply because it was not for her. This is where our wives must be careful to understand that God reserves the right to possess the very core of their husband's passions unto Himself. Do not yield to the spirit of jealousy. Instead, rejoice that your husband is pouring himself out to God. This is and can be a reason why many women are barren. Perhaps not barren from having children, but barren from having joy, peace and the simple attributes that God would bestow within their spirit. When a woman stands in the way of God possessing the core of her husband's passions, there will be consequences due to the fact that

God's claim is being challenged and such a challenge is one of contempt toward a Holy God.

To worship God, one has to maintain a constant vigil over their passions. It was due to David's abandonment of His passions being rooted and grounded in God that led to his reckless, adulterous affair with Bathsheba. Worshipping God has everything to do with our body as the channel of expression. This is why we must first present our bodies as a living sacrifice, holy and acceptable unto God which is nothing far fetched; it is reasonable. As soon as David refrained from presenting his body to God, he could not surrender his worship to God. Therefore, David's decision was made known when he yielded to the misguided passions of his flesh.

The culmination of unsurrendered affections will lead to the pursuit of seeking their fulfillment. Eventually, they will drive their subjects to extreme levels of sin and therefore, the consequences that come with them. David went on to commit adultery and then he murdered the woman's husband in order to cover up his sin and to have her. This is what David determined when he chose to abandon Divine Protocol in worship.

Though his need was legitimate in wanting to express himself through sexual relations, his unrestrained impulse drove him down a path that changed the course of his kingdom. The consequence was that David would never find his way back to God's original intent for his life. Though David was king and the promise of a king always being upon the throne of David would come to pass, he was wrong. His desires for sexual expression or the need to be received by a woman's love and approval did not give him the right to overrule God's protocol in relationships. Relationship has everything to do with worship and when we abandon God's order in relationships, we have done so also in worship.

The scripture reads:

> ***And it came to pass, after the year was expired, at the time when kings go forth [to battle], that David sent Joab and his servants with him and all Israel; and they destroyed the children of Ammon and besieged Rabbah.***

But David tarried still at Jerusalem. And it came to pass in an eveningtide, that David arose from off his bed and walked upon the roof of the king's house: and from the roof he saw a woman washing herself; and the woman [was] very beautiful to look upon. And David sent and enquired after the woman. And [one] said, [Is] not this Bathsheba, the daughter of Eliam, the wife of Uriah the Hittite? And David sent messengers and took her; and she came in unto him and he lay with her; for she was purified from her uncleanness: and she returned unto her house. And the woman conceived and sent and told David and said, I [am] with child. ***2 Sa 11:1 -5***

David chose not to worship God in battle where he should have been. It was at a time when kings go forth to battle, yet David had chosen to worship himself. Though he did not intentionally plot and plan to commit adultery and murder, he was where he should not have been which led to him doing what he should not have done.

Protocol in worship has everything to do with protocol in position. David arose from his bed (v.2) and walked upon the roof of his house. It was from there he saw Bathsheba. It was customary for women to bathe themselves during this time of day and David knew it. What possibly could have been on his mind after getting up off of his bed and walking to the roof to perhaps find a woman bathing? David's passions were driving him and he chose not to stop them. He was king and though he had wives and concubines, he yet desired what was not his; she who was bathing whose name was BathSheBa. Human nature has not changed. When passions go unrestrained in worship, there will be a dissatisfaction with what one has been already given by God. Excessiveness will be the result when the object of worship is anything or anyone other than Jesus Christ. This means we can take that which is good and through excess, experience harm instead of a closer union with God.

Hast thou found honey? eat so much as is sufficient for thee, lest thou be filled therewith and vomit it. ***Pr 25:16***

Please understand that this especially covers religious exercises of which Israel was very much involved in, yet their hearts were far from God. This spirit is very much alive today. If God's people cannot "feel" it in the flesh rather than perceive it in the Spirit, they are slow to respond.

***[Ye] hypocrites, well did Esaias prophesy of you, saying, This people draweth nigh unto me with their mouth and honoureth me with [their] lips; but their heart is far from me. But in vain they do worship me, teaching [for] doctrines the commandments of men.* Mt 15:7-9**

King David had lost control. This unspoken desire had been culminating inside of him due to the mismanagement of his passions. Restraints had been abandoned and thus, what had begun as a leak, led to a flood and David did not have the willpower to resist that internal tug any longer. Willpower cannot do anything in and of itself unless it is focused toward God's enabling. It takes the Holy Spirit's power to do everything. Therefore, David was led astray by his unrestrained passions. He jumped up from the bed, determined to have what he could not have. However, when this impulsive affair with the wife of another man resulted in her pregnancy, he relentlessly pursued to fix what could not be fixed. He called Uriah out of the will of God to entice him to sleep with Bathsheba, his wife. However, God used the words of this servant to rebuke the king for not doing what he should have been doing and not being where he should have been.

***"...the ark and Israel, and Judah, abide in tents; and my lord Joab, and the servants of my lord, are encamped in the open fields; shall I then go into mine house, to eat and to drink, and to lie with my wife? as thou (king David) livest, and as thy soul liveth, I will not do this thing."* 2 Sa 11:11**

This had to prick the heart of King David. It pricked his conscience, yet he refused to yield and repent before God and before this man at that very moment. David's lust for his self gratified passions was in full gear and satan's plan was finally taking shape through his weakness and abandonment of his emotions. His need to worship had been misdirected and could only be fulfilled through submitting to the foundation of the protocol of God's Holy Word. People who have lost restraint over their affections can do nothing to help you keep yours. Even when those who are leaders of God's people have fallen, they will entice others to do likewise if they have determined to justify themselves by covering up their sins. When a person has chosen to worship the core of self in all of its expressions, what do you think they will want you to worship?

We are clearly warned that if a man be overtaken in a fault to be very careful in bringing him to restoration. It is written:

> ***Brethren, if a man be overtaken in a fault, ye which are spiritual, restore such an one in the spirit of meekness; considering thyself, lest thou also be tempted.*** ***Ga 6:1***

I could continue to develop this scene for us to discover the extremes that our own hearts will go to in order to worship. The end result of David's decision was that the sword would never leave his house and the enemy would rape his wives openly before the people and before the sun (2 Sam. 12:11,12). What he did in secret, the Lord would do openly. It was David's own son who ended up raping David's own daughter. His own son murdered his own son. Solomon, the son he had with Bathsheba, gave himself over to many women and built high places to their gods. He even burnt incense and sacrificed unto them himself (1 Kings 11:7-8). The consequences of our worship go far beyond our life. They carry on into the life of our children and thus, their children.

There is an order that is correct in the dealings of God's kingdom for the man to be fulfilled in the realm of his passions as it pertains to sexual expression. When managed properly, there is a godly order that allows for a freedom of a sexual relationship with his wife to ensue with the presence of purity and holiness. Furthermore, those who will realize divine worship, have safeguarded their moral temperament by keeping the marriage bed undefiled and free from inordinate affections.

> ***Marriage [is] honourable in all and the bed undefiled: but whoremongers and adulterers God will judge.*** ***Heb 13:4***

> ***Mortify therefore your members which are upon the earth; fornication, uncleanness, inordinate affection, evil concupiscence and covetousness, which is idolatry:*** ***Col 3:5***

Many have fallen into immoral traps assuming that their marriage allows for any form of sexual expression. Though the bible does not speak specifically against certain acts that are not acceptable, it speaks clearly about what is natural and clean.

Wherefore God also gave them up to uncleanness through the lusts of their own hearts, to dishonour their own bodies between themselves: Who changed the truth of God into a lie, and worshipped and served the creature more than the Creator, who is blessed for ever. Amen. For this cause God gave them up unto vile affections: for even their women did change the natural use into that which is against nature:

And likewise also the men, leaving the natural use of the woman, burned in their lust one toward another; men with men working that which is unseemly, and receiving in themselves that recompence of their error which was meet. Ro 1:24 -27

But after thy hardness and impenitent heart treasurest up unto thyself wrath against the day of wrath and revelation of the righteous judgment of God; Ro 2:5

Those issues that abide at the surface of your conscience and accuse you is another means by which God uses to reveal his displeasure in certain forms of sexual gratification that will not work his righteousness in your life. On the contrary, it will build a resistance against the conviction of Holy Spirit's and establish deeper roots within your flesh that will only hinder God's deeper work in your spiritual man. Satan will go to extremes to hold your moral nature under some form of rule other than God's. Marriage is one of the most common relationships that he uses to trap God's people in vices which inhibit presenting their bodies as living sacrifices, both holy and acceptable to God. This presentation of our bodies and minds are so essential. Without a holy and acceptable body, one will not be able to ascertain the will of the Lord, for the mind refuses to be transformed from the world and the flesh.

Sexual temperance is a mandate for those who will walk in spiritual maturity and know the power of divine worship. There are countless issues that God has remained silent about in His written Word. However, the specifics of His will are revealed by His Spirit. He yet speaks in parables today so that those who have ears to hear and eyes to see will hear and see. There are certain areas in your life that you are looking for a direct order from God to give and you will not find it. Yet you believe that by His Spirit, the Lord is dealing with you about it. The bible does not specify not to watch television or not to eat meat or go to movies. However, the voice of the Lord will say to you, "My child, I have certain things I want to show you, but you must give up the television in order to see it. I have chosen you to walk with Me in a closer fashion and I simply am dealing with you about sacrificing these things for My kingdom that I may dwell with you closer. I realize that you have the legal right to eat certain things and watch certain things, but I am calling you to sacrifice them that you may see what others do not see. Would you surrender them to Me?"

When God appeals this way to us, it is not because He wants to take your meat or to interfere with your entertainment just for the sake of doing it. It is because He wants your spirit liberated from weights and distractions that inhibit His voice and His ways from being known intuitively in your spirit. He sees that your flesh has developed habits and dependencies that need to be brought under control. Therefore, He begins to require things of us that might not be literally expressed in His Word, but has a foundational base for them.

> ***And if thy right eye offend thee, pluck it out, and cast [it] from thee: for it is profitable for thee that one of thy members should perish, and not [that] thy whole body should be cast into hell. And if thy right hand offend thee, cut it off, and cast [it] from thee: for it is profitable for thee that one of thy members should perish, and not [that] thy whole body should be cast into hell.***
>
> **Mt 5:29, 30**

> ***Wherefore, if meat make my brother to offend, I will eat no flesh while the world standeth, lest I make my brother to offend.***
>
> **1 Co 8:13**

There are many issues that I have faced as a man. I have come to realize that the price to walk with God in a personal and intimate way must be paid in full. For those who have no intention in knowing God in an excellent way, they will always remain childish in the faith. The way you distinguish a child from an adult is by their actions, not their words. You can explain the gospel with expertise, or speak in tongues with interpretations following, yet if you still act like a child, you only possess "head knowledge" and are unable to eat the meat that you are discussing. Go back to sucking the breast of God's Word until you are ready to grow up and part with your childish ways and temperament.

When I was a child, I spake as a child, I understood as a child, I thought as a child: but when I became a man, I put away childish things. **1 Co 13:11**

There are many Christians who know enough to be adults but their ways and actions keep them as children. When we become legalistic with God and seek for ways to maintain our childlike ways instead of maturing in the faith, we might make it to heaven as by fire, but we will have few rewards to show for ourselves in the New Jerusalem.

JEZEBEL

While King David yielded to adultery as a result of not restraining his passions, King Ahab turns over his kingdom to Jezebel, which means, "Where is the prince"? Perhaps the answer is found in the Phoenician interpretation name meaning, "Baal is the prince." In other words, when a man gives over his passions to the worship of the woman, he does so by yielding to his lower nature. The only channel to express worship on a carnal level is through the channel of some form of sexuality. When sex is used in this form, it is perverted because it does not work the righteousness of God. It has one intent; self worship. It was not Jezebel who necessarily turned Ahab's heart toward this perverted worship; it was Ahab himself who chose to marry the daughter of a heathen king. Therefore, his heart was already turned toward such perverted worship.

The reality of Ahab's choice of such a wife answers why the object of worship was the god of fertility; namely, sex. Fertility worship attributes its success of the crop, land and herds to the sexual relationship of the supposedly "divine" couple. Theoretically, once this divine couple engaged in sexual intercourse, the gods were provoked to preserve the earth's fertility. Baal's resurrection came with the return of the rains. Therefore, when the prophet Elijah declared that it would not rain for 3 years and 6 months, he emphatically declared that Baal is not God. In essence, he was declaring to Ahab and his new wife Jezebel, "you all can have all the perverted sex you want; it still will not rain, because only Jehovah is God!" Can you imagine the orgies they must have had in attempting to induce Baal to produce rain? It was not until Elijah called them out of their orgy halls to meet him on Mount Carmel that he settled the issue once and for all regarding who was really God.

This Jezebel spirit is very familiar with sexual perversion through the various channels of sexual relationships that are not within the confines of marriage and that is pure and free of offense toward the conscience of the husband and the wife. It can and will lead to the extreme forms of idolatry that renders the man weak in his spirit and unable to lead the woman as a spirit led man. There will be manifestations of control which will arise, and only through excessive means, can godly control be regained. Do not play with this area of sexual impurity. It does not matter what form of sexual bondage you might be in; if you sincerely want deliverance, God will set you free! Curse such spirits in Jesus' name. Submit yourself unto the Lord and it will flee from you (James 4:7). Prepare for the attacks to continue for a season and if you fall, regain your position immediately and continue to fight until you obtain your freedom. Get in a word preaching and teaching church where holiness is declared and taught, and God will liberate both your body and your mind. Be sure to ask God to lead you to a church whose pastor is living as well as preaching holiness. The preaching will reveal the fear of the Lord while the teaching will reveal the way of the Lord. You need both for proper growth and development.

The examples given regarding the worship that Ahab and David portrayed are only two of many found in God's Word. Moses determined to worship God all the days of his life and was buried in the valley of Moab by God Himself. Elijah poured out his worship to Jehovah God and a chariot of fire came down to carry him home. Jo the Baptist determined to separate himself in the wilderness and came forth with blazing commitment to "be a voice of one crying in the wilderness", and found his joy in hearing the voice of the Bridegroom. Rahab determined to forsake her prostitute business and follow the God of the spies and worship Him. Esther placed her life on the line to preserve the people of God through approaching the king without being summoned. Reformers of all centuries determined that God would be their object of worship and they would walk in a way to preserve this worship at any expense.

Shall we now proceed to understand God's official order that is correct in the dealings of His kingdom in worship? Shall we set aside our religious traditions that we have labeled as worship and placed before God's people as worship? God seeks such as those who will worship Him in two ways; in Spirit and in Truth. All other worship is perverted or twisted and will not work His righteousness regardless of the method and the reasons to justify it. God has never changed his standard for a generation, and will not start with this one. He wants worship from you and from me, for nothing else will suffice Him but our whole heart, our whole mind, our whole soul and all our bodily strength.

SIN

Sin is a pouring out of ones self to another other than God. It is self-worship. In all of our doings, we are either preparing to worship, entering into worship, or worshipping. We are created beings that have an unquenchable thirst to worship and until we are fulfilled, we will worship anything, anyone and do it all at any expense. We will even worship to such a level of indulgence to where it finally brings death. And rightly so, for what is the wages of sin but death (Rom. 6:23)?

Man's existence hinges on worship. He will die if he does not have a channel to release worship. Satan's objective is to keep him totally occupied with the worship of the creation rather than the Creator, God. He will go to any extreme to keep you preoccupied with another other than the very person of Jesus Christ, the Messiah.

Who changed the truth of God into a lie, and worshipped and served the creature more than the Creator, who is blessed for ever. Amen. **Ro 1:25**

While we label sin many things, it is really one thing; the worship of anyone other than God. Of course, sin has many forms of expression, but its single aim is the worship of self. The substance of your life will be determined by what or who you worship - not what you intend to do, not what you say, not what you pray, but what you actually do. This is where your worship will be found.

***Know ye not, that to whom ye yield yourselves servants to obey, his servants ye are to whom ye obey; whether of sin unto death, or of obedience unto righteousness?* Ro 6:16**

***Whose end [is] destruction, whose God [is their] belly, and [whose] glory [is] in their shame, who mind earthly things.* Ph 3:19**

***Jesus answered them, Verily, verily, I say unto you, Whosoever committeth sin is the servant of sin.* Jo 8:34**

What many of us intend to do, we take for doing. Therefore, we deceive ourselves and as 1 Jo 1:6 declares, "if we say that we have fellowship with him, and walk in darkness, we lie, and do not the truth". There is a protocol in worship, and many of God's people have falsely assumed that you can have worship without obedience. It is my desire to explore this realm enough to understand that spiritual worship has laws which, if abandoned, is sheer noise and clutter that cannot find its way into the ear of a holy and sovereign God.

What is Worship?

There are many definitions of worship that do well to describe its general meaning and its prescribed method as revealed in the Bible. It is my hope, however, that God would allow me to shed light on the unspoken aspects of worship which reveals His intimate intention for this expression of spiritual life being experienced in unspoken passion called worship.

I will, however, lay a simple foundation by stating that worship is a human response to the perceived presence of the Divine; a presence which is holy. Worship in the Bible moves back and forth between personal experience and corporate experience. Personal worship and corporate worship are mutually interactive. Corporate worship is empowered by personal experience, but personal experience needs affirmation and interpretation in corporate worship. (Bible Dictionary p. 1421). Worship means to bow down. It is the bowing down of every area of our life that causes God to receive our worship.

It is with this awareness, among those who are born again and those who are not, that we strive to fulfill this inner thirst. Therefore, we give ourselves over to someone or something that is greater than our being. We have the need to be submitted to a spiritual force that moves us where we cannot move ourselves. It is a spiritual empowerment that enables us to have a completion about our existence that must emanate from another source far greater than us. We realize that all outer substance is unable to fill the void that echoes for God. Today's generation, both in the church and outside the church, must simply come to grips with the fact that it is only by one means that we and the world will ever experience this unfathomable intimacy with God that we call worship. It is through an order; a divine order that is correct in the dealings of His kingdom.

This worship that I am speaking of cannot be brought on by self will. It can not be manufactured by studios and the best Christian voices of our time. This inner realm of worship cannot be found at the most anointed conferences whose speakers are among the "who's who" of preachers and teachers. Nor will you discover it after studying for years at the seminaries around the world. Though the above mentioned is a part of the process in coming into worship, it is nonetheless not the depth of worship that God desires for us to know. Granted, though we might be where we have attained, we must yet realize that we have been called to press beyond where we are. Complacency in God's kingdom can and has developed into mediocrity in pressing into levels of intimacy with God that even sheer words fail to describe. We need to understand the phases of worship so as not to misinterpret processes as the actual expression of it.

There is an order in worship that perhaps many of us are not willing to sacrifice to know. Divine worship comes with a price that the many who are "called" will not pay. Rather, it will be the "chosen", who press beyond duty to taste the rarity of this realm. Though it is open to all, only a few are willing to suffer and bring their being under the influence and desire of a Holy God. Only through the purging of the Holy Spirit can one be a vessel met unto honor and fit for the Master's use (2 Tim. 2:20). Yes, there is even a separation of God's people among God's people.

Sovereignly, God has chosen one vessel for one purpose and another vessel for another purpose, yet He has called us all to the inner courts of worship. This is where we are capable of being one of the "few". It is by God's design that we all shall know Him, from the least to the greatest (Hebrews 8:10-11). Likewise, it is by God's design that we participate in this process by drawing nigh unto Him, for then He will draw nigh unto us.

> ***Draw nigh to God, and he will draw nigh to you. Cleanse [your] hands, [ye] sinners; and purify [your] hearts, [ye] double minded.***
> ***Jas 4:8***

This worship is as personal as a man and a woman becoming naked before each other while not being ashamed and then lying down to become intimate. For the act of intimacy to be joyous, there first has to be a joyous relationship outside of this worship, or else they will find themselves going through the motions and it will not bring the climax that God has designed sexual expression to bring. Though they experience a physical climax, the soul is yet left unsatisfied and this couple is unfulfilled where it is really needed; in the soul. The testimony often found among those who practice fornication is, "it felt great but I still feel empty". Even those who are married and have avoided building a proper relationship will find that sex cannot replace making love, nor can the process of worship replace the inner core of God and you becoming intimate through the unheard and unseen realm of spirituality.

More on Worship

On the other side of the holy form of worship, you will find that many forms of perversion are an alternative in attempting to use the process to replace the actual purpose of the process' intended design; to bring us into worship with God. Due to our fears, selfishness and misunderstandings, we fall short and remain in the outer courts of worship. We feel ashamed of being "naked" before the Lord, for we are unprepared and or unwilling in our minds and bodies to be wholly separate unto Him, not only in our will, but also in the act of obedient living, which is the highest form of worship in and of itself.

Therefore, worship is the act of two individuals giving and receiving of ones highest self in complete trust supported by a covenant of sinless blood initiated by the Greater of the two. Such worship is the worship of God and must be preceded by the lesser of the two submitting to the laws governing the covenant. The standard of the covenant will be set by the One whose blood was shed. This being true, no other Person known to man shed His blood for man and then arose from His death by His own power to declare Himself worthy to receive all of creation's worship and honor other than Jesus Christ.

Divine worship has a definite order that must be followed as outlined in the oracles of the covenant manual; the Holy Bible. Any deviation from this Word will result in improper worship. Let us endeavor to understand this New Covenant as it pertains to worship toward the divine goal of intimate communion between God and man.

THE NEW COVENANT AND ITS MESSENGER

For this [is] the covenant that I will make with the house of Israel after those days, saith the Lord; I will put my laws into their mind, and write them in their hearts: and I will be to them a God, and they shall be to me a people: Heb 8:10

And to Jesus the mediator of the new covenant, and to the blood of sprinkling, that speaketh better things than [that of] Abel. Heb 12:24

Many times when I am in church, I become so very aware of how many of God's people are not living under the power of grace, but rather, are still upon the isle of law. Many of our leaders are tempted with interpreting God's Word from a position of seniority of God's flock, rather than a position of being among them. Though the leaders are to receive honor as such, they are not to confuse their role within the scope of the New Covenant; to be the friend of the Bridegroom.

Jo the Baptist best demonstrated the protocol of a minister in declaring that we must decrease as the person being heard and seen in the lives of God's people and allow Jesus to increase as the Person upon Whom they trust. The people saw Jo, but they heard him speak of Jesus. They even wondered if he was the Messiah, but he made them to understand clearly that he was not by declaring that he was simply, "a voice crying in the wilderness to make straight the way of the Lord" (Jo 1:23). In essence, our role is to get people to a place of making the way of the Lord accessible. The New Covenant preacher must understand that his joy will be found in hearing the voice of the Bridegroom rejoice with His Bride. Nothing more. To go beyond and attempt to have a covenant relationship with the Bride is outside of the described protocol as written in the Word of God. It will only produce doctrinal error and spiritual consequences that will carry eternal dividends.

> ***Ye yourselves bear me witness, that I said, I am not the Christ, but that I am sent before him. He that hath the bride is the bridegroom: but the friend of the bridegroom, which standeth and heareth him, rejoiceth greatly because of the bridegroom's voice: this my joy therefore is fulfilled. He must increase, but I [must] decrease.*** ***Jo 3:28-30***

Many of our churches have produced Christians who are dependent upon the body rather than the Head of the Body. This system is not only unscriptual, but it will not bring believers into maturity or the bliss of divine worship. While it is certain that there is a level of dependency that Christians should maintain upon one another, they should never lose sight of their foundation; Jesus Christ.

The leaders of God's people carry a serious weight of responsibility in the entire scope of God's kingdom. God has delegated gifts to be given, and Christ gives them to men for the express reason of building up His Body (Eph 4:8-16) to come into an ever increasing knowledge of Himself, and to know Him like no man could ever teach you or know Him for you ((1 Jo 2:27; Hebrews 8:10). Yes, God has entrusted men to be gate keepers of His Word and some refuse to be after the joy of hearing His voice and being His friend. They are after you and yours; the Bride of Christ.

This is why Paul clearly declares that the man must be found faithful in small natural things in order to be trusted with spiritual things. If he is unfaithful to his wife, he will certainly be unfaithful to Christ's Bride. Our aim is divine worship, yet without divinely appointed men of God, there will be no divinely focused worship to Him. This is why men of God must be judged by the fruit of their character, rather than the endorsements of their colleagues. What an honest colleague might not see, their character will truly reveal.

Let us now press our way into the mind of God and allow the New Covenant to speak clearly in reference to the divine worship that the Holy Spirit so desires for you and I to know.

Let a man so account of us, as of the ministers of Christ, and stewards of the mysteries of God. Moreover it is required in stewards, that a man be found faithful. **1 Co 4:1-2**

But if I tarry long, that thou mayest know how thou oughtest to behave thyself in the house of God, which is the church of the living God, the pillar and ground of the truth. ***1 Ti 3:15***

THE NEW COVENANT - THE FOUNDATION OF DIVINE WORSHIP

The reason why the essence of the New Covenant is so crucial to worship is because it is the only means by which God will receive worship. The Old Testament and its priests have been relieved of duty and the New Testament Priest, Jesus Christ, Who lives forever, rules over the New Covenant. Therefore, He will never be replaced. A new system of worship has been instituted and without proper instructions, such worship will not be experienced. Even the Jews, who have refused to receive the witness of Jesus as being hailed the Messiah, grope in darkness unto this very day. However, those who accept Jesus Christ as Lord and yet remain under the systems of the law will enter into heaven, but will miss the essence of the New Covenant life and its privileges while in this lifetime.

The Apostle Peter speaks of God's divine power giving us all things that pertain unto life and godliness. These are given through a knowledge of Him. This knowledge implies that there is a responsibility to search it out at the expense of all that we have (Mt 13:44). The divine worship and the perfect will of God go together. It does not happen just to happen. These precious promises spoken of ensure us the privilege of being partakers of a divine nature, yet they are a direct result of our hungering and thirsting after righteousness.

> ***According as his divine power hath given unto us all things that [pertain] unto life and godliness, through the knowledge of him that hath called us to glory and virtue: Whereby are given unto us exceeding great and precious promises: that by these ye might be partakers of the divine nature, having escaped the corruption that is in the world through lust.* 2 Pe 1:3**

The divine nature must be lived in order to experience divine worship. Many of the problems experienced by Christians today center around trying to be made perfect in the flesh. In other words, we are determined to make the things of God work our way. This is a spirit of rebellion and as result, we remain under the law and not under grace. This is the very core of religion; man made, man controlled and thus man- the object of its worship.

The New Covenant is built upon a much higher order than the Old Covenant. In fact, Jesus is greater than Moses even as the builder of the house is greater than the house (Hebrews 3:3). Remember that "the law was given by Moses, but grace and truth came by Jesus Christ" (Jo 1:17). When dealing with the issue of worship, you must first of all deal with the issue of covenant. Do not say within yourself that you are born again and filled with the Holy Ghost and because of that, you will just claim worship, His promises and the results of the divine nature by faith, without doing anything to move toward these attributes. You must walk in covenant with God in order to possess the benefits of that covenant. To walk in the shadow of good things to come is not good enough. You must walk in the very image of the thing in order to know it.

For the law having a shadow of good things to come, [and] not the very image of the things, can never with those sacrifices which they offered year by year continually make the comers thereunto perfect. **Heb 10:1**

The law could not do what only Jesus did in dying and raising from the grave. The law could only point to the coming of the promise; it could not fulfill it with all its sacrifices which were offered year by year. Even today, in the name of Christ, many God fearing Christians attempt to offer sacrifices under the banner of traditions and the commandments of men, attempting to provoke the favor of God or establish a point or program that is not in keeping with God's kingdom. It will not work! We can conduct the most organized conferences and produce the most outlandish events, yet if they are not found within the heart of the doer in experience and seeking to cloak oneself inwardly with the divine nature to bring forth fruit met with repentance, it is in vain.

Please understand that when I say "vain", I say it in the light of "divine ordering". In other words, such works are permissible but not perfect. Today's Church has lived long enough in this stage. We must move on to the thrust of the New Covenant and produce mature men and women who are discipled to truly serve their King and His government by being taught the true meaning of FREEDOM. This is the power of His death and resurrection that many of our priests and prophets have not fully expounded to the sheep of His pasture.

The New Covenant is built upon the most hidden intimacy imaginable and the five fold ministry's responsibility is to usher God's people into that intimacy, while not becoming the object of that intimacy themselves. Naturally, Christ can only draw them, yet He has given ministers certain keys to unlock mysteries to others.

And he gave some, apostles; and some, prophets; and some, evangelists; and some, pastors and teachers; For the perfecting of the saints, for the work of the ministry, for the edifying of the body of Christ: Till we all come in the unity of the faith, and of the knowledge of the Son of God, unto a perfect man, unto the measure of the stature of the fullness of Christ:

That we [henceforth] be no more children, tossed to and fro, and carried about with every wind of doctrine, by the sleight of men, [and] cunning craftiness, whereby they lie in wait to deceive; But speaking the truth in love, may grow up into him in all things, which is the head, [even] Christ: From whom the whole body fitly joined together and compacted by that which every joint supplieth, according to the effectual working in the measure of every part, maketh increase of the body unto the edifying of itself in love. Eph 4:11-16

This body of scripture is absolutely powerful. Please read it again, slowly. Let it sink down deep within your heart, especially if you are a preacher. Are those who are called to declare the Word and teach to those who are babes in Christ "perfecting the saints"? Are we working the ministry? Are we edifying the Body of Christ? Are we bringing them into a closer unity of the faith? Do we have more knowledge of the Son of God? Or are we being tossed to and fro as children and carried about with every wind of doctrine by men who practice the cunning craftiness of deceit?

When you usher people into the protocol of the New Covenant, you do so with Christ being their stature of measure and not you, not your denomination, or your interpretation. You do so understanding that the body is fitly joined together only in Him.

Now of the things which we have spoken [this is] the sum: We have such an high priest, who is set on the right hand of the throne of the Majesty in the heavens; Heb 8:1

What is the sum of all that is being expressed in regards to the New Covenant? I believe that question can be best answered by the above scripture. We have such a High Priest Who is set on the right hand of the throne of the Majesty in the heavens. This Majesty in the heavens is God the Father and the sanctuary is of the true tabernacle which the Lord pitched and not man (v.2). Likewise, I speak of a worship that only God can unction a man to know and understand.

This is Jesus, Who has obtained a more excellent ministry, by how much also He is the mediator of a better covenant which is established upon better promises (v.6). Christ is our Mediator, not King Saul, who was a desire of the people. Not the popular pastor in the city. Not the TV evangelist. Jesus! Though the pastor can be preaching down heaven, and the TV evangelist preaching the unadulterated Word of God, many times it is God's people who make them the priests to offer up sacrifices. Next time you see them, look in their eyes. Do you see flames of fire? Look at their thigh and see if it has the inscription; KING OF KINGS AND LORD OF LORDS. Does his palm possess the nail scars? Are you able to thrust your hand into his side? If the answer is no, then cease from man whose breath is in his nostrils and turn your gaze upon the One Who is able to destroy both the body and the soul. Those who parade themselves as if they are the key to God's Kingdom are contrary to God's protocol and are tampering with the blood of this covenant.

> ***For this [is] the covenant that I will make with the house of Israel after those days, saith the Lord; I will put my laws into their mind, and write them in their hearts: and I will be to them a God, and they shall be to me a people: And they shall not teach every man his neighbour, and every man his brother, saying, Know the Lord: for all shall know me, from the least to the greatest. For I will be merciful to their unrighteousness, and their sins and their iniquities will I remember no more. In that he saith, A new [covenant], he hath made the first old. Now that which decayeth and waxeth old [is] ready to vanish away.***
> ***Heb 8:10-12***

We no longer need to await the permission of a man to worship God our Father. "For we have not an high priest which cannot be touched with the feeling of our infirmities; but was in all points tempted like as [we are, yet] without sin. Let us therefore come boldly unto the throne of grace, that we may obtain mercy, and find grace to help in time of need. "(Heb 4:15-16).

The key to divine worship is found in the newness of life that comes at the acceptance of the offering made by Christ once and for all (Heb 10:10) when by His blood, a new and living way was consecrated for us, through the veil that is to say, His flesh. What once separated us from the Divine Himself, Jesus hath removed by cleansing us from all sin and joining us to Him!

That at that time ye were without Christ, being aliens from the commonwealth of Israel, and strangers from the covenants of promise, having no hope, and without God in the world: But now in Christ Jesus ye who sometimes were far off are made nigh by the blood of Christ. For he is our peace, who hath made both one, and hath broken down the middle wall of partition [between us]; Having abolished in his flesh the enmity, [even] the law of commandments [contained] in ordinances; for to make in himself of twain one new man, [so] making peace;

Eph 2:12-15

Praise the Lord! The divine worship that I speak of will not come as a result of working ourselves up. It will not happen with all the fanfare and hoopla that money can buy. It has already been provided by that middle wall of partition being broken down between God and us. We have received the promise of first of all receiving His laws written upon our hearts. This creates in us a desire. At the same time, He writes them upon our minds. This gives us a spiritual understanding. We no longer need the tablets of stones, that is to say the shadow of what was to come, because the very image of the long awaited promise is here.

The spiritual worship that God longs for from His people will cost you everything. You have to let go of your tradition and the commandments of men that make the Word of God of none effect in your life. You have to abandon years of teaching that have done absolutely nothing for your spiritual growth. Whatever you need to do in order to position yourself to understand and exercise the principles of the New Covenant, be willing to pay that price. Worship will cease to become a reality because you are so resolved to really get into God. Though this is a blessing from God itself, the desire is not the enabling. It will be to those who rely solely upon the mercy of the Most High, for apart from Him, there is no ability in the flesh to attain or apprehend the worship of God.

The New Covenant's strength is found in Christ making possible all things by the power of His might. This gives you the blessed privilege to rest and no longer wrestle against this flesh and blood, but against the true enemy of our soul; the devil. Democracy in the Lord's house will always be a reality to deal with. The answer will not be found in leaving the worship of the community of God's people. Rather, it will be discovered as others see you bringing it with you in your own personal witness of its existence in your life. God longs to know us on an individual basis without the orchestration of men whatsoever, except it be as those appointed to equip us in the sowing and watering process.

When the people who witnessed Jesus' ministry determined to make Him King by force, He immediately withdrew Himself for He knew what was in man. The role that men do play is pointing your spirit to the orchestrator; the Holy Ghost. The Holy Ghost shall not be replaced by any teacher in your life. If you will not yield yourself to be taught by Him, you hinder yourself from entering into the dimensions of divine worship.

We must address a few important aspects of this New Covenant that are not only essential to worship but without such, one will not experience divine worship and will be in an ever constant struggle of gaining spiritual relevance and effectiveness in their life for God's kingdom. There are definites within the structure of this New Covenant that are instrumental in ushering you into the higher courts of divine worship which take you from glory to glory until we behold Him face to face.

MORALITY

As mentioned earlier, perversion means "twisted", "bent," or "crooked" and applies to persons involved in moral error. The channel of moral conduct is through the conduit of the body. In like manner, the channel of worship is through the conduit of the body. We lift up our hands, we sing with our tongue and we dance with our feet. It is in our conduct that we reveal what is truly our heart's desire and object of our adoration. The correlation here is obvious. We must first present our bodies as a living sacrifice that is capable of entering into worship. This capability is not due to its own righteousness, but due to its obedience to the righteousness that is of God. Worship is with, through and by a right relationship with the Holy Spirit of God.

Watchman Nee has phrased it wonderfully by stating: "*Faith in Christ makes one a regenerated believer; obedience to the Holy Spirit makes him a spiritual believer. Just as the right relationship with Christ generates a Christian, so the proper relationship with the Holy Spirit breeds a spiritual man"* (Spiritual Man, Watchman Nee, p. 18).

Therefore, perversion is an attempt to manipulate God's Official Order That is Correct in the Dealings of His Kingdom with respect to every aspect of God's creation. When dealing with worship, the result of perversion would be sensationalism rather than an emotional response to the genuine presence of Christ. What one must obtain through being in right relationship with the Holy Spirit in their body, they refuse by attempting to twist or bend around Him when they do not submit themselves to moral holiness. By doing so, we settle for (though it appears as though we have not), will worship; that which is manufactured by sheer effort and worldly wisdom and is void of true humility and intimacy which is built on the wisdom that cometh from above. In fact, it is a result of refusing the leading of the Holy Spirit that is speaking to us through the facility of our conscience (1 Jo 3:20).

> ***Let no man beguile you of your reward in a voluntary humility and worshipping of angels, intruding into those things which he hath not seen, vainly puffed up by his fleshly mind, And not holding the Head, from which all the body by joints and bands having nourishment ministered, and knit together, increaseth with the increase of God. Wherefore if ye be dead with Christ from the rudiments of the world, why, as though living in the world, are ye subject to ordinances, (Touch not; taste not; handle not; Which all are to perish with the using;) after the commandments and doctrines of men? Which things have indeed a shew of wisdom in will worship, and humility, and neglecting of the body; not in any honour to the satisfying of the flesh.***
>
> **Col 2:18-23**

To leave out the previous verses (18-22) makes it unclear as to what things have a show of wisdom in will worship and humility. Remember, our aim is to realize that outside of a correct relationship with the Holy Spirit in and through our moral behavior, divine worship will not become a reality. It will remain a distant desire that will continue to evade us as long as we insist on our tradition and our righteousness to bring us into its courts.

Paul is emphatically stating that if one is not holding the Head (Christ) from which all have nourishment provided, they must manufacture worship and develop their own interpretation of humility. They must base their reasoning upon their own intellect which has been derived from things they have not seen. The direct result is to worship angels, not Christ. These are the commandments and doctrines of men stemming from the wisdom of the world of which we are not to subject ourselves to. Furthermore, they have an appearance of wisdom but are of no value in keeping your body under control.

Worship that does not lead to moral sanctification is worship not born out of moral sanctification. Neither is there a mind to desire it. Worship that is perverted is worship that is born out of moral perversion. Such worship is not received by God, for we are worshipping what we have created; life-styles and ideologies that have no demands or order which reflect the righteousness and the holiness of God's character as well as His kingdom. The intention of love that we have for the Lord Jesus will always remain an intention until we turn from our wicked ways that are not pleasing in His sight. To love God is to keep His commandments and contrary to what we "feel" or "think", His commandments are not grievous, for whosoever is born of God overcometh the world.

For this is the love of God, that we keep his commandments: and his commandments are not grievous. For whatsoever is born of God overcometh the world: and this is the victory that overcometh the world, [even] our faith. 1Jo 5:3-4

It is this world, that is, the things that are in it and of it, to which we attribute much of our problems. It hinders us from pressing into the kingdom of God. This is why those who do obtain spiritual growth and communion with the Holy Spirit must do so with violence (Mt 11:22). This violence is not one of physical fervor or human intellect. Instead, it is a resolve to cast oneself upon the arm of the Lord and through faith, prohibit trust in the strength of the flesh or that which is acceptable among the multitudes. This violence is to hold dear the Holy Writ and to base ones decisions solely upon the witness of God's Spirit and the confirmation of this everlasting Word.

It is through such violent aggression of submission and suffering of the flesh that one is placed on the path of beholding this worship of which words cannot express. We have held to the opinion that worship is easy and costs little. We have limited our worship experience to just that; an experience rather than a living reality of everyday life. Divine worship is reflective of the "divine nature". If we fail to walk in this divine nature, why should we expect to have divine worship?

> ***Whereby are given unto us exceeding great and precious promises: that by these ye might be partakers of the divine nature, having escaped the corruption that is in the world through lust.***
> **2Pe 1:4**

We fail to experience this divine nature because we are unwilling to part with our lower nature. We want to dwell on our intentions. We stay in the same state for years waiting for a miracle to take place for us to change. It will not be a miracle, but a direct result of you "doing" the will of God. Salvation is acceptance of God's grace. Sanctification is cooperation with the Holy Spirit's work in you. It is doing God's commandments. You cannot accept by faith what you are to do by works. In fact, if you have no works, your faith resides under a tombstone (James 2:26).

> ***If ye then be risen with Christ, seek those things which are above, where Christ sitteth on the right hand of God. Set your affection on things above, not on things on the earth. For ye are dead, and your life is hid with Christ in God.*** **Col 3:1-3**

> ***Mortify therefore your members which are upon the earth; fornication, uncleanness, inordinate affection, evil concupiscence, and covetousness, which is idolatry:*** **Col 3:5**

> ***But now ye also put off all these; anger, wrath, malice, blasphemy, filthy communication out of your mouth.*** **Col 3:8**

> ***And have put on the new [man], which is renewed in knowledge after the image of him that created him:*** **Col 3:10**

Teaching us that, denying ungodliness and worldly lusts, we should live soberly, righteously, and godly, in this present world;
Tit 2:12

This is where those who emphatically teach the "once saved always saved" message error. For such a doctrine to be true, which declares that regardless of how you live God will welcome you into His kingdom, insinuates that He would have to abandon His righteousness. As Paul put it, "...if our unrighteousness commend the righteousness of God, what shall we say? Is God unrighteous who taketh vengeance? God forbid: for then how shall God judge the world?" (Rom 3:5-6). Are those who are saved and making straight paths for their feet (Heb 12:3) and working out their salvation in fear and trembling (Ph 2:12) while being sober (lest they have believed in vain and be as a dog who returns to its vomit) doing so for nothing? If so, such holy living would be futile, for there would be no need to be holy to see Him. What saith the scriptures? "Follow peace with all men, and holiness, without which no man shall see the Lord:" (Heb. 12:14).

This holiness cannot be presupposed by mere will. Though it is by faith, such faith proves genuine by fruit. This is, in fact, the way Jesus said we would know the real from the fake (Mt 7:16-17). Mere affirmation does not replace the commandment to bring forth fruit met with repentance.

There is a distinct difference in the morale of a sheep and the morale of a goat. Many of the goats thought they were going to heaven. It would be in our best interest that you and I understand that it will not be the hearers of the law who will be sheep, but the doers of the law which will qualify to enter into His kingdom (Romans 2:13). You see, the sheep hear the voice of their Shepherd and follow Him. Though the goats hear His voice and are even found amongst the sheep, they do not follow Him. In fact, goats are extremely destructive to vegetation and thereby contribute to erosion. Instead of just eating the plant, they tear it out of the ground. As a result, it is unable to grow again. It was customary to separate the sheep and the goats though they grazed in the same pasture, because the goats became hostile toward the sheep (Mt 25:32).

Morality on earth will determine much of our positions in heaven. Though certain acts of moral behavior will not keep one from entering into the kingdom of heaven, I nonetheless believe that though billions of souls are going to heaven, only millions will be recipients of its full blessings. Again, we are dealing with the issue of choice and will, both permissive and perfect.

> ***Know ye not that the unrighteous shall not inherit the kingdom of God? Be not deceived: neither fornicators, nor idolaters, nor adulterers, nor effeminate, nor abusers of themselves with mankind, Nor thieves, nor covetous, nor drunkards, nor revilers, nor extortioners, shall inherit the kingdom of God. And such were some of you: but ye are washed, but ye are sanctified, but ye are justified in the name of the Lord Jesus, and by the Spirit of our God. All things are lawful unto me, but all things are not expedient: all things are lawful for me, but I will not be brought under the power of any.*** **1Co 6:9-12**

> ***All things are lawful for me, but all things are not expedient: all things are lawful for me, but all things edify not.*** **1Co 10:23**

By the Spirit of God, Paul makes mention of some of the sins of the body (v.9-10), then emphatically declares that those who practice such sins will not enter into the kingdom of heaven. Verse 11 continues by reminding us that we used to be of that company, but we are washed, sanctified and justified in the name of the Lord Jesus and by the Spirit of our God! He then develops this issue more clearly by classifying all other things as lawful, however, those same things which are acceptable are not going to edify my life toward a closer walk with God. This is where the world, the flesh and the devil take specific aim to beset our strides for Christ (Heb. 12:1). We determine that since we are not practicing blatant sins, there is no reason for us not to experience the higher order of God's kingdom. We do not see a reason why we cannot be partakers of divine worship, even though our moral standard is dwelling as close to the line of compromise as possible. We want to yet be carnally minded in our mind, in our body and in our worship, refusing to adhere to the truth that "to be carnally minded is death; but to spiritually minded is life and peace" (Rom. 8:6).

The New Covenant has made provisions for us to overcome these entanglements of the flesh. "Walk in the Spirit and ye shall not fulfill the lust of the flesh" (Gal 5:16). You will not attempt to live by the rivers of carnality and become constantly barraged by the fiery darts of this world. The only way to become morally temperate is to submit yourself to the Person of the Holy Spirit Who abides within you. There is no negotiating on this point. You are the property of God through the transaction of His death for your life. This is what the contract of the New Covenant declares:

> ***What? know ye not that your body is the temple of the Holy Ghost [which is] in you, which ye have of God, and ye are not your own? For ye are bought with a price: therefore glorify God in your body, and in your spirit, which are God's.***
> **1Co 6:19-20**

> ***And [that] he died for all, that they which live should not henceforth live unto themselves, but unto him which died for them, and rose again.*** **2Co 5:15**

Worship will be the experience of those whose body has been surrendered, is being surrendered and shall continually be surrendered unto the Lord. God will not inhabit that praise of foolish living and careless behavioral conduct amongst those who, though they are saved, continue to live after the pleasures of this life. The scripture gives a clear warning of such consequences. It is written:

> ***But if, while we seek to be justified by Christ, we ourselves also are found sinners, [is] therefore Christ the minister of sin? God forbid. For if I build again the things which I destroyed, I make myself a transgressor.*** **Ga 2:17**

> ***But now, after that ye have known God, or rather are known of God, how turn ye again to the weak and beggarly elements, whereunto ye desire again to be in bondage?*** **Ga 4:9**

> ***Now the just shall live by faith: but if [any man] draw back, my soul shall have no pleasure in him.*** **Heb 10:38**

For if after they have escaped the pollution's of the world through the knowledge of the Lord and Saviour Jesus Christ, they are again entangled therein, and overcome, the latter end is worse with them than the beginning. **2Pe 2:20**

Nevertheless I have [somewhat] against thee, because thou hast left thy first love. **Re 2:4**

Imagine the loss that will be experienced because one refused to surrender the desires of this life in order to have works that would withstand the testing of God's fire. Before one can present their works, they must first be able to present their bodies as "a living sacrifice, holy, acceptable unto God, which is your reasonable service" (Rom. 12:1).

Now if any man build upon this foundation gold, silver, precious stones, wood, hay, stubble; Every man's work shall be made manifest: for the day shall declare it, because it shall be revealed by fire; and the fire shall try every man's work of what sort it is. If any man's work abide which he hath built thereupon, he shall receive a reward. If any man's work shall be burned, he shall suffer loss: but he himself shall be saved; yet so as by fire.

Know ye not that ye are the temple of God, and [that] the Spirit of God dwelleth in you? If any man defile the temple of God, him shall God destroy; for the temple of God is holy, which [temple] ye are. **1Co 3:12-17**

The issue of morality in the scope of divine worship will never cease to confront us. Only through mortification of the flesh with a mindset to endure the process that it will bring, shall one begin to walk in the holiness of God. As holiness becomes your character, worship will be its result. By presenting your body a living sacrifice and renewing your mind, you will be able to know what the will of the Lord is. This is Divine Protocol in worship: God's Official Order that is Correct in the Dealings of His Kingdom.

Your Body - The Temple of God

Most of the time, our greatest struggle is with this body. When God calls for worship, He is, in essence, calling for our body to give Him honor. The notion of going to service to worship should be understood as going among God's family to worship together. This fact is clear due to the reality that we are already worshipping alone in His presence on a continual basis through the conduct of how we maintain and carry our temple.

Every person has their own personal struggle when it comes to the temple of this body. Food, sex, television, clothes, or the earnest quest for material possession presents a serious struggle in the lives of many Christians today. When it comes to the body, it is constantly striving for the mastery over you and against God, "for the flesh is enmity against God" (Gal 5:17). The devil knows that without a body being presented, worship cannot be offered. Your enemy will not stop you from preaching, singing songs of praise, or lifting up your hands and shouting. His mission is to keep your vessel contaminated through allowing your voice to gossip, your hands to sin and your feet to dwell where they should not. The issue of sexuality will be a prime target for satan to entrap your life and passions as well.

> ***Who shall ascend into the hill of the LORD? or who shall stand in his holy place? He that hath clean hands, and a pure heart; who hath not lifted up his soul unto vanity, nor sworn deceitfully.***
> ***Ps 24:3 -4***

The devil knows the "ins and out's" of the New Covenant and he will legally keep you from being qualified to experience the intimacy of divine worship by holding the temple of your body in some form of bondage.

The key here is being acceptable to the Lord in practice that you may be accepted of the Lord in worship. The Lord does not receive the wonderful sounding voice you have. He does not look upon your beautiful dance. He does not take notice of how sharply dressed you are. Contrary to perhaps many of God's people, your speaking in tongues is not evidence of being filled with the Spirit. There are tongues of men and angels that are void of a holy unction. If you do not exemplify the simple fruit of love, kindness, long-suffering and meekness, then your tongues are as a sounding brass and tinkling cymbal. Tongues are a gift of the Spirit. Love is fruit of the Spirit. Jesus said we would know them by their fruit, not by their gift. Satan can counterfeit gifts, but he cannot fake the fruit!

What the Lord beholds is how you have regarded His Word with the instrument of your voice before you sing, where you have placed your feet before you dance, and how you have conducted your body before you dress. It is the manifestation of the fruit of the Spirit through your temple that God beholds, which determines the effectiveness and the genuineness of His spiritual gifts.

For all those [things] hath mine hand made, and all those [things] have been, saith the LORD: but to this [man] will I look, [even] to [him that is] poor and of a contrite spirit, and trembleth at my word. ***Isa 66:2***

And rend your heart, and not your garments, and turn unto the LORD your God: for he [is] gracious and merciful, slow to anger, and of great kindness, and repenteth him of the evil.
Joel 2:13

The height of outer worship is based on how lowly you are before the Lord's throne. It is determined by how much you respond to His Word. We all have some degree of rebellion in our heart until we are brought to the end of ourselves. Even when we attain to a degree of spiritual maturity, we have to live a sober life to keep what we have attained, lest we allow the spirit of pride to deceive us.

In the last chapter of Isaiah, God declared that the heavens are His throne and the earth His footstool. All of creation is a result of His making. But who shall be those who will be found worthy of receiving His look? We feel awed when we are looked upon by some celebrity in or outside of the church. But the eyes of the Almighty beholding you is worship that is received and pleasing in His sight. These are the things that are not capable of being celebrated with the masses. This is called intimacy between you and God. It is the height of all experiences through the atonement of Jesus Christ that we might experience the union of being one with God, even as Christ is One with Him.

Worship is not as we have been led to believe. It is not singing and going to musicals. It is not Christian concerts or expressing yourself in any form of bodily movement. As I have stated previously, though these things are a part of the process (and some are nothing but the flesh), in and of themselves, they are not worship!

Worship - The Very Act

When you have taken an assessment of your life at certain intervals, you begin to realize that what really matters is how much of God has been a part of your life. How often have you sat in His presence? Is it a habitual part of your everyday life? Your assessment takes you through a maze of events that flash before your eyes. You see yourself waking up every morning to go to work, captured in a vice of the temptations of trusting in the system. You wonder sometimes if this is the most that you will ever accomplish at the workplace; a Christian who is on time, does not provoke anyone, has a nice savings account with a mortgage that is almost paid off and the children's educational fund in tact. This is truly acceptable but has God's kingdom really advanced through your life to impact others? How much of your labors will truly withstand the rigorous fire of God on judgment day? What will be your argument to justify minimum involvement in the worship of God and the call to kingdom advancement? Better yet, while you live in this maze, you hunger for more of God and yet you are afraid of the cost. The Holy Spirit tirelessly pursues your attention, yet you are easily distracted by this week's event.

Perhaps your maze is a religious one. Every Sunday your eyes pop open and you flip on the radio to listen to some great Christian music! You dress with care and are proud of your new hair style. The children must hurry up and eat the latest chemically laced cereal and be ready for more junk food at church. You finally arrive and are happy to see all the brothers and sisters and everyone putting on their best "bless you, I'm doing fine" show. We pay our money, perhaps are touched by the preaching and then we gather to our cars and race to dinner at the restaurants that line our streets. We then spend the rest of the evening reading the days garbage in the community newspaper, or watching men play games on the tube. In fact, some could not make it to church because of the game. Others went, but could hardly wait to get home and push play on the VCR.

Or you are a preacher and your maze is a trying one. You preach your heart out to the people and they seem enjoy it, but there is no evidence of conformity to the preached Word of God that even angels long to look into, but has been reserved for the human race (1 Peter 1:12). Everyone has an idea and it is your desire not to be offensive, so you take the time to be dumped on by everyone. By God's grace, you survive this weight of His people and get before God to receive His direction.

The ministry is constantly trying to define you by all the agendas of men and denominations. Your own desires are attempting to define what God wants of you. You see the need and feel the unction of God to take a stand on certain issues. Yet you realize the price that comes with it. Do you suffer the consequences of telling God's people their wrong? Or do you, through silence, condone it religiously believing that God will work it out, while you just pray. You think, "let someone else say it and I will jump up and say AMEN"! You read the latest magazine searching for insight on your present trial. You locate a few articles that addresses the issue facing you, yet there remains an obvious void within your spirit that indicates you need more.

Perhaps you are just fed up with the Body of Christ and its condition of compromise and obvious struggle to recapture the fire of God and the impact that is needed upon your country. You do not have a lot of patience for those who refuse to grow up and for preachers who are content with a dry bone word. You see through the self orchestrated services and you want to drink from a well that has fresh water, refreshing you each time you drink. You simply want more in your Christian walk from leadership and you go from church to church searching for it. In the meantime, you place your membership somewhere until it happens. In other words, you are there, but you are not there. You are passing time waiting for God to speak.

The mazes of life are countless and some of them are not as difficult as others. We all have them and our struggle is to work through them until the maze becomes a line that gradually climbs upward to spiritual bliss and purposeful living on a daily basis. What will remedy our dilemma? WORSHIP!

The precise act of worship cannot be articulated or described in any human terms. It is only revealed and known by the Spirit.

> ***God [is] a Spirit: and they that worship him must worship [him] in spirit and in truth.*** ***Jo 4:24***

Divine worship has many aspects to be understood, and only One Person can teach you them. That is the person of the Holy Spirit. I shall now devote the remainder of this chapter to sharing spiritual insights to worship; the act of two individuals giving and receiving of ones highest self in complete trust backed by a covenant of sinless blood initiated by the Greater of the two.

When you are alone with God and just begin to love Him, something happens. It is a very personal, peaceful and powerful union which captivates the soul like no other person or element that we as human beings know. There is an awareness that God grants you of Himself which is a result of you truly wanting and desiring the Lover of your soul to manifest.

What begins as a quest for spiritual renewal first of all develops into small meetings that are viewed as times of reflections or thoughts that we dwell on for a few seconds. While contending with our maze, we find ourselves laying aside our tinkling with trying to fix it, to just looking up at God and asking, "how long Lord, how long?"

But then God, in His mercy, begins to reveal Himself. First, He shows that the purpose of the maze was good and that it has an end. He does this by allowing you and I to come to the end of ourselves and to simply quit the games that we play in trying to write the pages of our lives for whatever reason. It is when we give up on ourselves that God gives us Himself. The maze makes us ready for rest. The maze causes us to want the true worship of God. We come to grips with the fake and the feigned to where we see this life for what it really is. We desire to know God in His fullness. Through the maze, we become prepared to pay the price. We are not afraid anymore; we just want God and we dare anything or anyone to hinder us from the highest expression of life.

But the question that remains is; will we exit the maze when God reveals to us that its purpose has been fulfilled and it is time to come out? Or will we justify it another day, week, month and year that everything will work out in time? For those who come out, they will enter into the private corridors of their heart and position their mind, bodies, strength and soul to worship. They will make the changes necessary for God to come near them. They will remove the idols of their hearts and tear down the altars of humanism and wait for Jehovah God to reveal Himself. The will afflict themselves with fastings and remove themselves from the vanities of men and welcome whatever suffering they must endure for the God Who made them, to simply reveal Himself.

The scriptures takes on a new meaning of refuge and hope. They no longer look to it for a "word". Rather, they look to it for God revealed in His Son, Jesus Christ. Their day is ordered around the preparation for the worship of God. This time it will not be for just a day or maybe a week at the most after a conference. Again, in His mercy, God is enabling you to desire and set yourself to worship.

As you press into the chambers of your heart, you become aware of Him and you lose your awareness of time. It is through this pressing that your deliverance breaks forth. It is through this pressing that you discover the satisfaction that you have so desired. It is through this pressing that the desire of other things that has so demanded of you dries up because the desire of your total being is being fulfilled. When fulfillment comes, the lust for other things loses its pull. As you build your life daily in this realm, you will reflect on how such filthy and vile practices could be desired. For the first time, you begin to experience fulfillment and through the fulfillment of your soul, you begin to desire the fulfillment of His will.

Your emotions are touched; not overwhelmed to the point that they rule and dictate this union, but they are simply touched. You begin to understand issues regarding your life that were not previously clear. You begin to pray prayers of devotion that you never heard before. You begin to see the future the way you never saw it before. You begin to desire God in ways you never desired Him before. You are worshipping and the response of God is flooding your mind with His mind, your will with His will and your hope with His hope. You begin to rest with His rest and rejoice with His joy. You have tasted the intimacy of Divine Worship and you will never settle for anything less again in your life. Hallelujah and Amen.

Chapter 7

Dealing with the Demonic

satan will not cast out himself nor can those who have given place to him do so

his chapter is not designed to deal with the intricate aspects of demons. I will not focus so much on their hierarchy as found in Ephesians six. The purpose of this chapter is to prophetically articulate the relevant mind of God for this generation in following Divine Protocol in their warring against demonic forces that will no longer be held back by the hand of God. It is a prophetic warning to the church that the battle cry of warfare is upon us and the small amount of time that we have is enough to prepare for this confrontation, if ones house is divided and thus, not prepared.

Whatever a child of God has to do to align themselves with His righteousness, now is the time to do it. Whatever sin that you have justified, now is the time to repent and let it go. Whatever doctrine that has deceived you from pursuing the advancement of His kingdom and has lured you to the acquiring of things in this kingdom (earth) food for the belly, pleasures for the eyes and knowledge for the mind (Gen. 3:6), must be rejected with all sincerity and godly repentance, lest you be found ill-equipped to face the enemies of God's kingdom that shall no longer be withheld. The days of speculation of what is doctrinal and what is not will cease when the days of demonstration of God's kingdom with power opens. Behold, it is suddenly upon you! The kingdom of God is at hand!

As we approach the last moments of time and prepare to confront the kingdom of darkness, dealing with the demonic realm will become a public display of kingdoms clashing not only for the souls of men, but also their minds, bodies and wills. Those who are not ready for the confrontation will respond one of three ways.

And he was casting out a devil, and it was dumb. And it came to pass, when the devil was gone out, the dumb spake; and the people wondered. But some of them said, He casteth out devils through Beelzebub the chief of the devils. And others, tempting [him], sought of him a sign from heaven. Lu 11:14-16

When people observed Jesus casting out a devil, some of them simply wondered. They were baffled at such power and could not fathom the reality of the spirit world. Perhaps they had so accepted demons and the problems that inflict as such a normal part of life, that they did not want the knowledge of a way to be delivered. In any event, these people wondered.

Then you had those who were exposed for having no relevant power to break yokes. Their only way to save face was to accuse Jesus of being the chief agent of demons. Instead of submitting to this power and being endued with it by following the protocol of God's kingdom, these people chose to attribute to satan what only God could do. If they were to give God the glory, they would also have to admit that they do not have the answers and that Christ was indeed the Messiah. They would rather give the devil credit.

Even as we behold the manifestation of power upon certain vessels, there will be others who accuse them of being in league with the enemy. This is dangerous on an eternal scale and as Jesus said, ye are in danger of eternal damnation and unforgiveness in this life and in the life to come (Mk. 3:28-29).

The third response is to show contempt by demanding a sign from the heavens that verify such a person is of God. If people are not as foolish to blame the devil, they will then ask you to provide some supernatural evidence that you really have been anointed by God to cast out demons.

Whatever the response may be, should you be chosen to this confrontational work of casting out demons, prepare yourself for a combination of responses. Some leaders will reject you, others will question you and yet others will attempt to exalt you. Dealing with demons brings a life of dealing with people on a variety of levels. Only through possessing a sober life acquired through fasting and prayer, will you be able to deal with people and not be provoked one way or the other.

In His mercy, God has greatly limited satan from manifesting himself in many ways. Very seldom do we even see demons disrupt a service as they did throughout the ministry of our Lord. Nor do we observe mocking spirits, who interfere in the ministry of salvation. Such spirits must be told to "be quiet".

Spirits that have crippled people or allowed them not to speak or hear are possessing millions of souls that are saved as well as unsaved. Spirits that torment the mind and take control of bodies that defile themselves in unspeakable ways, are running rampant in our country with very little opposition from the church. God is about to start a fight and those who say they are anointed preachers, prophets and ministers of righteousness, had better be found free from demons in their own life, in their own habits and in their own mind. Otherwise, when such spirits begin to mock them, there will be no power to command them to, "COME OUT OF HIM AND BE QUIET"!

One of the methods that God has always used amongst His people to cause them to become serious about serving Him was war. In the Old Testament, it was war that caused His people to fall on their face and seek deliverance. It was war that caused soberness to become the norm and not the exception. God allowed a foe from the north to bring His people looking for Him like nothing else would. While there was peace, prosperity and victory parties going on, His leaders became intoxicated on their security in their systems. They become over confident in themselves to answer every problem that they faced. God had blessed Israel with surpassing wealth so that they wanted for nothing. Yet as long as they were threatened with war, they never had a problem with fasting and prayer. They never had an issue with being at peace with each other. Racism was totally swallowed up because everyone's life was a stake and as long as you were willing to fight for the God of Abraham, Isaac and Jacob, you were family.

When Rahab decided to reject her own people and side with Israel, she was identified with Israel. A war was getting ready to start.

When the Gibeonites heard what Joshua had done unto Jericho and to Ai, they did work wilily (deceit), says the Word of God in Joshua 9:3-4. They deceived Joshua and the princes of the congregation to make them sware unto them peace and make a league to let them live. A war was happening. Fear drove them to survive and through deception, they caught Joshua and the princes of Israel off guard. Though Joshua and the princes of Israel asked the Gibeonites questions after the flesh, Joshua yet did not seek spiritual counsel of the Lord (Joshua 9:14).

When the early Church witnessed Ananias and Sapphira drop dead for holding the Spirit of the Lord in contempt, great fear came upon the Church in such proportions that people who were not real dared not to join themselves to the apostles. The Church was in the height of warfare and the demonic realm was being invaded. As a result, spiritual warfare was in full manifestation, demonstrating that there is a God and all power is in the name of His Son, Jesus Christ.

These are a few examples of what happens when there is true spiritual warfare. People align themselves with whoever has the power because they want to live. Even enemies will become friends when they realize that without one another, they both are going to perish. Walls fall down when destruction is certain. Leaders of all groups unite their minds, resources and wisdom to stand for one purpose; survival.

As we enter the next century of Christianity, God is going to allow war to bring His church together. The times of peace are the times to prepare for war. The test of our Christianity is upon us. It will not have anything to do with how you spell faith, where the book of Hebrews is located in the Bible, or what is the shortest scripture. Being able to give me the Greek interpretation of grace and the Hebrew meaning of salvation will be to no avail. Those who have built works on the words of the Bible and not the Spirit of the Bible are going to face some serious consequences when the battle cry of warfare is sounded throughout this country. These things will happen before the return of our Lord and Savior Jesus Christ.

Am I trying to cause God's people to fear? Heaven, yes! For all the issues that have allowed the Church to become sidetracked and distracted from the real work of God's kingdom, there is no more time for us to get it together on our own accord with our own motivations. Though there are many declaring what needs to be done, only a few are doing it. What is going to cause the many to join in with the few is WAR - war with the devil and his demons in a fashion that our generation has never seen. God is forewarning you to get ready to demonstrate what you have been living, for the Gospel is not of talk, but of power!

Many people declare that they are Christians because they do not associate being a Christian with casting out devils or even healing the sick. The healings that we observe today are shrouded under questions of whether they were really healed. Though I believe people are being healed to some degree, there is coming a time and day that the world will witness dead people get up, withered hands unfold, blind eyes open and doctors bewildered at the undeniable miracles that shall unfold. It is not my intent to come across as fanatical or to excite through mere sensationalism. It is without question that we have had enough hype in the Church today. I am simply declaring that God is going to demonstrate to our generation that Jesus Christ is Lord even as He proved to that generation that He is. New Agers are going to denounce what they believe because the evidence of Christ and His power will be so overwhelming. Of course, you will have those who yet deny Him, however, it will be obvious that the miracles could only be done by God.

The purposes for God allowing the confrontation of demons are multifold. Those that are relevant to me, by God's Spirit, are first of all to cause the heat of warfare to bring the Body of Christ together. It will melt our differences away and cause the Body to become complete as well as expose those who have done nothing but talk and therefore deceive many of God's people. To exalt some and humble others in one day. To convict the world of sin and to demonstrate that Christ is the only Begotten Son of God. It will be a great moment in history to watch millions turn from their worship of demons and desire the worship of God through Jesus Christ and finally, to truly prepare the Body of Christ to meet their Lord in the sky. Once again, these are not conclusive in and of themselves. There are many other reasons that God will allow confrontation.

Dealing with Demons

And the scribes which came down from Jerusalem said, He hath Beelzebub, and by the prince of the devils casteth he out devils. And he called them [unto him], and said unto them in parables, How can Satan cast out Satan? And if a kingdom be divided against itself, that kingdom cannot stand. And if a house be divided against itself, that house cannot stand. And if Satan rise up against himself, and be divided, he cannot stand, but hath an end. No man can enter into a strong man's house, and spoil his goods, except he will first bind the strong man; and then he will spoil his house. **Mr 3:22-27**

For those who possess the Spirit of the Lord and are His, there is no need to fear demons. They are fallen angels who lost their first estate and realize they are going to hell where they will spend eternity. They are such enemies of righteousness; our minds cannot comprehend the vile hatred they have toward Jesus Christ and His saints. They are manipulators, liars and inventors of degradation to such a degree that human reasoning or intellect is worthless in trying to assess it.

Demons represent a kingdom whose prince is satan, also know as beelzebub, and they work based upon kingdom laws that have been established by God. They recognize these laws and abide by them. They have no respect to any other laws whatsoever. When spiritual righteousness is present, they must obey. When spiritual righteousness is not present, they work evil to the fullest extent of their rights. To the degree that God's people have aligned themselves with His protocol in dealing with demons, is the degree to which they will be able to deal with them when God allows the days of demonic warfare to unfold once again upon the earth. Keep in mind that although all righteousness has been fulfilled during a certain dispensation, such warfare will not yet unfold until it is time. Even at the age of 29, Jesus could not confront demonic spirits for... "His time had not yet come." Spiritual wisdom will be so important to prevent becoming presumptuous or hasty as well as being hesitant to following God's leading.

Those who are religious will fight those who have the power. They will say to them, "you have the devil in you and that is how you can do what you do". It is here that Jesus lays the protocol for understanding and carrying out demonic warfare.

While they accuse Him of possessing the prince of the devils, He takes their own words to reveal just the opposite. Verse 23 says that He called them over to Him and asked them a question. "How can satan cast out satan? How can the devil in me, cast out the devil in you? How can the ruler of one kingdom cast himself out from that kingdom? How can darkness cast out darkness"? Jesus is clearly establishing one of the first rules of protocol; a person cannot cast out what they themselves possess. As a Christian, if satan has a place in your mind, your body, your appetites, your eyes and your beliefs, then it is impossible to cast him out of someone who has the same strongman residing in them. Though as a Christian, you cannot be possessed with the devil, you nonetheless can be oppressed and controlled by the devil. Regardless of how much you can preach, teach and pray, if the devil has a place in you, that is all he needs to render you powerless in casting him out. This is why Jesus declared that satan had nothing in Him.

Hereafter I will not talk much with you: for the prince of this world cometh, and hath nothing in me. ***Joh 14:30***

Jesus went on to speak with them. He declared:

And if a kingdom be divided against itself, that kingdom cannot stand.

Your kingdom consist of the laws by which you govern your life. Every kingdom has a set system of how to judge and administer. Jesus is Lord of lords and King of kings. This reveals to us that we are seen as gods who are capable of choosing our way of determining what will be in the sphere of our domain.

America is a kingdom that has set laws for its citizens. We pay taxes. If you rob a bank, you go to jail. If you go to college for four years, you get a degree. At least at one time in this country, people did not choose their occupation, it was chosen for them. It was called, *slavery*. They did not live where they wanted to live; they lived where they were told to live. Every nation is likened unto a kingdom that has set rules by which it makes decisions and operates. If that kingdom is divided in any form or fashion, it will fall. Perhaps not right away, but the fall is guaranteed. We even observe how many kingdoms have fallen, not because another kingdom was stronger, but because that particular kingdom was divided against itself.

As Christians, our kingdom individually as well as corporately is made up of the laws that we use to make our decisions. Our kingdom is divided if we are mixing God's laws with pagan laws. Our kingdom is divided if we mix Phosophies with spiritual truth. Our kingdom is divided if we substitute our righteousness for God's righteousness. Our kingdom is divided if we declare doctrines that talk about holiness, but we walk in a habitual carnal life-style. Our kingdom will not stand if we have a form of godliness (talk) but deny the power thereof (walk). If our kingdom operates off of a double standard, we will not be able to stand against the coming onslaught of demons.

And if a house be divided against itself, that house cannot stand.

Your house is the result of what your kingdom stands for. What you do in your house is a result of the rules you have established. Your house is the demonstration of whose kingdom your kingdom is built upon. It is the most powerful declaration of who is your lord and who is your king. There are only two kingdoms in the world - God's and satan's. They both are manifested inside the home.

This is why those who are called to the ministry must prove themselves faithful first at home. Their home will reveal what kingdom they represent. Inside the home, we demonstrate what we really believe. Our eyes are viewing that which is contrary to godliness or that which is godly. Even our kitchen will determine who really possesses our bodies. A great many people have made their belly their god. They eat anything they want to anytime they want to eat it. No moderation whatsoever. Obesity has been accepted as normal and not as an indication that somebody is eating too much. If you are in the ministry and your belly is blocking your eyes from seeing your feet, it should be clear to you and to everyone whose kingdom is ruling your home. A house that is divided will not be capable of dealing with demons!

If your children are permitted to carry on and entertain themselves with things that are contrary to God's kingdom, your house is divided. If you have objects that represent satan's kingdom, no matter how innocent you might think it is, your house is divided. When you sit down and spend two hours per night viewing sitcoms that make light of the family as well as movies that exploit your mind, YOUR HOUSE IS DIVIDED! The devil knows how to allow a little leaven to work its way into your environment and eventually his objective is level your whole lump!

Demons are very organized and they know if they have a root in your house. If they do, you have no right to confront them, until there is godly sorrow that worketh godly repentance. You can confront them, but they know that your house is divided and as a result, you can do nothing to cast them out of someone else's house. Even as they must adhere to Divine Protocol, so must we. Satan knows how to discredit your ministry by simply dividing your house.

Married couples must not be deceived into thinking satan cannot divide their house by how you carry yourself sexually toward one another. The marriage bed is to be undefiled. That means it can be defiled (Heb. 13:4)! Though you are married and you have become one flesh, that does not nullify God's first rights to your body as His temple. Marriage is rooted in God's kingdom and if His kingdom laws are not governing your marriage bed, then perversion will be the result of satan's kingdom governing it. Demons know when you are living a perverted life and they also know that you cannot confront them because they have something in you.

And if Satan rise up against himself, and be divided, he cannot stand, but hath an end.

The success of satan's kingdom is based on one principle. As long as he can have some kind of claim to your kingdom, your house, or your body, he can survive with you around. He realizes that as long as he is in that person's life, no matter how small it may be, he cannot be confronted when told to leave someone else's life. If this was not true, then there would be no way for satan to even maintain a stronghold. Nor would we be able to for the principle is the same for both kingdoms.

Divine Protocol; The Order of God's Kingdom, is to have every aspect of your life under His rule, under His reign and under His righteousness. This position renders satan totally ineffective in resisting the demand to vacate any property that you demand him to leave. These truths all coincide with God's timing and God's purpose. Though these principles are true, they only operate according to His will and not our own.

No man can enter into a strong man's house, and spoil his goods, except he will first bind the strong man; and then he will spoil his house.

This is the qualifier for waging successful warfare over demons. You cannot enter into a strongman's house and salvage his goods except you first bind the strongman. The binding of the strongman must first take place before you can have benefits of the goods in the house. The first house he must be bound in is our house. The first goods we need to acquire are our own goods. Many are trying to get the minds of other people set free and the strongman has their mind. Satan is meticulous in finding ground to maintain his position. Forgiveness can alter the outcome when dealing with the devil. Lusting after a woman with ones eyes is enough to give place to the devil which in turn renders that person ineffective in warring against demons.

To first bind the strongman means removing his influence completely from your kingdom and your house. This takes time to the point to where the house has been filled with the proper goods and there is a godly mode of operation there. If there is not a life-style of godliness, then although the strongman is gone, he will return to attempt to occupy his original habitation. Until he returns, accompanied by others seven times worse than him with him, then the process is incomplete. The Word says he must be bound. Bound means completely defeated.

The protocol that God is calling the Church to is simply to get the devil completely out of your life. God will bestow all the grace necessary for this strongman in the life of all His children to be totally bound and cast out. Until then, dealing with demons will only be a theoretical observation. It will be a mere discussion but never demonstrated. As I have stated earlier, the days of demonic confrontation are upon us and this small dialog that Jesus had with the scribes is the scriptural foundation for being found prepared to deal with demons. As well, please understand that the information shared here is not conclusive. You should not presume authority to confront demons simply because you are free of them and or are living an upright life before the Lord to where you have attained. Though Jesus lives in you, that does authorize you to do what He did in the full scope of His works. There has to be a mandate and calling on your life to receive this unction. There will be those who take upon themselves this work without being directly instructed by God. Contempt can be a result of a deliberate action or a sincere mistake. Whatever the case, contempt is contempt.

My prayer is that those who can hear through the Spirit would properly discern this issue and simply prepare for the coming warfare of God's people against satan's kingdom. There will also be a level of contending with those who are the children of the scribes. They will be religious leaders that people would less expect to reject this sovereign move of God. Even as they accused Jesus of being Beelzebub, so will they accuse you. However, everyone will be justified by their fruit. Ask them what Jesus asked the scribes:

> ***And if I by Beelzebub cast out devils, by whom do your sons cast [them] out? therefore shall they be your judges. But if I with the finger of God cast out devils, no doubt the kingdom of God is come upon you.*** ***Lu 11:19, 20***

In other words Jesus is stating, "Your sons have never cast out a devil because they have devils. Therefore, by their works they will judge that you have devils too. But the fact that I have cast out devils with just the finger of God, it is certain that the kingdom of God has come unto you".

In conclusion it must be clear that these are the only spiritual laws that demons will submit to. They are not into the personalities of men. You either will yield to the Spirit of God by obeying His word and will, or through neglect of doing so, you will be automatically yielded to demonic forces whose sole purpose is to destroy the Christian life and work.

Fasting and Prayer

There comes a time when it appears that no amount of rebuking the devil works. He stubbornly maintains his hold upon his victims and in many situations, there is only one answer for such resistance; fasting and prayer.

When the disciples were confronted with a man whose son was heavily demonized, they proceeded to utilize the authority that Jesus had just given them in the beginning of Luke chapter nine. They themselves were perplexed as to why this demon would not remove itself from its victim. They asked Jesus why they could not cast it out. No matter how many disciples there were at this particular scene, they could not cast out the devil from this young man.

It is insightful to note Jesus' first response when the man came to tell Him that His disciples could not relieve his child from this demon.

> ***And wheresoever he taketh him, he teareth him: and he foameth, and gnasheth with his teeth, and pineth away: and I spake to thy disciples that they should cast him out; and they could not.***
> **Mr 9:18**

Though I want to focus on prayer and fasting specifically, we need to understand the type of characteristics of demons who must be addressed in this fashion.

First of all, they have full control over their victims. "Wheresoever he taketh him" . This reveals that such a person has housed this spirit for years. They have no say in where they go. Furthermore, this reveals that the will is paralyzed from exercising choice. This can happen in a variety of ways. Allow me to simply state that though this victim was possessed from a child, there are some cases where the victim has willingly allowed satan to slowly possess and take over their being by participating in sin knowingly. In such a case if there is a willful consent from the victim, fasting and prayer may not remove the demon from them. The only breakthrough that can take place is enough freedom for the victim to repent of their wrong and renounce the devil. Then the demon can be cast out.

Those who are playing around with sin begin to give up their will in where they go. It increases every time they yield to the demonic influence. Those who open themselves to pornography soon want to visit men's clubs, porno shops and X- rated movies. Those who give themselves over to liquor go to the liquor store and bars. Those who give themselves over to gluttony are found at the buffets where they can feed that demon until it tells them to leave. Those who yield to fornication are out at dance clubs looking for those who are fornicators. There are many people that are being taken to places where they would not want to go. This is why many people admit that they should stop this activity but cannot. If there are Christians yielding to these kinds of devils, they need to simply confront that spirit and tell it to come out of their mind and to release their will. Spirits are always talking to get into the minds of Christians and too often, we take it for a thought that is floating by. Before demons can get into your body, they have to get into your mind. If you are not saying, "satan get thee behind me, for it is written..." a minimum of four or five times a day, you are yielding to his persuasions.

An example I had when confronted with a demon inside of a young man clearly illustrates the power of will. While I was taking offering at a church, this young man comes forth and stands directly in front of me declaring that he wanted to get saved. I was, of course, moved and proceeded to ask him a few questions. As soon as I held his hand to pray, his entire countenance changed and the demon inside of him totally objected to the Spirit of God taking residence through the new birth.

It must be noted that when engaging in warfare, do not expect these devils to simply say, "sure I'll leave." They are being evicted from their residence and the only place they can go is dry (arid) places. If the sheriff has to come evict people when they must vacate the premises because the landlord does not want to take the risk of being entreated violently, how do you think demons have to be approached? With legal ground to put them out and then the authority to enforce those legal rights!

Immediately, the young man stiffened a gave me a look of repulsive hate as well as violence. I confronted this demon and commanded him to come out. Needless to say, he spit up blood, went from wall to wall, threatened to spit in my face, (I told that devil that he had better not) held on to my feet (by this time those who previously boasted of their authority were standing behind me pouring globs of anointing oil all over my hands), wallowed on the floor and resorted to his last alternative; it turned to the pastor and begged, "tell the preacher to leave me alone." I could not believe it. I stood there totally baffled. I expected the pastor to back me up. The pastor said, "Brother Owens, he'll be alright". The young man sat down next to the pastor in total confidence that I could do nothing else. That demon found legal ground through the covering of that church to stay and as a result, I let it.

I have met people who know that Jesus loves them and readily admit that they are wrong. On one occasion while ministering to a homosexual I simply asked him, "you enjoy what you do, don't you"? He looked at me with such excitement and said, "YES!". He went on to say he liked his sin and did not want to leave it even though he knew he was going to hell! If people do not want to literally repent (turn around), they are saying, "I want to keep my pet devils so leave me alone". If there is no godly sorrow, there will be no godly repentance (2Cor.7:10).

My point in communicating this story is to make plain that fasting and prayer clearly enables a confronting of demons, yet the legal aspect of those demons coming out has to be established first. This young man surrendered himself under the authority of that pastor and obviously there was a relationship already established between them that caused that demon to find legal ground to stay. His will was still unmoved; therefore, so would that demon be. The young homosexual wanted his demon and all the authority of heaven would not cast it out.

In the previously discussed parable, the father of this demon possessed son also noted these characteristics; "he teareth him: and he foameth, and gnasheth with his teeth, and pineth away". While it is obvious what some of these terms mean, there are several I would like to focus on specifically. "Pineth" literally means to shrivel, dry up and wither away. "Teareth" means spasmodic contraction, to mangle, to convulse with epilespsy. These traits clearly denote a strong uncontrollable spirit who causes their victim bodily harm, whose goal is to work havoc upon their victims until they totally dry up or "pineth" away. At such a level, there is a physical manifestation of abnormality that must be contributed to spiritual wickedness. This was no ordinary case. It was a public display of satan's kingdom working havoc upon a son of Abraham and Jesus was establishing the protocol of confronting such levels of demonic activity. This was no ministry of explanation. It was clearly one of demonstration. Jesus only explained what was necessary to bring change and that by spiritual words. His method of teaching His disciples was by performing the Gospel, never by merely talking about it.

Finally, let us notice that this is a young boy whose father is interceding on his behalf. Later, Jesus asked the father how long the boy had been like this. He responded, "from a child". Obviously, his age was older than that of a child at this point. It appears that this victim was not responsible for this possession. Jesus inquired enough to realize that this young man was truly a victim of another person's ignorance, whether intentionally or not and his father, representing him, repented of unbelief. The rest was history. Jesus confronted the demon to come out and it did.

We now come to the issue of why the disciples could not cast them out and then why Jesus declares that only through fasting and prayer shall this kind come forth. We have defined "this kind" to a degree. Let us now look more closely at the issue of fasting and prayer.

He answereth him, and saith, O faithless generation, how long shall I be with you? how long shall I suffer you? bring him unto me. **Mk 9:19**

Before the Lord deals with His disciples, He first deals with this generation. He declares that it remains faithless even though He has been amongst them long enough for them to realize that the devil and his demons are responsible for all misery and that Christ alone can deliver. He asks Himself how long He would be willing to put up with such unbelief. The Church today is falling into such belief by yielding to society's diagnostic views of problems that the devil is directly responsible for. He knows how to hide under human reasoning and logic so as to allow remedies that are void of God's finger to cast him out. Psychology, medicine and deep forms of therapy and counseling that is even labelled "Christian" are of no avail when dealing with demons if God's agents are void of power to cast the devil out. What appears as deliverance is simply maintenance. Unless the devil is cast out, though measures are taken to make the victim comfortable through sedation and human means, the devil is still in. The way you know the devil is gone is that the victim changes. Unless change has taken place, the strongman is yet in the house. You can talk about their history, get them to cry, hug them, pet them and feed them. Devils will play along and even have a conversation with you over dinner. Clear and concise measures must be defined according to scripture in establishing the protocol for setting captives free.

Jesus was vexed in His spirit at the slowness of heart for His generation to believe that the cause was the devil. "How long must I be with you! Bring the boy to me - SATAN... COME OUT!"

Toward the conclusion of this event, Jesus finally reveals to His disciples why they could not cast the devil out. He knew they believed, yet they were still unable to bring deliverance to this young man.

And when he was come into the house, his disciples asked him privately, Why could not we cast him out? And he said unto them, This kind can come forth by nothing, but by prayer and fasting. **Mr 9:28-29**

The disciples finally get Jesus alone to inquire as to why they were not successful. This is excellent advice for ministers who have no power in the word as well as in the demonstration of the Gospel with power. Get alone with Jesus and ask Him why things are not happening! Quit winging it with a dry bone word and a humanistic message that is old, stale and late. Go to a mountain privately with Jesus and stay there until He reveals your problem to you. He will tell you only if you humble yourself and ask. If you already know why and refuse to obey, stop preaching and laying rebellious hands on God's people lest some demon jump on you. Such rebellion is dangerous and the consequences are heavy for that servant who knew the Master's will and did not do it.

Jesus said unto them that there is no other way this demon will budge unless you fast and pray. The question we must endeavor to answer is, "exactly what is effected by the fasting and the praying? Us, the demon, or both"?

I believe both. Let us first look at ourselves. The disciples were willing to pray but nothing happened. I believe however, that deep within their spirit, they did not have a belief that was beyond doubt. I believe they were confronted with a fear that was a result of what they saw and a realization of the magnitude of what confronted them.

Fasting and prayer develops an unspoken depth of faith that goes beyond Hebrews 11:1. It brings that vessel into a spiritual relationship with Christ that surpasses the norm. It is not weird or of such a heavenly origin that such a person is incapable of living life or relating to people, but such closeness provides a true understanding of God and God's enemy; satan. Fasting causes the callous surrounding the spiritual man to fall off. It removes the dross that hinders the faith of God from manifesting through the instrument of His people.

Fasting provides a source of spiritual strength that food cannot provide. One has to find their strength in one or the other. I believe that the kind of fasting that Jesus was speaking of was more a life-style than a causal acquaintance. Without a habitual form of exercise in anything, one can never build enduring authority. Those who lift weights for a profession do so everyday. Even their diet is centered around the main objective; muscles. Those who declare themselves ministers of the Gospel should likewise be found centering their diet around their profession and not their profession around their diet.

There is a certain benefit one derives from eating foods that are strong in protein and carbohydrates. Likewise, there are numerous benefits found in eating that spiritual meat which is of a divine orgin. Fasting opens a spiritual corridor that enlightens spiritual understanding to such an extent that a person can operate with this understanding. I have met many people who understand, but cannot cast a flea off of a dog. This is only head knowledge. Though ones knowledge of demons and the understanding of the method of casting them out are present, they yet lack a quickening that cannot be presumed. There is much presumption in the Body of Christ today that will be revealed as outright foolishness. Many have foolishly presumed scriptures, offices and ministries that are based on the letter and are void of Divine Protocol. There is no order in their diet and therefore, they live by bread alone.

When one has a lifestyle of fasting, it reveals their consent to living after the things of God. It is a declaration of submission and a surrendering of their strength as the means by which they will operate. Fasting in and of itself is futile. There exists many religions whose followers fast and are doing nothing but going hungry. Yet for the vessel whose conscience is clear before the Lord and is walking where they have attained in knowledge, fasting with sincere and pure motives moves them closer to God. I recognize that we usually say, "God moves when you fast." I understand the implication and it is true. However, we have failed to clearly articulate who is moving. God is moving us. God is always moving with or without our involvement in His kingdom. Through fasting, we voluntarily surrender ourselves and a moving that is continual and progressive evolves that takes a person to a level of dealing effectively with demons of this sort.

Fasting is truly a mystery. The only part we probably can relate to well is that the feeling is painful, uncomfortable and simply revealing of just how pitiful we are. I am sure everyone's perception of fasting is as different as everyone's place within the body of Christ. It is my opinion that not everyone has been called to deal with demons. Jesus gave authority to specific persons who walked closely with him. While I am not discouraging a Christian from exercising the authority of a believer, I am clearly decreeing that such authority should not be presumed. It should be clearly delegated from Jesus by His Spirit. If He has anointed a person for such a ministry, it will involve a lifestyle of fasting. There is not much to really talk about when it comes to this topic simply because it is more a demonstrative expression of God's kingdom than an oratative expression. There are many secrets of the kingdom that God will not reveal in words. They must be deposited and through an ordained fast that is based on relationship and obedience, such deposits are made.

Prayer enters into this domain once fasting has been clearly defined as a habitual part of life. Satan's kingdom revolves around stealing, killing and destroying. Those who move in the high realms of authority continually pull down strongholds. This form of prayer is as high as this form of warfare. Such warriors are not asking for jobs, money and the carnal necessities of life. We are admonished not to even seek after them. Rather, there is intercession for God's kingdom and righteousness to become a reality upon the earth that is the focus of those who enter into this kind of fasting and prayer. Jesus declared that without such prayers, one cannot remove devils of this sort. Quite frankly, our society and churches are full of them. As I said earlier in this chapter, God has protected the Church against itself and has not allowed the increase of spiritual warfare on such levels for the simple fact that we are not ready. Yet, even as those who read this truth and other revelations that God has released upon the Church, excuses will not be found any longer and lack of power will only reveal lack of commitment.

Prayer of this sort can involve days, weeks and even months. It is not as though you isolate yourself away from God's people. I simply mean that such vessels maintain an undisturbed watch and attitude of warfare that is focused and intense. This intensity should not be confused with legality or to such a state that there is no sensitivity towards life in general. Jesus was intense but He was yet human. He could laugh one minute and rebuke the scribes and Pharisees the next. He was intense, yet He was able to maintain a disposition that allowed

Him to be among masses of people and divinely feed them with five loaves and two fish.

Many times, fasting from certain foods is as effective as total abstinence. Whatever your pallet craves and drives you to is what you need to abstain from. Many preachers are captive to meat. They have trained their mouths to live by it. Whether it is steak, pork, or chicken is not really the issue. When meats are a constant form of food, it will hinder this form of spiritual life and authority. I simply do not believe that a preacher's diet can consist of meat everyday and enable him to have power on Sunday. In fact, as we enter the next millennium, those who are going to move forward with God had better accept heavy eating as a thing of the past. We will not have time to run to a closet and fast and pray while the demon possessed is waiting at the altar. Gluttony is a definite reality within the courts of ministry and it does not mean this is geared toward only toward those who are overweight. There are those who eat what they want and due to their metabolism, you would never know. The issue is that unless you are suffering in the flesh to an extent, the flesh is not under. If the flesh is not under, the Spirit is.

Allow me to clearly state that there is a time for rejoicing and the breaking of bread. There is nothing like good food and friends to share it with. I believe it is important. The holidays would not be what they are without good cooking. It is not my intent to create some farfetched idea about fasting and prayer that is legalistic and imbalanced. My objection is to establish that fasting and praying is the norm for those of the coming millennium and not the exception.

Another benefit of a life of consecration are the health benefits. When you trace the ministry of Jesus on foot, there are days He and His disciples covered 30 miles to get to the next city. There is no human way possible the disciples and Jesus could have endured such bodily demands and maintain a diet that is obviously for the enjoyment of the flesh. I observe men of God today who are greatly overweight and not doing anything about it. I am even aware of how many people do not drink half of the amount of water they should, let alone eat correctly to live and enjoy life without the pains of sickness due to eating for the pallet and not for the spiritual man.

Those who practice natural medicine will readily tell you that all disease starts in the colon. The related illnesses that can be contributed to eating habits would be found to consist of all of them. Those who are physically sick in the Church and in leadership can be found as a result of a deliberate neglect of their eating habits. Even those who are well are found sluggish and void of stamina due to their diet.

The benefits of fasting in this regards speak clearly as to the rest and kindness that is shown to the body. It allows it to endure and a lightness to progress in the natural realm that those who over indulge cannot find the ability to do. There is a saying that will hold true for every living soul when it comes to eating according to the dictates of the flesh. It goes like this: "Thousands of people are digging their graves with their teeth with what they eat".

This is Divine Protocolin the arena of fasting and prayer.

The Bible reveals how fasting and prayer directly affects demons. The Gospels record a constant reactionary effect that Jesus caused when He simply appeared on the scene. Demons were petrified when they saw Jesus for one primary reason; torment.

And, behold, they cried out, saying, What have we to do with thee, Jesus, thou Son of God? art thou come hither to torment us before the time? **Mt 8:29**

And cried with a loud voice, and said, What have I to do with thee, Jesus, [thou] Son of the most high God? I adjure thee by God, that thou torment me not. **Mr 5:7**

When he saw Jesus, he cried out, and fell down before him, and with a loud voice said, What have I to do with thee, Jesus, [thou] Son of God most high? I beseech thee, torment me not.
Lu 8:28

They know their torment has been decreed by God and they recognize that when Jesus appears on the scene, by His word they can be sent to such torment immediately. Though this torment is not that which is final for satan and all his demons as well as those who rejected the love of the truth, they are yet sent under darkness being reserved in chains until their appointed time of judgment.

> ***And the angels which kept not their first estate, but left their own habitation, he hath reserved in everlasting chains under darkness unto the judgment of the great day.*** ***Jude 1:6***

When servants of God live a life of consecration, they too will experience a reactionary effect when they encounter the presence of demons. When demons do not sense light, they are unfettered and comfortable. Yet when the brightness of light is present according to the purposes and seasons of God, they react. Such are the effects that a lifestyle of fasting and prayer will have upon demons.

In closing, be prayerful in your fastings and rejoice not that the demons are subject to you in Jesus' name, but rather, that your name is written in the Lamb's book of life.

Chapter Eight

Divine Mandates

*The Next Millennium will
be Ruled by Divine Mandates*

pon the inauguration of the New Testament, a profound freedom of spiritual rule was released upon mankind. Jesus, our Lord, demonstrated this freedom by tearing ferociously into the systems and democracy of the scribes and Pharisees. The scriptures reveal that many times, the very purpose for Him healing, casting out a devil, or simply eating with unwashen hands, was to declare that system, man, angel, demon or denomination would rule God's kingdom and God's servants except God!

I declare to you today, most soberly and seriously, that the sons of the scribes and Pharisees are still busy hindering those sent to fulfill a specific task for God's kingdom. They are those who sit in Moses' seat and yet do nothing to delegate the works of Moses. They make their living from widows and like Saul, use the strength of the young man for their own agenda which is centered around the bleating of the sheep and the sparing of the enemy. Their works are the works of men. Indeed, they appear to be righteous but inwardly they are full of dead men's bones and all uncleanness. Such hinderers of the move of God's Spirit upon His chosen servants will compass sea and land to make one proselyte. When he is made, such is twice the child of hell than they are.

These ungodly deceivers understand the way that men must go to enter into the kingdom of heaven. They neither enter in themselves nor do they allow others to enter. These modern day sons of satan truly know how to pray long prayers just for a show and therefore, they shall receive greater damnation in the day ofjudgment. Again, to men, they truly appear to be in good standing with God, but within, they are full of hypocrisy and iniquity. Jesus declared that He would send to such serpents and generation of vipers prophets, wise men and scribes and they would kill them, beat them and even crucify them. They would persecuted from city to city.

I have just expressed truths that many of God's people are not ready to face. The above word is a prophecy, a declaration and a warning based on Matthew 23:13-36 that is yet relevant for our generation today. We have excused away the reality of imposters and those who parade upon God's flock without the slightest concern of judgment. Those who are prophets are not prophesying what thus saith the Lord. Those who have mandates are not minding them and as a result, fools, dumb dogs and gluttons are raping God's people both spiritually, financially and even physically. Oh, but the Spirit of the Lord shall no longer wink for He hears the cries of His people and God is stirring Himself to work!

Listen, ye who love the Lord with all that is within you, to what Jesus had to say about these bastards who are indeed without Father. When He secluded the disciple Jo whom He loved on the isle of Patmos, He told him to "Write the things which thou hast seen, and the things which are, and the things which shall be hereafter (Rev 1:19)". The seven churches that were addressed can be viewed in many ways. Yet, this verse allows the discerning and sober child of God to understand it is for us today and others tomorrow, as it was for them yesterday. These seven churches that Jesus addressed contain characteristics that can be found to some degree in most churches in our generation. While maintaining my course in dealing with Divine Mandates, it clearly behooves us to identify the enemies of such heavenly sent commandments. I shall not go into great detail concerning the warning that Jesus gave those in Asia Minor. It will suffice me to state that if you have purposed to answer the call of the Divine Mandate upon your life, you must prepare to deal with the characteristics of those who will oppose it. Do not waste your time in attempting to understand it, explain it or ignore it. We wrestle not against flesh and blood but against the devil and his demons. We have been called to liberty and this liberty has been purchased by the blood of Jesus Christ Who is the Chief Cornerstone by Whom all things hold together.

I know in my spirit that the Holy Ghost of God is grieved at the many mandates that He has inspired within thousands of young men which have gone undone because of democracy. The vastness of God's kingdom has been defined and controlled by a few. Well argued doctrine has infiltrated the spirits of God's servants and paralyzed them from following the leading of God's Spirit. Many of us have become armor bearers for the wrong leader and are fighting the wrong battle. This is why our weapons are not working and our joy not real. We are polished and groomed and articulate and can present the word, yet we are not picking a fight with the devil! We are not snatching souls from the pit of hell nor casting demons out of the oppressed and stirring up conviction amongst the spiritual lethargic and lukewarm saint. We're bored stiff! We are faking it and getting fat because fasting and prayer is not necessary for those who abide upon the shores of ease while they do what they please. REPENT!

Where are the audacious prophets today? We need "permission" to say what GOD said say. We are all guilty. I'm am as guilty as anyone because no one can do what God called me to do. We discern the heartbeat of God and ask God to make it clear because we are afraid to be alone. Afraid that we will have no friends. Afraid that they will talk about us. Especially afraid that they will misunderstand our hearts. "Please God, I can't say that, I won't have a place to preach! Is there any other way I can say it?" We escape to Tarshish and cast off to hide. We present an option to God doubting that God can do what He pleases. God can knock a man down with a look and replace him with a blink! Our fear reveals that we yet need to press closer and realize just Who we are serving. It reveals that we have not sanctified the Lord as our fear and dread (Isa. 8:13). It is the acid test of those called of men and those who are called of God. Our fear reveals that we savourest that which is of man and not that which is of God. In essence, it reveals that we are not committed to a Divine Mandate from heaven.

Divine Mandate. An order. A directive. A commandment. A charge. God has spoken for His bidding to be done and He expects His behest to be fulfilled with a zeal. A Divine Mandate must be responded to with a fervent mind and a excellent execution coupled with a godly fear that refuses to rest or draw back until that vessel can declare, "It is finished!".

The origin of a Divine Mandate is God. The mediator is Jesus. There is no other man necessary for a Divine Mandate to be given. There is no other permission necessary for a Divine Mandate to be carried out. God only uses men to confirm by the Holy Ghost what He wants done and through whom it shall be done. Whether or not man consents does not void what God has spoken!

> ***Let no man despise thy youth; but be thou an example of the believers, in word, in conversation, in charity, in spirit, in faith, in purity. Till I come, give attendance to reading, to exhortation, to doctrine. Neglect not the gift that is in thee, which was given thee by prophecy, with the laying on of the hands of the presbytery.*** ***1Ti 4:12-14***

Timothy had not been fulfilling all the responsibilities of verse 13. This gift was given to him by prophecy; that is, through utterance of some a prophet(s), the church was informed of the divine enablement granted him. It was the laying on of the hands of the church elders in recognizing the fact that God had called Timothy to the ministry and had gifted him for it (notes from The King James Study Bible on 1 Tim. 4:14).

> ***As they ministered to the Lord, and fasted, the Holy Ghost said, Separate me Barnabas and Saul for the work whereunto I have called them.*** ***Ac 13:2***

Again it was the HOLY GHOST who said, "separate". It wasn't the deacon board, the bishop, missionary JoJo, or prophet Smitty. It was the HOLY GHOST!

Let it be established by three scriptures lest some Pharisee call me a liar.

> ***And no man taketh this honour unto himself, but he that is called of God, as [was] Aaron. So also Christ glorified not himself to be made an high priest; but he that said unto him, Thou art my Son, to day have I begotten thee.*** ***Heb 5:4-5***

The scriptures are clear as to Who decrees who. Christ Himself received the greatest of all Divine Mandates and even He did not take such an honor unto Himself. But He too was called of God. Christ did not glorify Himself to be made our High Priest, but His Father before ordained that He should be so and decreed that "...The zeal of the Lord of hosts will perform this" (Ps 2:7; Isa 9:6-7).

Threaded throughout the Word of God we behold the movements of God within and upon man and even those true women who were divinely appointed by heaven. We also see the contention against such from those who had received a Divine Mandate and refused it or those who never had been called by God to begin with. In any event, the call of Divine Mandates are relevant for our generation and we shall behold a going forth of such that will cover the earth with a demonstration that God has the plan.

Characteristics of a Divine Mandate

If God has called a person, that call is a Divine Mandate. He has no other kind of calls. He is Divine, therefore, everything He does is Divine. We are partakers of the Divine nature according to the working of His Divine power that we should neither be barren nor unfruitful with the knowledge He has given us (2 Pet 1:3-4, 8). God never calls a person to a fulfill a Divine Mandate with their undivine self. When He calls us, we are unqualified and He begins the process of qualifying us through character. development

It must be clear that a true Divine Mandate does not rest upon the one who has been called to fulfill it. The evidence of God's divine workings manifesting upon that vessel testifies of the authenticity of a Divine Mandate. Though a person might be truly called to fulfill a mandate given by God, the manifestation of it must yet come to pass within and without that person. This reveals the problems we have in leadership today. Though they have been called, they have not been made in likeness of that call. Though the voice of God has been heard, the character of God has not been developed. To move on the voice of God and not the character of God is zeal without knowledge.

> ***Lay hands suddenly on no man, neither be partaker of other men's sins: keep thyself pure.*** ***1Ti 5:22***

When Paul addressed Timothy regarding the ordination of elders by the laying on of hands, he cautions him against hastily doing so. Otherwise, he would be a partaker of this unqualified elder's sin if he acts irresponsibly in office. Timothy's safeguard to keeping himself pure is by refusing to place such men into office prematurely. This should speak volumes to leadership at the sort of preachers we have ordained in our generation. Paul goes on to declare how Timothy can know the difference.

> ***Some men's sins are open beforehand, going before to judgment; and some [men] they follow after. Likewise also the good works [of some] are manifest beforehand; and they that are otherwise cannot be hid.*** ***1Ti 5:24-25***

There is an obvious manifestation of sin declaring in advance (beforehand) the judicial decision to be passed upon them by God in judgment. Even so, there are the sins of others that are not so obvious, but will catch up (they follow after) with them in judgment. Similarly, the good works of some are easily seen (manifest), while those of others are not; nevertheless, even these good works will be eventually be made known in judgment. The point is that when complete examination is made in exposing all deeds; good and bad, known and unknown, such shall bear witness to Divine Mandates.

This profound application allows for a righteous judgment to be rendered regarding the appointment of vessels of God. By careful examination of vessels who have declared that a Divine Mandate has been issued them, their true character and fitness for that office will validate that mandate from heaven. There is no need for human agents to approve one or disapprove another based on their wisdom which is foolishness to God. God forbid that one should take upon themselves the approval of mere clay to engage is spiritual warfare. Defeat awaits those who go in the name of any other except the name of the Lord!

> ***Not that we are sufficient of ourselves to think any thing as of ourselves; but our sufficiency [is] of God;*** **2 Co 3:5**

> ***For we dare not make ourselves of the number, or compare ourselves with some that commend themselves: but they measuring themselves by themselves, and comparing themselves among themselves, are not wise.*** **2 Co 10:12**

Therefore, as mature saints of God, we come to understand that the character, testing, temperance and other perfecting characteristics that should be in you and abounding are the evidence of not only a Divine Mandate but the approval to carry it out (2 Peter 1:5-10)! All other reasons are presumptuous and such efforts will not withstand the attacks of the enemy, of men and of ones own conscience.

Conscience and Mandate

"*Another thing one must guard against is the blocking of his conscience. It often loses its normal operation through a kind of blockage. When we are surrounded by those whose conscience is deadly numb, ours may be numbed also through their argument, conversation, teaching, persuasion, or example. Beware of teachers with hardened consciences: beware of man-made consciences: reject all attempts of man to mold yours. Our consciences must be responsible directly to God in all regards. We ourselves must know His will and be responsible for executing it. We will fail if we neglect our conscience to follow that of another*" (The Spiritual Man, Watchman Nee pp. 126-127).

How clearly and powerfully written by Watchman Nee the standard by which God leads His people. The conscience is God's property. It does not listen to your arguments of persuasion, your excuses in justifying or the many Phosophies that are presented to quiet its power when it accuses us righteously for not obeying the voice of God. Whether it's eating a certain food, taking a certain job, or trusting in someone or something other than the Lord, your conscience will be the witness for or against you regarding the will and pleasure of God.

God directs His people through their conscience. Our conscience is made up of the knowledge we have and even the knowledge that we don't have. God judges us by what we know, not by what we are ignorant of. Should we remain ignorant intentionally, He will judge us for willful ignorance.

When dealing with Divine Mandates, you must deal with the power and the privacy of conscience. No one knows what God has told you to do like your conscience does. You can justify it with the best of arguments. You can find others who will tell you that you are right. You can avoid the hand of God by throwing yourself into forms of indulgence; religion, knowledge or sin. Your conscience will yet declare the same thing: God's mandate. When a person no longer has a conscience, they are in trouble. It is evident that God is finished dealing with them. He has given such a person over to their lust and they are ignorant of it.

> ***And even as they did not like to retain God in [their] knowledge, God gave them over to a reprobate mind, to do those things which are not convenient;*** **Ro 1:28**

> ***Speaking lies in hypocrisy; having their conscience seared with a hot iron;*** ***1Ti 4:2***

> ***They profess that they know God; but in works they deny [him], being abominable, and disobedient, and unto every good work reprobate.*** ***Tit 1:16***

Many who have been given a Divine Mandate are currently dealing with their conscience like never before. God is tugging and speaking so heavily sometimes they can barely handle it. They need to get away from their environment until it gets clear. Take a leave of absence from your job, from your church and from your food and let the Holy Ghost recapture your conscience! Retreat to a mountain where it's quiet and simply rest and be still. No television, phone or music; simply God, Jesus, the Holy Ghost and YOU!

Others are surrounded by people who keep you captive with arguments. They realize God's call upon your life because you are always talking about it hoping they understand and embrace you. They just look at you and nod their heads. They then come forth with vain Phosophies and deceit to put that blazing mandate and unfeigned faith out. They need you for *their* program. You are the reason they can afford the life-style they have. You feed their pride, stroke their ego and are the topic of their light headed conversation amongst their fellow serpents.

> ***Beware lest any man spoil you through Phosophy and vain deceit, after the tradition of men, after the rudiments of the world, and not after Christ.*** **Col 2:8**

> ***As many as desire to make a fair shew in the flesh, they constrain you to be circumcised; only lest they should suffer persecution for the cross of Christ. For neither they themselves who are circumcised keep the law; but desire to have you circumcised, that they may glory in your flesh.*** **Ga 6:12-13**

> ***But of these who seemed to be somewhat, (whatsoever they were, it maketh no matter to me: God accepteth no man's person:) for they who seemed [to be somewhat] in conference added nothing to me:*** **Ga 2:6**

The most dangerous position a servant of the Lord can take against the devil and man is to follow his conscience to the degree of complete obedience. Organized religion has masterfully hindered man's conscience that it would appear it has not. Satan has legally arrested the conscience of millions of warriors who are fulfilling careers upon the earth rather than Divine Mandates from heaven. The devil has ever so subtly deceived even those with knowledge from obeying their conscience by sound and theological rhetoric. Knowledge puffs up but love obeys! If satan can't keep you down, he'll just wait until you get up and knock you off! Our enemy is a smart one and no human can win playing with him with their own wit and strength. Only Jesus has single handedly brought lucifer down and only through Jesus can we.

A strong conscience, coupled with strong character and mature fruit, equips one to possess the evidence of a Divine Mandate that is calling for fulfillment. It is certain that the human agent of man plays a vital role. Consent to what God has decreed. The Body of Christ must repent in crossing over into the directives of God for another person. Leadership has twisted certain truths to fit their own fears and therefore, has placed weights on those whom God has called. I say to those who are weighed under such oppression that you are FREE! There is no need to explain anything to anybody. Let your character and your conscience bear witness in the Holy Ghost that you are moving after the leading of God!

***I say the truth in Christ, I lie not, my conscience also bearing me witness in the Holy Ghost,* Ro 9:1**

Be not angry against any person. Forgive and forget and get busy fulfilling the Divine Mandate upon your life!

Mandate and the Next Millennium

As we have witnessed the knowledge of God poured upon the earth for the greatest move of His Spirit that mankind has ever witnessed, we shall also see a company of warriors marching to battle with Divine Mandates given directly from the throne. They will be men and women who know their place and shall not thrust one another. They will keep their ranks and do exploits for the Lord!

Like the noise of chariots on the tops of mountains shall they leap, like the noise of a flame of fire that devoureth the stubble, as a strong people set in battle array. Before their face the people shall be much pained: all faces shall gather blackness. They shall run like mighty men; they shall climb the wall like men of war; and they shall march every one on his ways, and they shall not break their ranks:

Neither shall one thrust another; they shall walk every one in his path: and [when] they fall upon the sword, they shall not be wounded. They shall run to and fro in the city; they shall run upon the wall, they shall climb up upon the houses; they shall enter in at the windows like a thief. The earth shall quake before them; the heavens shall tremble: the sun and the moon shall be dark, and the stars shall withdraw their shining:

And the LORD shall utter his voice before his army: for his camp [is] very great: for [he is] strong that executeth his word: for the day of the LORD [is] great and very terrible; and who can abide it? ***Joel 2:5-11***

The next Millennium will not allow dictatorship. We will witness those ministries that became who they are through dictatorship fall. They will be stories of the past. When the Body of Christ beholds the glorious movement of freedom amongst those who are arrayed in battle armorment and their cry is one of battle, they will never again settle for the religion of men. God's people are going to run from camps which have refused to allow them to express His full purpose for their lives. They will be liberated from leadership based on fear of them failing to leadership full of faith for them succeeding!

This next move of God is going to be beyond concept for those who do not transform their minds toward heaven and warfare for God's kingdom on the earth. Even as computer technology has increased in capacity so shall the Church. What took ten computers to perform five years ago, one can perform today. Even so, there will be Divine Mandates that will be led of God to go forth and conquer with two today what took the Church 2000 yesterday. God will lead this army. The word "committee" will never be heard again. There are only three votes that count in this hour; The Father, The Son and The Holy Ghost!

Through supernatural evidence, God will silence the mouths of those who bring accusation against this fearless army. They will be too busy to answer their critics. If they do address it, it will be by the unction of the Holy Ghost and then God's power will fall to bear witness of Himself.

The Church had better prepare for a division. There will be a fight within the house of God in these last days and only the truly committed will be found standing. There are imposters who have no plans in letting God's people go forth to worship Him. They are Pharaohs disguised as apostles and pastors. They have gotten fat off of God's people and God is about to pull the plug! There is coming a foe from the North that will be used to humble this high and haughty spirit that would have accused God of being out of order! The Church has behaved itself like a silly dove and God is going to wake it up with a slap upon the cheek. When it's over, that which is silly shall be drunk on its own folly. However, that which is truly an eagle shall become sober through repentance and soar, oh, so high. They shall run and not get weary, they shall walk and not faint (Isa. 40:31).

Divine Mandates shall have Divine resources. The current method of financial dependency has been allowed by God but will have to change overnight. When God sends this wake up call, the Church will then search out those who know how to move with God. Though they have been fought against in the past, they will become valuable in the future. They will respond with love toward every sincere desire to move with God. Even those who have misjudged them and spoke evil of them will be forgotten and forgiven.

Those leaders who were in error and chose not to repent will yet have opportunities all along to get their systems in order. Prepare your men by setting them free to follow the voice of God. Hold no man back. Make sure they are with you because God told them to be. This will only ensure a strong house when the storms of the next millennium begin to rage. The angel of the Lord is being sent out in war regalia and those who are found drinking water like dogs, eating like hogs and sleeping like bears are going to suffer loss. Prior to experiencing the times of warfare, there will be a short season for saints to prepare and out of love, God is going to expose many of His servants. It will be the best thing for them. Through this exposure, correction will come. Though they suffer loss, they will yet be able to capture the original purpose that God had in His mind for their life.

As I close this chapter, I do so realizing the last few pages have been prophecy. My heart is totally free in knowing that I have written what the Spirit of the Lord has instructed. Many of the words I have written in this chapter is going to truly cut many of God's people. It will not feel good, but they know that it is the truth. There will be many attempts to explain this word away but to no avail for God's word is like a hammer that will dash the rocks (hardened hearts) to pieces. His word is like a fire that will purge away the dross.

[Is] not my word like as a fire? saith the LORD; and like a hammer [that] breaketh the rock in pieces? Jer 23:29

Divine Mandates must be fulfilled and God will use any means necessary to awake the giant that sleepeth the giant whose name is the Body of Christ.

Chapter Nine

Results and Rewards of Divine Protocol

When The Results are In
The Rewards will Reveal Them

he areas of Divine Protocol extend far and beyond ones ability to grasp. The reasons for this are as endless as the realm of the Divine itself. The essence of the moment is not to explore every facet of life to define Divine Protocol to the core, but through prayer, we internalize its principles and that by a sincere and unfeigned desire to simply walk with God as a friend.

We all are certain that one will reap whatever one sows, whether good or bad. It is equally important to comprehend that when sowing righteous seeds, there is a correct and incorrect way to do so. May we not deceive ourselves with illusive contentment through rationalizing with our fleshly minds which determines to find comfort in our own methods that we call order. We are quick to declare "I don't sow wickedness and at least have a few good efforts toward the kingdom of God". Church attendance three days out of the week, coupled with a "spirit filled" workshop seminar thrice yearly is not God's expected reasonable service from us. We are hungry for strong meat in our walk with God, without realizing that it is the very meat discovered in doing the greatest work in life; believing on Him Whom He has sent.

The Bible speaks clearly of the results and rewards to be expected of those who have fulfilled Divine Protocol in the kingdom of God, as well as those who opted for the pursuit of the temporal life and its pleasures.

Every man's work shall be made manifest: for the day shall declare it, because it shall be revealed by fire; and the fire shall try every man's work of what sort it is. **1Cor. 3:13**

On the day of Judgment, there shall be a revelation of the results of our labors. We ourselves need not say a word, for the fruit of our labors will reflect the one or the other; the standard of Divine Protocol, or the protocol of man.

It is interesting to note that the Apostle Paul places this scripture in context of the Corinthian church being divided because of man. This very fact is the motive for him clarifying that there is only one foundation.

For other foundation can no man lay than that is laid, which is Jesus Christ. **1 Co. 3:11**

The scriptures attest to the fact that we can readily identify in this life what our results will be for the labors we put forth while in this body. God is not hiding from us what will be required to inherit all that He has reserved for those who loved not themselves even unto death. I believe that many Christians who barely make it into glory will slap their heads with amazement when they are enlightened to the fact that heaven was never designed for a moment of idle living while on earth. Every act that we carried out in the earth will have a consequential result in heaven. The rewards that we receive in heaven will be greatly determined by how we conducted ourselves in this life. God has given us the right of way.

The young man saith unto him, All these things have I kept from my youth up: what lack I yet? Jesus said unto him, If thou wilt be perfect, go [and] sell that thou hast, and give to the poor, and thou shalt have treasure in heaven: and come [and] follow me. But when the young man heard that saying, he went away sorrowful: for he had great possessions. **Mt 19:20-22**

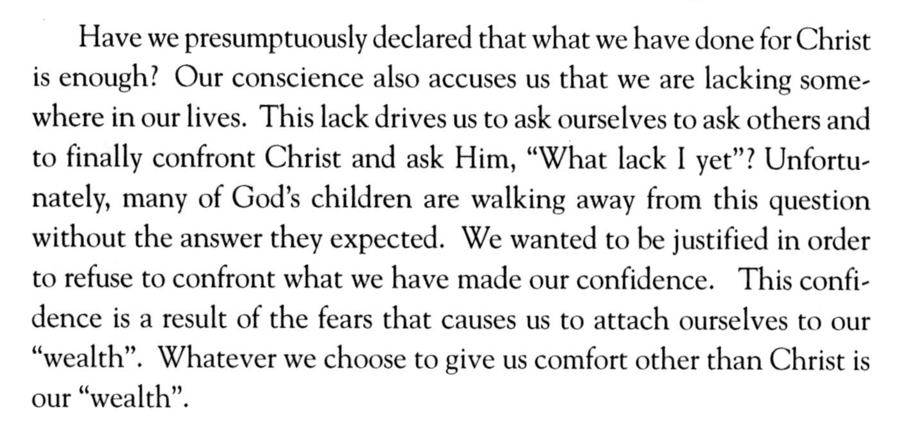

Have we presumptuously declared that what we have done for Christ is enough? Our conscience also accuses us that we are lacking somewhere in our lives. This lack drives us to ask ourselves to ask others and to finally confront Christ and ask Him, "What lack I yet"? Unfortunately, many of God's children are walking away from this question without the answer they expected. We wanted to be justified in order to refuse to confront what we have made our confidence. This confidence is a result of the fears that causes us to attach ourselves to our "wealth". Whatever we choose to give us comfort other than Christ is our "wealth".

Yet, Jesus begins to speak to us in clear, concise words. "If you will be perfect". Perfection comes by way of death. Death comes by way of the cross. The young ruler refused his cross. He went away broken hearted believing that it did not require the relinquishing of his father's wealth in order to be made perfect. It was not the money that Jesus was dealing with; it was the young man's security in money which hindered him from trusting totally in Christ. It is not necessarily the thing that God is dealing with. Rather, it is your heart that is controlled by the thing that God is dealing with. If you will be made perfect, you must confront what you have made your trust, your hope and your wealth and allow Christ to be your sole reward. You can confess your perfection until the return of Christ. Until you experience the pain of the cross and death is complete, you are refusing Christ the right to be Lord. There is no other way around the cross. Those who avoid the pain of the process through their humanistic argument will walk away from Christ or insist on following Him their way. I encourage you to allow the cross to prepare you for God's purpose. It has an end. Eventually, the pain passes and the perfection of Christ in you is the reward. Divine Protocol becomes a way of life and the understanding of His kingdom flows clearly within your spirit.

You want to know the bliss of entering into heaven with a perfect record. It will be an indescribable reality that will only be known by those who sold that one thing that would have hindered them. The treasures in heaven that Jesus has promised are real. We tend to be more concerned with the treasures of this earth than with those in the heavens which cannot be corrupted or stolen. Jesus knew that this rich young ruler could relate to treasure. The things that we refuse to relinquish are things that Jesus has correctly prepared for us as it pertains to the rewards of His Kingdom. If we concern ourselves with following Him, He will concern Himself with building our mansion in His Father's house. He will guarantee that the results are Divine. The question that we must face will be, "do we go away sorrowful because of the great possessions that we must surrender"? I sometimes wonder what happened to that rich young ruler. I can assure you that the joy that he had before he met Jesus was never found again. Why? Because he came in contact with Joy Himself and refused it. Do not entrust your results to yourself. Walk in the Divine Protocol of God's Kingdom and you will have great treasure in heaven that will be awaiting you for eternities to come.

Throughout the Word, we are admonished to "take heed". This implies that God will give unto you exactly what you have given unto Him. If we knew the possibilities of our place in the scope of God's eternal kingdom in a literal way, we would esteem our present country and its rewards as highly as we do. Prophetically enough, there are those who esteem their country highly who lightly esteem the kingdom of God!

> ***These all died in faith, not having received the promises, but having seen them afar off, and were persuaded of them, and embraced them, and confessed that they were strangers and pilgrims on the earth. For they that say such things declare plainly that they seek a country. And truly, if they had been mindful of that country from whence they came out, they might have had opportunity to have returned. But now they desire a better country, that is, an heavenly: wherefore God is not ashamed to be called their God: for he hath prepared for them a city.***
>
> ***Heb. 11:13-16***

The results of Divine Protocol will only be realized by those who start and continue in faithful service to God. To die in faith is a true commitment unto the Lord. To assume that we have died in faith is a foolish commitment to ourselves when we are void of the scars of the cross in our character.

Our rewards directly reflect our results. While by faith we believe that God is a rewarder of those who diligently seek Him through the simplicity of observing His Word in sincerity, we can yet know whether our results are those of gold and silver, or of wood or stubble. Faith is not blind concerning the spiritual realm. Faith is not ignorant. It is spiritually intelligent based upon eternal truths that have been deposited within your spirit by communion with Almighty God.

Why, through mental reasoning, should we settle for the crumbs of this life with persuasive excuses that are masterminded to avoid giving our best to the Lord with the utmost expression of passionate love and adoration? Is it not obvious that we are in the eleventh hour of time? It behooves us to realize that if our results for today prove that they will not endure the test of God's fire, then we must, with haste, redeem the time. By no means should we respond presumptuously, but rather efficiently and quickly in the quiet abode of our spirits in most earnest, repentive prayer.

When we have set ourselves to pursue Divine Protocol, we will be confident in knowing that whatever we have entrusted to Him shall be kept and revealed on that great and terrible day.

I challenge you, saint of God, to reflect on your labors! What do they reveal? Come on, face it. Eternity is too long to cut yourself short from receiving all that God has prepared for you. Some of those tears that will be shed in heaven will be shed from those who realized what they missed for gaining a few extras on earth that are now forever gone. The parables of Jesus extensively revealed the consequences for ignoring the results of Divine Protocol. Such ignorance is a choice that we make, not a direction that God has purposed.

> ***By faith Moses, when he was come to years, refused to be called the son of Pharaoh's daughter; Choosing rather to suffer affliction with the people of God, than to enjoy the pleasures of sin for a season; Esteeming the reproach of Christ greater riches than the treasures in Egypt: for he had respect unto the recompence of the reward. By faith he forsook Egypt, not fearing the wrath of the king: for he endured, as seeing him who is invisible.***
>
> *Heb. 11:24-27*

The results of Moses' daily life revealed his reward. Likewise, so shall ours. Moses simply chose! Again, he chose to follow Divine Protocol - God's way. Let it be clarified that those who continue to seek shortcuts and ways that are void of bearing a cross will suffer loss (1 Cor. 3:15), if not be altogether as a dog returning to its vomit (1 Pet. 2:21,22).

Christianity demands results. God clearly states that those who yet refuse to bear fruit will be cut off from Him (Jo 15:2, Rom. 11:22). To adopt the view that one cannot lose their salvation based on grace and God's unchanging love is to render God completely void of character and integrity and to subject himself to the willful lusts of man. I believe that this doctrine, supposedly based on "God's love", has undermined Christians far and wide. If this doctrine was sound, then based upon God's holy writ, He is found to be a liar! Without veering from the subject at hand, I must address this doctrine, for it is contrary to Divine Protocol and directly opposed to obedience and responsibility. The servant who chose not to bring forth results was called wicked and cast into the fire (Mt 25:24-26).

He that despised Moses' law died without mercy under two or three witnesses: Of how much sorer punishment, suppose ye, shall he be thought worthy, who hath trodden under foot the Son of God, and hath counted the blood of the covenant, wherewith he was sanctified, an unholy thing, and hath done despite unto the Spirit of grace? **Heb. 10: 28-29**

For it is impossible for those who were once enlightened, and hath tasted of the heavenly gift, and were made partakers of the Holy Ghost, And have tasted the good word of God, and the powers of the world to come, If they shall fall away, to renew them again unto repentance; seeing they crucify to themselves the Son of God afresh, and put Him to an open shame.
Heb.6:4-6

Sinners will be spewed out of the mouth of God, but rather, those who have some of God and some of the world. The scriptures, speaking of the church of Laodicea, are proof that they were nigh unto total rejection.

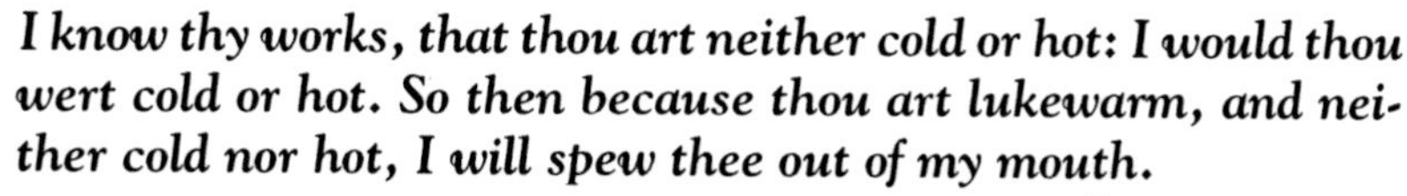

I know thy works, that thou art neither cold or hot: I would thou wert cold or hot. So then because thou art lukewarm, and neither cold nor hot, I will spew thee out of my mouth.
Rev. 3:15-16.

I will readily agree that no man can pluck anyone out of my Father's hand (Jo 10:29), however, be assured that He Himself can cast you from it!

Behold therefore the goodness and severity of God: on them which fell, severity; but toward thee, goodness, if thou continue in his goodness: otherwise thou also shalt be cut off. **Ro. 11:22**

When the scripture declared...

For it had been better for them not to have known the way of righteousness, than, after they have known it, to turn from the holy commandment delivered unto them. **2 Pet. 2:21**

...it clearly meant just that!

Our results will reflect just how we lived! To buy into the deceitful lie that you can sow evil in Jesus' name and reap heaven is to be deceived by a demonic spirit through possessing a motive that is carnal and contrary to godliness. A demon cannot deceive a person unless they want to be deceived by believing a lie.

Just one more note. "Once saved, always saved", has absolutely no room for faith, abstaining from sin, or direction toward obedience. There is no need to fear God, no space for conviction and thus, no way for God to even condemn sin and judge the world.

But if our unrighteousness commend the righteousness of God, what shall we say? Is God unrighteous who taketh vengeance? (I speak as a man) God forbid: for then how shall God judge the world? For if the truth of God hath more abounded through my lie unto His glory; why yet am I also judged as a sinner?
Ro. 3:5-7

If God has to ignore my willful iniquity at the expense of His blood, then why should He condemn the sinner if we are just alike? If my results are worse than a sinners results seeing that I know the truth, what need is there for God to even separate the goats from the sheep?

If I say I know Him but my results unveil darkness, I lie and the truth is not in me (1 Jo 1:6). Please spare me for the indignation is kindled against such unholy protocol! My beloved, God has purposed for our results to shine and light the world and not draw back unto perdition with carnal excuses (Heb.10:39).

Shall we not pursue Divine Protocol and flourish like a tree planted by the rivers of living waters and not as a pig which returns to the mire? Resist the devil's venomous doctrine and cleave to that which is holy and just. As a good soldier of Christ, prepare your heart and fulfil all of what God requires of you, for such results will bring forth a reward that eyes have not seen, nor ears heard!

REWARDS

Every organization known to man from Shanghai to Ohio is aware of the desire for rewards. Despite the economy of the most famished nation, the slightest relief offers a reward for patient endurance.

Americans are more acquainted with rewards than any other country in the world. From the hospital through school, on to college, then our careers, we all experience an array of certificates, trophies, plaques, money and the praise of men. This country is so engulfed with this form of commendation that it has become an idol; a form of pagan worship whose orchestrator is satan. From box office stars to basketball gods, soap opera queens to sitcom kings, this country has found someone to reward.

Though most Christians are not dependent upon the systems of the world to reward them for service toward God, we yet are seeking for a natural alternative to rewards. Our natural man is constantly suggesting ideas and methods that will produce a reward for self regardless of the cost we must pay. We even look to others to provide some form of reward when we labor with them and for them. We thrive on the thrill gained when rewards are in our view. The natural man is hesitant to be involved in any pursuit unless one question has been carefully answered, "What's in it for me?" At times, it literally takes an act of God for the human mind to surrender its rights and efforts in pursuing the carnal road to rewards.

Those who have been called into the citizenship of the kingdom of God must renew their mind toward understanding Divine Protocol pertaining to that of rewards. We must, through heartfelt prayer, refuse the ideologies which present temporal forms of rewards which distract our view from heavenly ones.

Through lack of rhema understanding of God's rewards, many of us yield to fear of the future. Many Christians have pierced themselves through with pursuits that have no value toward spiritual growth or even a place in God's will for their lives. One of my biggest mistakes was taking my entrepreneurial abilities and assuming I was to be a business man in the arena of my choosing. I recognize the gift and truly had the desire to use it for God's glory, but the direction in which I was using it absolutely had nothing to do with God's will and it led me away from the divine flow that God's will brings. It was not easy in breaking away from this 'good' idea in my mind. This mindset was a result of not trusting God's plan for me in business. I justified myself and tried to do in the natural what God could had purposed by His Spirit. I stood in unbelief that God would reward my efforts in using this enabling for His will of which would provide those things that I needed and were desired for my family. Evenso, God has used these experiences to teach me and to bring me to an understanding that our gifts must operate in a divine order that they may bring divine results not only in the arena of finances, but doing so without adding sorrow to our lives. With this understanding, I now operate in the business arena according to His very detail plans which where far greater than mine. We can never out do the purposes that God has established for us.

This is not to say that if you are called to preach you should not have anything to do with the business world. God has many men and women who have been called to the business world for His glory. Each person's conscience that should determine their involvement in issues outside their specific purpose of preaching and teaching the gospel not matter how financial beneficial they may be.

God's very nature is to reward those who are obedient to Him. It is so much a part of Him that He even extends it to the unthankful and evil.

...for he is kind unto the unthankful and to the evil.
Luke 6:35b

After the disciples heard Jesus declare that it is easier for a camel to go through the eye of a needle than for a rich man to enter into the kingdom of heaven, they quickly responded with, "Who then can be saved?" Peter went directly to the point when he stated that they had left all - families, houses, jobs and friends and had become the target of many attacks as a result of following Him (Christ). In essence, he said, "We are being talked about, and never know when or what we are going to eat, where we are going to sleep, nor the security of our future, and you are telling me that I have no possibility of experiencing wealth in my life (Mt 19:23-27)! Peter failed to understand that the system of God's kingdom operates totally by faith and the rewards follow after one has submitted all to the Lord. Jesus plainly declared that except a corn of wheat fall to the ground and die, it abideth alone, but if does die, it will bring forth much fruit. Peter was very much alive and he did not want to die unless he had enough evidence in the natural that his reward was certain.

At one time or another, we all have experienced this attitude toward God. Perhaps many of you still do. Let us be assured that with ourselves, all things are impossible, but with Him, all things are possible. Jesus was declaring the truth regarding rewards gained outside of the scope of Divine Protocol for your life when He said that one cannot serve both God and mammon. You will serve one or the other. We cannot entrust God with spiritual things while we are insuring the carnal things. He will either be Lord of all or not Lord at all!

Shall we clear away the cobwebs of confusion and doubt regarding His faithfulness to reward us in this life and the life to come? We should certainly kill the spider, for such webs shall surely return if we take a temporal approach toward the eternal systems of God's dividends and how they are paid.

We should not question God's rewards, but rather our willingness to strive for them. The rewards of Divine Protocol are real. They extend much further than the scope of ones natural ability to compute a return. Contending for this faith is truly a warfare greater than anyone has ever fought on a natural level. It is the only one of its kind. If satan cannot keep you from heaven, he will do his best to see to it you get there by fire, void of eternal dividends.

Those who succumb to struggling for earthly gain outside the scope of Divine Protocol, have, in essence, cast away their confidence in God. They are also ashamed or wary of those who are pursuing God's rewards through faith. This they demonstrate by their lack of compassion of understanding how God has dealt with faith filled saints, or in how they distance themselves from genuine fellowship. Frequently, they refer to such warriors as "too deep". It is not that they are "too deep". Instead, it is because immature Christians are so fearful of the water that they are dressed to swim, but are on the shores of complacency making castles. They are trying to avoid their crossing of the Jordan.

> ***For ye had compassion of me in my bonds, and took joyfully the spoiling of your goods, knowing in yourselves that ye have in heaven a better an enduring substance. Cast not away therefore your confidence, which hath great recompence of reward. For ye have need of patience, that, after ye have done the will of God, ye might receive the promise. Heb. 10:34-36***

The recompense of reward or the requital of ones labors pursues you when your single focus is doing His will. Anytime we pursue it, we are not minding the will of the Lord. God's official order pertaining to rewards is to simply patiently seek first His kingdom and everything would automatically be added. We are told that if we observe to do all that is written therein and not veer to the right or to the left, success is inevitable.

> ***Only be thou strong and very courageous, that thou mayest observe to do according to all the law, which Moses my servant commanded thee: turn not from it to the right hand or to the left, that thou mayest prosper whithersoever thou goest. Josh. 1:7***

To be strong and very courageous pertaining to His revealed will for our lives should be our focus and meditation. When we attempt to pierce into the established order of His rewards, we have done so in unbelief.

How many people have refused to follow Jesus as the rich young ruler did? How many Christians are yet not pursuing the excellence of serving God due to the doubt of no reward or the misconception of it? Why have we allowed America, a country that is steeped in moral decay and abandonment of God in Whom it says it trusts, to be our standard of successful Christian living? This country is a ticking time bomb waiting to explode on a number of issues, ranging from racial tensions to international war. A country with laws to protect the eagle so they can procreate is the same country passes laws designed to kill its human babies that its citizens procreate. America exists solely for God's purpose and in time, shall receive God's judgment. Why do we pattern ourselves after any country other than the one Whose Builder and Maker is God? Such a view only reveals spiritual immaturity and shallowness to equate God's present and eternal rewards with earthly merchandise, financial advantage and heathenistic systems. Carnally minded Christians desire gain for vain reasons, are deceived by the cunning craftiness of men who have no heavenly vision or desire.

> ***Beware lest any man spoil you through Phosophy and vain deceit, after the tradition of men, after the rudiments of the world, and not after Christ. Let no man beguile you of your reward in a voluntary humility and worshipping of angels, intruding into those things which he hath not seen, vainly puffed up by his fleshly mind.*** ***Col. 2:8, 18***

> ***Perverse disputings of men of corrupt minds, and destitute of the truth, supposing that gain is godliness: from such withdraw thyself. But they that will be rich fall into temptation and a snare, and into may foolish and hurtful lusts, which drown men in destruction and perdition. For the love of money is the root of all evil: which while some coveted after, they have erred from the faith, and pierced themselves through with many sorrows.***
> ***1 Ti. 6:5,9-10***

If the saints of God would but seek first the kingdom of God and His righteousness and seek it second, third, fourth and fifth, the wiles of the enemy would be quenched by our shield of faith and the sword of the Spirit. Believers who possess an aggressive violence in their relationship with God will enter into the reward system of God's kingdom.

God alone can enlighten you to this profound truth. One can sow, the other water, but it will yet remain a mystery to all who have not sought the very person of Jesus Christ and the express will of His Father at any and all expenses.

There are extremists on each side; Christians who pursue money outside of God's direction, and Christians who believe that if you stay poor, you will remain humble. The balance is found in those who have a personal rhema of rewards while striving toward complete obedience in this life and a hope of rewards to be realized in the life to come. They neither pursue money nor deny its place. They pursue the will of God, accepting the protocol of God's provisionary ways in bringing finances and rewards to pass in their lives. They truly have no needs because Christ is their full reward. Whatever state they are in, they have learned the secret and power of being content (Ph 4:11).

I am a firm believer in financial wealth. God is going to bless many of His people with it in tremendous ways simply because it is His will. Others will not even think along the lines of financial issues simply because it is not in the will of God for their life. The vision that God has given some of His people will require money to become a reality. God created currency for the purpose of His kingdom, not for our own self centered desires. Money is for the furthering of His will in the earth. While He blesses us to partake in rewards, we are warned not to be snared by them nor to love them, but to love Him, for such is the secret of contentment (1Tim. 6:6).

The ultimate objective of Divine Protocol is receiving the eternal rewards of all your labors while you were upon this earth as a child of God, as well as those that will be given in eternal life. The knowledge given, joy and peace in the Holy Ghost, the fellowship with the saints, the power of God over the devil and the keys to the kingdom, are all "right now" rewards that are commonly overlooked, taken for granted, and misplaced in our value system.

In the days in which we live, perilous times will increase and opportunities for the rewards of men will arise only to distract God's people from the eternal dividends that He shall provide to His saints. Unless

Christians purpose in their hearts to submit under the hand of the Lord, rejection of Divine Protocol of rewards of God's kingdom will result.

Throughout this writing of Divine Protocol, I have been rewarded beyond expectation and I know many others have been as well, for it is the Lord's doing and not mine own. My only prayer is for you to be changed in the inner man; for you to seek the Lord for the reality of His order to be manifested in your life.

Imagine heaven! Imagine the saints at your mansion. See Jesus walking in to tell everyone about your life on earth, about your faithfulness, about your labors of love and trials of suffering that you endured for His will. He will testify of how you handled His wealth that He entrusted to you whether financial or spiritual. How detailed would He be in describing your obedience toward Divine Protocol? What testimonies would reveal your supreme commitment to the kingdom of God or your lack of it? The knowledge of God will always be pursued, even in heaven. Will you be a teacher or pupil? There is no time like the present to tenaciously seek God. Divine protocol will then be rhema knowledge that continually unfolds.

Our time upon this grain of sand called earth is a vapor. Do you realize how quickly your life is when viewed against the backdrop of eternity? Our opportunity in this life will never be seen in the life to come. Divine Protocol then will be different for faith will be done away with. To obtain the full measure of Divine Protocol in the life and world to come, Christians must fulfil Divine Protocol in the life that we presently live in.

Do not put this book down and allow yourself to be the same. Don't allow the excuses of any kind - job, wife, pastor, deacon, denomination, illness and the many other excuses - rob you from perceiving and walking in Divine Protocol. It is for such divine ordering that God made you. You are made out of God's image and when He put His Spirit in you, He enabled you to know Him and the ways in which He governs His kingdom and His people.

I command you in the name of Jesus to reach for God through His Son, Jesus Christ. Do not be content with your last success. Ask God for more of His ways to be revealed to you. Pay the price of walking with God. You will clearly see His ways and hear His voice. Avoid idle religion and vain persons. Submit yourself under the leadership of true men of God that have proven to be examples in word and in deed and will be encouragers of your faith and not controllers of it.

Divine Protocol is demanded of me, of you and of all who are called in this chosen generation.

> ***But ye are a chosen generation, a royal priesthood, a holy nation, a peculiar people; that ye should show forth the praises of him who hath called you out of darkness into his marvelous light.***
> ***1 Pet. 2:9***

Let us not turn back our affections to what God has brought us out of. If we do, we will fall away from the faith and be found without God in the end.

I believe in you! I know God has a purpose for your life. Do not listen to the opinions of the devil through the mouths of unbelieving people. Whatever vision God has anointed you to fulfil can come alive through adhering to the principles of Divine Protocol. Do not allow a day to go by without applying yourself to His will. If all you can do is pray, then pray. Listen and appropriate. From His throne, God will impart in you His desire for your life. Begin to study those desires in God's Word and the growth of the vision will become tangible, impacted with a confidence in your spirit that will be imparted directly by God.

Alas, to follow Jesus within the guidelines of Divine Protocol - the Order of God's Kingdom, is a joy unrealized by many. Yet, I am confident that as one of the few who know it, you will be among that number!

> ***And behold, I come quickly; and my reward is with me, to give every man according as his work shall be.*** ***Rev. 22:12***

Please review books on the following pages published by Higher Standard Publishers. You may also learn how you can distribute these fine books in your community and earn up to 50%. You may order and inquire on-line at www.higherstandardpublishers.com

"The Authority on Ethnic Christian Book Publishing"

HIGHER STANDARD PUBLISHERS, LLC
P.O. Box 440131
Kennesaw, GA 301160

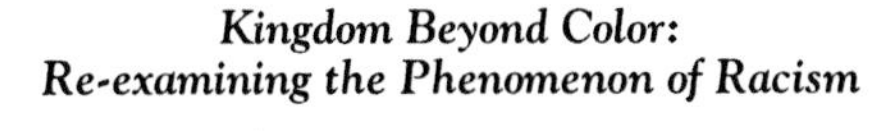

Kingdom Beyond Color:
Re-examining the Phenomenon of Racism

By Dr. Leonard Lovett

Dr. Leonard Lovett places the onus of responsibility for social change on every member of the Faith Community, to lead the way in the social redemption of North America, from the ravages of the demons of racism who now have a new address and zip code. Lovett views North America as lion country where only those who are intentional will survive racism. The truth provokes, yet enlightens. You may be offended should you take this work seriously, but you will also be liberated. *Topics Include: The Perennial Problem of the Color Line, Racism: Demons With a New Address and Zip Code, Can We All Get Along? White Denial and Black Rage, and much more.* ***200 pages $21.95***

Bastards In The Pulpit! - Part 1
By William Owens

What happens when Church leadership rejects the fatherhood of God. How it happens, how to deal with it and how it affects our families *Foreword by Dr. Leonord Lovett, Ph.D*
140 pages $14.99 **ISBN: 0-9658629-0-9**

Wisdom: The Principle Thing: *Get It!*
by William Owens

The generation of our young people need wisdom. Without wisdom, the decisions necessary to secure a powerful life as an young adult will be impossible. A verse by verse commentary on Proverbs 8. It will both bless and challenge the young adult.
72 pages $5.95 **ISBN 0-9658629-8-4**

Helpmeet: *The Power of A Wife to Give Her Husband Help By Selena Owens*

Learn the wisdom of how a wife helps her husband the way God has ordained and decreed.
140 pages $9.95 **ISBN 0-9658629-1-7**

Keep The Vision Alive: Make, Don't Break, The Man of Vision

When God has placed a visionary in your life, there are experiences that will make you or break you. Mrs. Owens is very familiar with working with a visionary and in this book, she brings to the forefront the call of wives to empower their husbands in fulfilling the vision. *Topics include: Characteristics of a Man of Vision, Understanding the Vision, Selfishness, Pride, Prayer, Support, A Time to Sow. Workbook included inside of book.*
108 pages $10.95 **ISBN: 0-9-658629-3-3**

Basusu
By Dr. Peart

The power of Africa is revealed in the resolve of a young named Basusu. After being captured by slave traders he eventually comes to realize his choice to triumph in the face of separation from his country, his family and his culture will completely be determined by his response to the God who made Africa. You will be raptured into Part 1 of this all inspiring Trilogy written by Dr. George Peart. Basusu is determined to have the family and the future that every man is entitled to. Discover how his dream becomes a reality in this breathtaking novel.

Coming Spring 2004

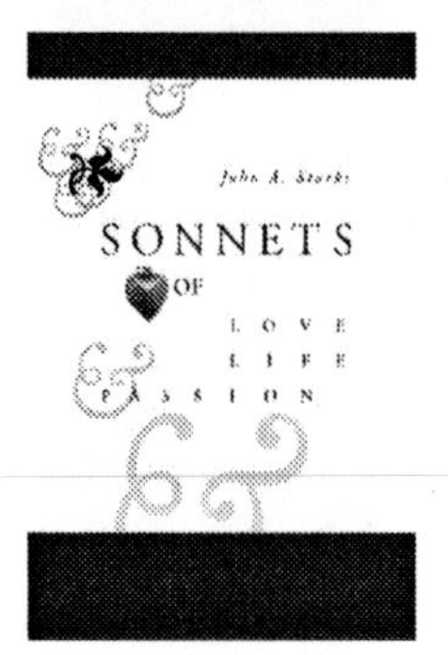

Sonnets of Love, Life and Passion
By John Starks

The ability to express ones heart, mind and soul through the art of sonnets is a rarity. We introduce to you the first ever published works of John Starks. Prepare to be enraptured with words and expressions that will compel your soul to give deep thought. Sonnets of Love, Life and Passion. This work will be cherished and shared by all.

Coming Fall 2003

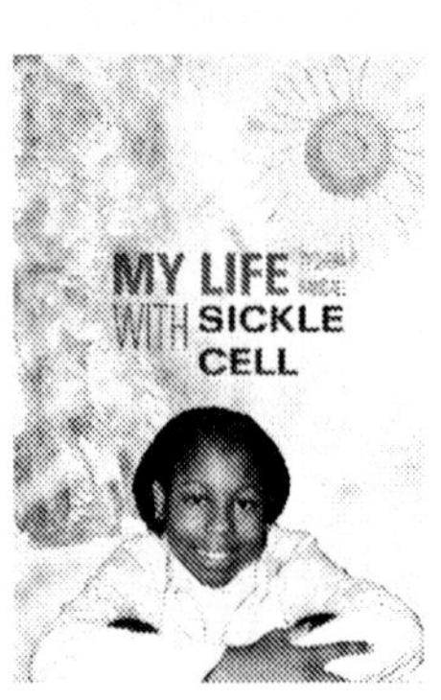

My Life With Sickle Cell
By Tasheba Randall

One of the most misunderstood conditions among black Americans is Sickle Cell Anemia. After being ask time and time again by her friends, what was wrong with her, Tashiba Randal decided to write a book about it. She determined that people should know what SCA was and how it affected her daily life. You will be educated and deeply impressed by this story of courage, endurance and joy as you read the life of Tashiba Randal in My Life With Sickle Cell.

Coming Fall 2003

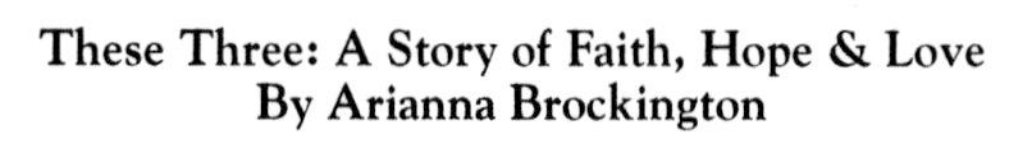

These Three: A Story of Faith, Hope & Love
By Arianna Brockington

When Faith Campbell returns to her hometown after years of avoiding it, she feels anything but at home. Although motivated by her love for her sisters to return, she can't forget the darkness in her family's past that she left to forget almost 10 years ago. Still not reconciled with the past, she struggles to fully enjoy the present time with her sisters. Will her shattered faith be healed before she allows the inner turmoil it has caused to tear her and her family apart? This is a poignant Christian novel that reveals God's power to heal and love for His children.

120 pages $11.95 **ISBN: 0-9658629-7-6**